INTRODUCTIONS TO GERMAN LITERATURE

GENERAL EDITOR: AUGUST CLOSS

VOLUME I

LITERATURE IN MEDIEVAL GERMANY

CONTENTS

LITERATURE IN MEDIEVAL GERMANY

By

PAUL SALMON, M.A., Ph.D.

Reader in German in the University of London
(Birkbeck College)

BARNES & NOBLE, Inc.

NEW YORK

PUBLISHERS & BOOKSELLERS SINCE 1873

Published in the United States
in 1967
by Barnes & Noble Inc.
New York, N.Y.

Printed in Great Britain by
Butler and Tanner Ltd, Frome and London

THE GENERAL EDITOR'S PREFACE

Literature must be seen in relationship to life in general. Any attempt to give a comprehensive account of literature must include at least some discussion and evaluation of such subjects as architecture, painting, sculpture and music as well as economics, history, sociology, science and philosophy. It is imperative to see not only the past but also the present in its proper perspective. These are the considerations that underlie the conception of *Introductions to German Literature.*

The history of the past and its literature can be of essential value if (as is particularly the case in German) it reveals characteristic trends of expression, e.g. in his *History of Modern Germany* (London, 1965) Hajo Holborn points to the 'lasting effects' of the High Middle Ages on Germany: (*a*) the creation of a national consciousness, and (*b*) the establishment of the dependence of the princes on the estates (of prelates and nobility) and the rising power of the cities, finally (*c*) the creation of a secular culture. Medieval roots or references can still be traced in literary images of our age.

In his cycle of finely woven poems, *Die Bücher der Hirten- und Preisgedichte*, *Der Sagen und Sänge und Der Hängenden Gärten* (1895), Stefan George endeavours to recapture the spirit of Greek serenity and the spirit of the Middle Ages: e.g. themes like the vigil, Parzival mood, the young knight, the dawn-song. Yet in moulding his historical and cultural heritage into timeless utterances Stefan George projected into the Middle Ages some meanings which are not to be found there. His poem *Die Gräber in Speier* (*Der Siebente Ring*, 1907) recalls the contests between Pope and Emperor and conjures up amongst the illustrious names of German rulers the memory of 'the greatest of the Fredericks': Emperor Frederick II, the Stupor Mundi:

Zum Karlen- und Ottonen-plan im blick
Des Morgenlandes ungeheuren traum.
Weisheit der Kabbala und Römerwürde
Feste von Agrigent und Selinunt.

. . . His gaze unites the plans of Ottos, Karls,
With his own boundless dreams of the Levant,
Wisdom of Cabalists and Rome's decorum,
Banquets of Akragas and Selinus.
[tr. by Olga Marx and Ernst Morwitz, 1949,
Univ. of North Carolina Studies]

Another incisive effect on the history, thought and poetry of modern Europe, and particularly Germany, was created by the Crusades. In the eleventh century Pope Gregory VII (Hildebrand) had summoned Christendom to fight the paynim, thereby enabling his successors to weld all the chivalric ideals and ambitions of the West into *one* formidable weapon and place it into the hands of the church where it was soon found useful for purposes other than that of subduing Islam. Ruthless greed for the earthly 'golden' Jerusalem besmirched the Crusaders' cause. The capture and desecration of Constantinople (1204), the Byzantine capital of Christian civilization for centuries and the guardian of priceless ancient Greek art treasures, proved an outward victory which brought dishonour to the spirit of European Christianity. According to Sir Steven Runciman (*The History of the Crusades*, 3 vols, 1954/5, Penguin 1965) the Venetians seem to have been the 'most rapacious ones', but the French and the Flemings, too, destroyed much. 'There was never a greater crime against humanity than the Fourth Crusade.' Although the Crusades in the end led to a vast fiasco from which the Moslem power emerged triumphant, they had brought about the creation of three military orders: the Templars, the Hospitallers of St John, and the Teutonic Knights. In 1235 these Deutschordensritter were directed by Emperor Frederick II to the Baltic regions where they conquered and christianized the pagan Pruzzen (Prussians), but this domination of the

Northern Slavs began to weaken in the fifteenth century and has, in our time, been completely reversed by the events of the two World Wars.

The above examples, quite apart from the impact of the age of Reformation and Humanism, will amply demonstrate how past and present are inextricably interlinked in our contemporary scene. An interpretation of the totality of German literature cannot ignore the changing milieu and the interrelationship between philosophy and economics, etc., of a special period, the religious, intellectual and social events at work in Germany and indeed in Western civilization as a whole: e.g. the effect of the Thirty Years War on German literature, thought and society; nor can it ignore mysticism, Leibniz's monadology, the influence of Baroque art and music, the French Revolution and the Wars of Liberation, Hegel's concept of the State as the embodiment of national spirit which is subject to the laws of absolute universal history, Ludwig Feuerbach's and Karl Marx's materialistic philosophy, National Socialism, Communism, and the many other physical and intellectual forces which are reflected in the mirror of present-day Germany, Austria and German-speaking Switzerland. Not least of these is the influence of World-Literature (a term coined by Goethe in *Art and Antiquity*, 6.1.1827), from the Bible, Homer, Dante, Shakespeare, Cervantes and Racine to Sanscrit, Russian, Chinese and other literatures. From earliest times German literature has been heavily influenced by foreign literatures, indeed, some of the earliest Old High German works were glosses. We trust that all these interrelationships will be highlighted by the extensive bibliographies as well as the discussion.

The arrangement of material in these four volumes has been modelled on that in the *Introductions to English Literature*, edited by Professor Bonamy Dobrée. Apart from vol. I, where more space is allowed to the general introductory section covering seven centuries of early German literature, about one-third of each book is taken up by the Introduction dealing with the literature of the period in all its genres and forms, connecting it with the other arts and with religious, social, philosophical and political movements of the time. The remaining two-thirds of each book provide a 'Student's Guide': a general reading list of recommended books dealing with the period as a whole, and also a critically selected bibliography referring to the various categories of works under discussion: poetry, fiction, drama, chronicles, literary periods, etc., and individual authors and their texts. Historical data, references to leading journals, biography and recent scholarly criticism are also included. In view of the vast amount of research published in Europe and America, only the most important relevant studies can be listed in the bibliographies. Naturally, British research is stressed. Wherever possible, modern translations of German literature into English are mentioned, too. The final choice in the selection of the whole material is left to the discretion and considered judgment of each contributor.

The presentation of the *Introductions to German Literature* in four volumes (instead of five) necessitated a drastic restriction of space allotted to the literary works, genres and movements under discussion: vol. I roughly covers the period 800–1500: Old High German, Middle High German Minnesang, Epics and Romances, the Mystics and movements leading up to the Reformation; vol. II the period: 1500–1700: Reformation, Renaissance, Baroque, and Aufklärung trends; vol. III is dedicated to the two centuries mainly under Goethe's influence: Enlightenment, Storm and Stress, Classicism, Romanticism, Jungdeutschland, Poetischer Realismus, up to Nietzsche; vol. IV deals with German literature from Nietzsche to our day, i.e. fiction from Thomas Mann, Hermann Hesse, F. Kafka, R. Musil, A. Döblin, etc., up to H. Böll and G. Grass; drama from Gerhart Hauptmann, F. Wedekind, F. Bruckner, G. Kaiser, etc., up to B. Brecht, C. Zuckmayer, M. Frisch, F. Dürrenmatt, R. Hochhuth, P. Weiss and contemporary Hörspiel authors; poetry from Arno Holz, R. Dehmel, Chr. Morgenstern, R. M. Rilke,

Stefan George, H. von Hofmannsthal, G. Trakl, to G. Benn, R. Hagelstange, G. Eich, H. M. Enzensberger, and P. Celan, etc. We felt justified in devoting a whole volume to the artistic achievements in German literature of our age.

A work of art, such as *Tristan*, *Parzival*, *Faust*, states UNIVERSAL TRUTHS, as does scientific research. But there is a fundamental difference between aesthetic and scientific TRUTHS. If on 4 October 1957 the first Sputnik had not been launched into space, sooner or later it would have been done by the force of technological progress. The same argument would make nonsense in creative art. Without Beethoven we would never have had the *Ninth Symphony* (whatever the human and scientific progress), without Shakespeare no *Hamlet* or *Lear*, without Mozart no *Don Giovanni*. These creations are no Homunculus-productions but aesthetic truths and human self-revelations which vindicate Hölderlin's proud word at the end of his *Empedokles*-tragedy where Empedokles says to Pausanias: 'What are the gods and their spirit if I do not proclaim them?' a phrase which reminds one of the mystic expression by Angelus Silesius (Johann Scheffler): 'God does not live without me: I know that without me God cannot live an instant'.

It is through language that the poet proclaims. Language is the key to literature. Through language we reach the reservoir of man's inmost resources; language preserves the imperishable treasures of the human mind and the human heart; language guarantees the continuity of man's spiritual existence. Ludwig Wittgenstein in his *Tractatus Logico-Philosophicus* remarks: 'The barriers of my language are the barriers of my world'.

In fact, every literary creation is translation, i.e. translation of experience into language. In his *Fragmente* the German Romantic Novalis pointed to the importance of translation. He differentiates between three kinds of translation: grammatical (i.e. literal renderings from one medium into another), interpretative (creative), mythical and symbolical in the highest sense. Novalis saw the whole universe as a symbol: 'Die Welt ist ein Universaltropus des Geistes' (The world is a universal trope of the spirit). To Novalis, Greek mythology is a 'translation' of a national religion into art. In a similar way the modern cult of the Madonna (mother, virgin, and goddess) is seen as the translation of a myth into a symbol.

Much has in the past years been written about the so-called 'willing suspension of disbelief'. In our view, it is not at all necessary to apply this strictly as a condition to art-appreciation. It is quite possible (cf. Bernard G. Heyl in *New Bearings in Esthetics and Art Criticism. A Study in Semantics and Evaluation*, Yale University Press, 1943, 1957 fourth printing) for an atheist to appreciate Rembrandt's *Christ's Supper* (Christus in Emmaus) intuitively. Moreover, we are not asked, as T. S. Eliot has rightly pointed out, to share Dante's theological creed in order to grasp the poetic greatness of the *Divina Commedia*. One could argue similarly about the revolutionary epic *The Twelve* (1918) by the Russian poet Alexander Blok: the twelve soldiers of the Red Army are not heroes; they are bestial, yet guided by a higher destiny. Christ Himself marches with them. Even Nature is symbolical: 'The wind strolls, the snow dances, / A party of twelve men advances.' Likewise, W. B. Yeats's *Sailing to Byzantium* (1927) reveals a vision of a spiritual empire to the reader without necessarily a 'willing suspension of disbelief': 'That is no country for old men . . . caught in that sensual music all neglect / monuments of unageing intellect . . . gather me / into the artifice of eternity'.

H. von Hofmannsthal mocks at the seekers of profundity, whom he contrasts with Goethe: 'The important Germans seem to swim continuously under water; only Goethe, like a lonely dolphin, moves along the shining surface' (*Tagebuch-Aufzeichnungen*). Goethe is, of course, not the only exception. Where surface and depth, the outward and inward worlds merge into an artistic unity, perfection is achieved, e.g. in

Goethe's *Mailied*, Mörike's *Mein Fluss*, Rilke's *Die Flamingos*, George's *Teppich des Lebens*, or Heinrich von Morungen's:

> Ich hôrt ûf der heide
> lûte stimme und süezen sanc.
> Dâ von wart ich beide
> fröiden rîch und trûrens kranc . . .
>
> I heard in the field
> a clear voice, a sweet song,
> whence my sorrow grew light,
> and my joy waxed strong.
> [tr. by Margaret F. Richey in *Medieval German Lyrics*, 1958]

to mention at random just a few examples, which express poetic truths.

W. B. Yeats is right when he states: 'We can create truths, but we cannot scientifically "know" them'; and Saint-Exupéry says: 'We do not discover truth, we create it.'

The poets, however, who are over-anxious to capture the *Zeitgeist* by using up-to-date scientific nomenclature at any price, are far away from poetic truth. The ineffectiveness of mere actuality is obvious. Neon-lights instead of oil-lamps do not make the poem more original! There is no shortage of topical events: the opening of the first railroad from Nürnberg to Fürth in December 1835 and the first railway journey from Leipzig to Dresden a few years later caused sensation and aroused heated controversies about the 'iron beast'. To Jungdeutschland the locomotive became the symbol of a new era which supplanted Romanticism. Heine's attitude to the 'iron beast' (das eiserne Vieh) is expressed in his *Pferd und Esel*: the horse and the donkey look with melancholy at the new monster. The noble horse is obviously the loser, but the poor ass will survive.

A glance at later versifications of technical achievements (mostly by the time of Impressionism and Expressionism) will prove the outdatedness of such literary effusions. Here are some German examples (apart from many other ones such as W. Whitman's poem on a locomotive in the winter): D. v. Liliencron: *Die neue Eisenbahn*, G. Falke: *Im Schnellzug*, Gerrit Engelke: *Lokomotive* and *Auf der Strassenbahn*, H. Lersch: *Die Lokomotive*, Otto zur Linde: *Bau der Untergrundbahn*, R. Dehmel: *Drohende Aussicht*, H. Carossa: *Der Eisenwagen*, Günter Eich: *D-Zug München-Frankfurt*, A. Petzold: *Der Werkbahnhof* and *Bergfahrt*, G. Kölwel: *Bahnfahrt durch den Vorfrühling*, A. Wolfenstein: *Fahrt*, René Schickele: *Ballade von unserer Lieben Frau im Coupé*, E. Stadler: *Fahrt über die Kölner Rheinbrücke bei Nacht*, G. Benn: *D-Zug*, Th. Fontane: *Die Brücke am Tay*. With a few exceptions, e.g. Fontane's and Benn's poems, almost all the above poems are either forgotten now or live on as specimens of outdatedness. Landscape is still a dominant factor in many of those poems. In our epoch of scientific laboratories and engineering triumphs, the natural order and humanistic scale of Nature have disappeared from ultra-modern works in favour of an intellectual pattern which claims to be impersonal but also anti-historical and anti-ptolemaic.

It would be misleading to assess twentieth-century literature by measuring it solely with the standards of Goethe's concept of organic form and universality of outlook. Instead of totality we now have fragmentation, accompanied by signs of a temporary retreat from language, cf. *The Retreat from the Word* (G. Steiner, *Listener*, 1960). The indisputable fact remains that the 'universal' image is shattered. In his *Second Coming* W. B. Yeats, surely the most inspired European poet of our age, expresses the present dilemma:

> The falcon does not hear the falconer,
> things fall apart; the centre cannot hold . . .

Instead of the 'total' view of poetic vision we are offered pieces of images, like pictures in a kaleidoscope, by rotation of the metal tube. The self-sufficient artist's ego is dethroned or absorbed into the web of bewildering patterns of events, ambitions and manifestations.

Basically, the shattering of the Goethean 'universal' images signifies not only the loss of a once generally accepted world-order, but it also triumphantly declares the supremacy of linguistic artistry over an apparently chaotic fragmentation of the universe. Yet, we should remember that in the creative literature of a nation the resources for renewal are inexhaustible. It is therefore unrealistic to speak of a complete 'tabula rasa', however strongly such a mood must have been felt under the stress of Germany's apocalyptic downfall in and after the last War. But we heartily welcome bold experiments which emerged on the German literary scene since 1945.

To *this* present our thoughts and efforts are directed. In *this* present lie the seeds of our future. Allowing for some variation of the theme, Gottfried's words (which actually refer to the community of the noble hearts, the 'edele herzen') in his 'Prologue' to *Tristan und Isolt* may lend expression to what is our deepest concern:

> . . . dem lebene sî mîn leben ergeben,
> der werlt will ich gewerldet wesen,
> mit ir verderben oder genesen . . .

> . . . To this life my life be dedicated,
> To this world let me belong,
> With it to perish or be saved . . .

A. CLOSS

AUTHOR'S NOTE

A brief *Introduction* like the present one has to be selective. It is hoped that concentration on what are agreed to be the most significant works will enable it to do two things—to give guidance to the serious student of medieval German literature in the often bewildering mass of writings produced by current reinterpretations and revaluations, and to provide a first introduction for a more general reader. It is with such a person in mind that so much attention has been given in the bibliography to translations and that the illustrative passages in the text are given in English renderings. The originals of these quotations are, however, reproduced at the end of the book, together with references which will enable the reader to pursue the more detailed allusions to medieval texts.

The views expressed do not invariably tally with received opinion, but I hope I have made it clear when I deviate from a generally-held view or hazard a conjecture of my own.

When the *Introduction* was written, I held an appointment at Royal Holloway College, University of London. I should like to take this opportunity, as I move to another college, to record my gratitude to colleagues and students there for fifteen years of pleasant association. My thanks are also due to the generous spirit of the General Editor of this series, to whom I owe most valuable suggestions; also to Miss Josephine Annable, for undertaking the arduous task of checking the entries in the bibliography. The errors and omissions which remain are my own.

PAUL SALMON

London, August 1967

I

THE EARLY LITERATURE OF GERMANY

Introduction

By comparison with English, German vernacular literature made a slow start; what is preserved of native tradition is mutilated, and what was produced in the vernacular in the interests of Christianity is at best derivative, and would probably be ignored completely if there were more original compositions to be read, or if the texts had not provided such a valuable quarry for historical dialectologists. Yet German writing antedates French; the earliest document which uses the French language contains the oaths sworn at Strassburg in 842, when the followers of rival Frankish kings, descendants of Charlemagne, but already distinctively German and French, swore a pact of non-aggression, each in the language of the other, before their assembled warriors. By that time, writings in German, on the evidence of texts which have survived, had a century or so of growth behind them. Resemblances between Latin and French were great enough for Latin to survive much longer in French-speaking than in German-speaking parts, as the language of official business. Christianity was not consolidated in German territory until the eighth century, and there could be no pretence that German speakers could understand Latin by the light of nature. Hence much that came to be written in German is directly concerned with the dissemination of the faith, and every piece of evidence of a pre-Christian culture that is preserved owes its existence to some cleric's enthusiasm for pagan letters. But Christianity in Germany was too precarious in the eighth and ninth centuries to permit literary development on the scale of English achievement, and more than one preface to a Latin or a vernacular work speaks of effacing the memory of rude barbarian song.

Only fragmentary traces remain of specifically German poetry from preliterary times; but it appears to share features of expression and content with other Germanic literatures like Old English and Old Icelandic. The Old High German *Hildebrandslied* goes back to a legendary version of Ostrogothic history for its background. This is in itself some evidence of the relative homogeneity of Germanic culture, and a justification for assuming that fragments of evidence in classical and post-classical Latin texts for the existence and nature of Germanic poetry in general apply also to German in particular. Evidence for some sort of mnemonic verse goes back as far as Tacitus, who mentions poems about gods and heroes, and also the *barditus*, apparently some kind of battle song. Jordanes, the historian of the Goths, speaks of the deeds of former times recited to the accompaniment of the harp; Gregory of Tours mentions in his history of the Franks a harpist sent by Theodoric at the request of Chlodowech; Paulus Diaconus' history of the Lombards gives a hint of subject-matter. From casual mention in the Fathers it has been possible to deduce various *genres* of poetry, but little, apart from heroic matter, is preserved in any of the Germanic languages, and hardly anything even of this in any of the dialects which contribute to German.

No one dialect attained pre-eminence in the Old High German period. In part this is a reflection of political circumstances, for seeds of the later particularism were already present in a system of inheritance which split possessions among the heirs of a king, and there was never a lasting continuity of overlordship; the title of King of the Germans and Emperor passed from one region to another, and no region held power and prestige long enough to establish its dialect as unquestionably superior. For practical purposes it may be taken that Old High German dialect boundaries, determined largely by reaction to a series of changes in the consonantal system known as the High German Sound Shift, conform fairly closely to those of the present day lying to the west of the Elbe. Districts further east were colonized in the eleventh and twelfth centuries to about as far as the Oder, but as the settlers came from various parts of Germany, dialect features in eastern districts tend to be less marked than those in the west. The northern part of this western strip, approximately modern Westphalia and Saxony, still has *Plattdeutsch* or Low German spoken dialects; Old Saxon is also specifically not a High German dialect, but it contributed one of the most notable single monuments—the *Heliand*—to early German literature.

The most important single group—neither so loose an association as a tribe, nor so formally organized as a nation—was however the Frankish. The central homeland of the Franks is identified by the name of France; their German domains were in a way originally an offshoot. In Merovingian times (fifth and sixth centuries) they had occupied romanized Gaul, and like the Romans before them turned their faces east for the preservation of the Rhine frontier and, with less success at first, for the preservation of the *limes* (Franconia and Bavaria). Salian Franks had established themselves in the Rhineland in the sixth century, but were less successful in dominating the Thuringians to the east, the Saxons to the north, and the Alemannian and Austro-Bavarian tribes to south and east. The Carolingians of the eighth century had family possessions in the Rhineland, and were more interested than the Merovingians had been in the lands to the east of the Rhine. Their hold on their neighbours was reinforced by the ties of religion, and the eighth century is characterized by missions in Franconia and Thuringia, in which the influence of Anglo-Saxon missionaries was decisive. Charlemagne's military campaigns against the Saxons were effective if costly; the Bavarians were held by the more peaceful means of civil and ecclesiastical administration, some effects of which are seen in the preservation of vernacular doctrinal and edifying works in southern dialects. Under the later Carolingians, the frontiers of Germany took on their characteristic shape of medieval times—bounded on north and east by the Elbe and the Böhmerwald, on the west by Alsace and Lorraine. Devolution of power within the kingdom came about as a result of external pressures, especially from Danes in the north and Magyars in the east; to ensure a state of readiness against external threats the duchies came into being, largely as a kind of regional defence. These were Franconia, Saxony, Bavaria and Swabia. In the rivalries between these, and in the Frankish practice of dividing up territories like private domains among a ruler's heirs, lay the seeds of much of the confusion and disruption which characterizes German history throughout the Middle Ages and after. The kingdom was stable for a time under the Franks, and the nobility, particularly in the southern lands, made themselves indispensable and ensured that they alone could attain to positions of temporal and spiritual authority. The election of a Saxon king (Heinrich I) when the German Carolingian line died out provoked some resentment in the south, especially among the Bavarians, who had never been incorporated into the Carolingian empire by conquest, but who were brought to acknowledge overlordship at the expense of concessions in the sphere of ecclesiastical patronage. Heinrich was successful in warding off external enemies, and he secured the election of his son as Otto I to a strengthened kingdom. Otto was also successful in keeping the duchies under control, but he did so at the price of quelling an armed rebellion in which his younger brothers joined with dissident Franks. The subsequent reconciliation is the matter of a short commemorative poem in mixed German and Latin.

The impact of outward events on literature was, however, slight; indeed, the time of the Saxons is sometimes seen as an age of regression from the promising beginnings of the Carolingian era. It is true that the language of the kings was different, but this should not have been enough to bring about the end of a literary tradition, if there had been a vigorous one in existence. It is not even necessarily the case that vernacular literature showed a relative decline because of the increasingly strong position of the church, for what records we have of the earliest German literature were preserved, even if only accidentally, through the agency of the church. Favours shown by the Saxon house to the church took the form very largely of making over to cathedrals and abbeys domains vacated by the extinction of temporal succession. It became accepted that the royal benefactor had the right of presentation when sees became vacant—a source of future contention between kings and popes. The defence of these ecclesiastical properties and the performance of military obligations to the crown were put in the hands of the *Vögte*, but the church authorities were granted privileges and immunities, including the establishment of markets and the exaction of tolls, which provided the beginnings of cities.

In the middle of the eleventh century, under the Salian Franks, the position of the church was exploited in a more direct way, when Heinrich IV succeeded as a minor and came under the tutelage of Archbishops Anno of Cologne and Adalbert of Bremen. Favours given to the church estranged the aristocracy; the crown came to rely more and more on the lower nobility and the *ministeriales*—the latter in the employment of the church for the administration of temporal possessions, and a new social pattern began to emerge. Outside Germany, favours given to the church had consolidated the power of the papacy, which now disputed the right of kings to appoint church dignitaries. Matters were brought to a head when Heinrich bought off rebellion only at the price of complete capitulation to papal demands at Canossa. Participation in the First Crusade did not of itself bring about unity, and Heinrich IV continued inactive in his Lombard kingdom while his son, having joined the rebels, ruled in Germany and in some degree restored the dignity of the crown, including in his achievements a compromise, the Concordat of Worms, which restored royal rights to endow ecclesiastical dignitaries with their temporal possessions.

At first sight there seems to be surprisingly little connection between life and letters in the Old High German age. Certainly some documents reflect the interests of the church in the conversion of the Germans and the maintenance of the faith. The growth of faction among the nobility in the tenth and eleventh centuries may be one reason why so little was written in German at that time. The church might have been expected to foster learning, but not the creation of independent works of literature in the vernacular. Nevertheless, it is to the antiquarian interest of monks that we owe the few scanty relics of pre-Christian writing in Germany, of which the first examples give a fascinating, if tantalizing, view of prehistory.

Charms

Perhaps the most primitive form of verse preserved in German is verse of a private rather than a public nature—the charm. The working of a charm, a kind of sympathetic magic, belongs to the realm of folklore rather than literature. The incantation itself is a mystery, not for general consumption; late examples of the *genre* in Old High German speak of whispering the spell in the ear of the patient, in this case a horse.

The importance of the horse in early cultures may be gauged from the spread and persistence of essentially the same charm; the one just mentioned is a late christianized version of a very prevalent incantation, preserved in several forms in German, including one pre-Christian version mentioning one known god and one known goddess of the Germanic pantheon (Wotan and Freia), besides other names less readily identifiable. But what is essentially the same charm may also be traced back to Vedic Sanskrit; there are later medieval versions, and Scandinavian versions from the sixteenth and seventeenth centuries. This is the second of two charms preserved on blank spaces in a ninth-century Merseburg missal. The two texts together number a dozen lines, and may be presumed to owe their survival to the antiquarian spirit of an unknown monk. The horse-charm tells (i) how the horse of the god Balder/Vol went lame when he was out riding with Wotan, (ii) how two groups of goddesses conjured the horse, apparently without success, and how Wotan took over, implicitly with success, and (iii) the formula of words used on this occasion. This pattern is taken as the essential form of the charm, though in fact few of the others preserved in Old High German give such a full account of the 'historical' precedent. A christianized version is found in a Trier manuscript of the tenth century, in which St Stephen and Christ are the horsemen and Christ performs the cure. In another version a man is walking disconsolately and pulling his foundered horse along by the rein, when Our Lord meets him and cures it. In the latter of these versions the paternoster is to be recited three times before the incantatory formula.

The three versions of the horse-charm have similarities shared by the versions in other languages. Indeed, the survival of charms into much later times suggests a subculture powerful enough to resist great changes in overt behaviour, beliefs and social organization. Later charms are almost all of medical or veterinary import; some of them, notably those concerned with the stanching of blood, remain obscure, as though the incantation had preserved its secrets even against the investigation of scholars. The other Merseburg charm is also rather enigmatic; it is generally held to be a charm to secure the release of a comrade-in-arms who has fallen into enemy hands. In this case, the narrative part is used to establish the precedent for the incantation; the precedent for the incident which made it necessary is left to be deduced from the instructions to the 'patient' to leap from his fetters and escape his enemies.

Apart from their evocation of primeval superstition, the antiquity of the two earliest German charms is attested by the verse form in which they are written—an alliterative long line, generally similar to that found in Old English and Old Icelandic, divided into two half lines of variable length, each containing two prominent syllables and a fairly fluid number (from two to six) of less prominent ones, and with at least two of the prominent syllables alliterating across the caesura according to fairly rigid principles. This type of verse is peculiarly well adapted to the Germanic languages, since they have a strong regular stress on root syllables, but the form survived less strongly in German than in the other related languages, and alliterative verse, whatever its subject-matter, yielded in the ninth century to rhyming verse probably adapted from the form of the Ambrosian hymn.

The 'Hildebrandslied'

But there are texts besides the charms in alliterative verse. The most important is the *Hildebrandslied*, important in its own right as a poem and as evidence for the short poem on a quasi-historical theme in a West Germanic language. The events which form the basis of this poem are the exploits of Theodoric the Great, King of the Ostrogoths (d. 526). His career brought him from the position of a subject-king of the East Roman emperor at the end of the fifth century A.D. to the conquest of Italy, the treacherous murder of his vanquished opponent Odoacer (496) and the establishment of a kingdom in Italy, which like so many Germanic kingdoms, barely survived its ruler. In the course of his rule he found it necessary to execute Boethius, the philosopher and 'last of the Romans' and author of one of the most influential books of the Middle Ages—and after. Theodoric's career was too meteoric to pass unsung, but the Theodoric of legend, familiarly known in Middle High German as Dietrich von Bern (Verona) from his royal seat, bears little resemblance to the historical figure. Boethius' *Consolatio philosophiae*, translated into German by Notker III of St Gall some 200 to 250 years later than the *Hildebrandslied*, gives in its preface an account of affairs which is much closer to historical fact, but even this 'historical' account shows the beginnings of legend-making. A statement that Theodoric was invited to Constantinople as an honoured guest seems hardly to tally with the fact of existence as a minor at the court as a surety for his father's good behaviour, though it is apparently true that he did find favour. The legend as it develops in literature blends these two accounts. As in history, Theodoric's absence from home was involuntary; as in the preface it was the mature Theodoric who went away. But what sent him away became a treacherous attack by Odoacer, who seized Theodoric's kingdom. By the time the legend had reached the form in which it was known to the author of the *Hildebrandslied*, the exile lasted thirty years and was spent at the court of Attila. From this earliest recorded version of the legend and on through the German Middle Ages, Attila is regarded as hospitable and friendly, in contrast with the historical assessment of his character, an unfamiliar view derived from a period of alliance with the Huns. The dates of Attila (d. 453) and Theodoric (d. 526) are sufficient indication of the extent to which history became garbled in the creation of legend.

The legend becomes further modified in later times, but the form sketched here is that which supplies the background to the *Hildebrandslied*. Dietrich is not a protagonist in the *Hildebrandslied*. Hildebrand, here as in later literature, is Dietrich's right-hand man; but the place of Dietrich, and for that matter the scene of the poem, emerges only from the words of the protagonists. As Dietrich's army enters Italy, it is met by hostile forces, but before or instead of a pitched battle, two champions are to meet. Dietrich's representative is Hildebrand; against him stands Hadubrand, who, the reader is told at the outset, is Hildebrand's son. The champions are unknown to one another. From their preliminary parley the father deduces the relationship between them; he tries to establish his identity, but the son interprets this as an attempt to gain an unfair advantage, taunts the old man with cowardice and makes a fight inevitable. The account of fighting is brief: lances are flung, swords hack the shields down to the nave—and the poem breaks off.

The *Hildebrandslied*, a fragment of 68 lines, was written

(about 800) on spare pages of a devotional work. If the entire poem had been greatly longer probably no attempt would have been made to write it out in such a confined space, so we probably have nearly the whole poem. Unfortunately we have to supply the conclusion from other sources, and their evidence is contradictory. The earliest of these is the minor Eddaic poem which records a lament of Hildebrand, in which he claims to have killed eighty opponents, and to have taken, unwillingly, the life of his own son. The second source is also northern—the *Thidrekssaga* of the late thirteenth century, a prose account of the deeds of Dietrich (Thidrek), written down in Norway from the oral accounts of German merchants. According to this account, Hildebrand, after a long struggle, has his son (here called Alebrand) at his mercy, and prepares to receive the latter's sword in token of surrender when Alebrand lunges at his outstretched hand. 'Your mother, not your father, taught you that stroke', exclaims Hildebrand; and he asserts that he will spare the young man only if he will acknowledge his lineage, which, at the point of death, he does. Hildebrand then reveals himself as Alebrand's father, and the pair are reconciled. The sixteenth-century ballad, the *Jüngeres Hildebrandslied*, appears to have a similar conclusion, for though the nature of Alebrand's blow is not specified, a similar taunt is made.

This evidence seems to suggest the following end to the Old High German poem: the old man wins, and the young man, after a gesture of surrender, attacks again, leaving the father no choice but to kill an unworthy opponent. What is missing is unlikely to have been very extensive; there was probably little more detail about the actual fighting, and the interest of the poem lies in the presentation in speech of reactions to a rapidly changing situation.

One would like to think of other poems of similar compass combined together to make a corpus like the heroic poems of the *Elder Edda*, but there is little evidence, and such as there is has to be pieced together rather in the way of the conclusion of the *Hildebrandslied* itself, but with even more imponderables. But if this minor incident, involving no historical figure as an active participant, was preserved in song, the deeds of Theodoric himself must have been remembered—indeed, it is only through oral tradition that the material could have been supplied from which the later stories of Dietrich arose.

Besides being incomplete, the *Hildebrandslied* is preserved only in a very corrupt text; whole lines fail to fit any acceptable plan of alliteration, and even this defect is insignificant in comparison with the dialectal confusion of the whole. Linguistic evidence suggests a superficial Low German surface on a text which is primarily Bavarian. A Bavarian original would agree well with the provenance of the legends about Dietrich; but there may have been an earlier version of the story in Langobardic—received by these neighbours of the Goths when Theodoric's kingdom collapsed.

The *Hildebrandslied* is the unique example in Old High German Literature of the heroic view of life. It cannot be compared with book epics like the Old English *Beowulf*, for it is concerned with the outcome of a single incident; it comes closest to the heroic lays of the poetic *Edda*, though some of these have moved towards the ballad. Like them it uses the minimum of description and reflection, and concentrates on dialogue; the style is laconic, and at its best depends on memorable utterances in a highly charged situation. Even in poems better preserved than the *Hildebrandslied* details of the action have to be reconstructed, for the poet could rely on his audience to fill in the details from their knowledge of an oft-told tale. Yet brevity is combined with a kind of expansion, a practice of giving the same content in different words—a means of giving prominence where most required particularly suited to the declamatory style of the alliterative verse in which this poem was written. The *Hildebrandslied* is too short to permit many conclusions about poetic diction, but there are traces of an international heroic vocabulary.

Although no heroic poetry is preserved in German between the *Hildebrandslied* and the *Nibelungenlied* some four hundred years later, it must be assumed that heroic figures of the past continued to be celebrated in song. The *Jüngeres Hildebrandslied* is a tantalizing instance of the survival of a legend; there must have been intervening stages, but they can be restored only by appeal outside the German language.

The Poetry of the Conversion

After the Hunnish incursions and the great movements of population in the fourth and fifth centuries (the *Völkerwanderung*), there was a need to convert those Germanic tribes which had not previously inhabited parts of the christianized Roman Empire. Celtic monks, like Gallus and Columbanus, set up their cells at St Gall and Reichenau respectively in the sixth century, but they did not achieve mass conversions. There was some infiltration of Arianized Christianity into Austro-Bavaria from an Ostrogothic refugee population, evidenced by items in the German vocabulary which survive to the present day. Other terms, however, show a striking similarity to those of Old English, and provide the clue that much of the edifying literature of Old High German is indebted directly or indirectly to missionaries from England. The most important of these was Winfrith Boniface (d. 762), the founder of the monastery of Fulda, which became a centre of learning whose influence is felt in a surprisingly large number of Old High German Christian texts. Englishmen, most notably Alcuin, were prominent among the advisors of Charlemagne, and Charlemagne was instrumental in pursuing, not always by the most peaceable means, the conversion of his peoples. Royal edicts may be connected with dialogue versions of baptismal vows, and with the numerous confessions which are preserved from the ninth and tenth centuries. Catechetical works and vernacular exegeses of the Paternoster may also be connected with the same process of conversion. The dialectal distribution of these texts extends into Bavarian and Alemannic, dialects remote from the immediate influence of the Anglo-Saxon missionaries. They owe their preservation to monasteries, and their creation appears to rest on local monastic initiative within the framework of a royal directive. Among the earliest of these texts is a version of Isidore's *Tractatus contra Judaeos*, not at first sight a text which would obviously call for translation, but accountable also as part of the work of conversion: it is interesting to note that the word *Judaei* is consistently rendered as *ungalaubiun* (faithless), and the work may be seen as Christian apologetics in the form of answers to doubters' objections. Doubters did not presumably read Latin, and probably not German either, so that a work of this nature must have been in the hands of the faithful—we have to imagine the user as a missionary who still needed help with an abstract text in Latin. The language of the tract is considered adept, but some of the constructions lean too heavily on the Latin original. The same may be said of the fragments of German translations of the Gospels from Monsee, mostly preserved in Vienna. They certainly mark an advance on interlinear versions of hymns or of the Benedictine Rule, both of which are preserved in southern dialects. Texts such as these provide the evidence of active missionary work against which early Christian poems may be seen.

Two incomplete southern texts may be associated with the earliest phases of Christianity in Germany; they are concerned with first and last things, and seem to be designed to combat previously-held pagan ideas. An early ninth-century manuscript from Wessobrunn contains, again on an odd page, nine lines of alliterative verse and a prose prayer. The verse itself may be subdivided into two parts, almost as though the poem were to be regarded as a compilation rather than a composition. The first words are an epic formula, disclaiming, like the opening of the *Hildebrandslied*, any untoward originality. The succeeding lines, in which the absence of the material world is presented by negative enumeration, are the most archaic part of the text, and strikingly resemble some lines in the (later) Eddic *Völuspá*. The second group of four lines specifies that before the created world existed, God and the angels were present. The use of a rhyming formula marks out these lines as later in origin. Finally the prayer is an appeal to be granted faith and strength to resist evil. The text has superficial Bavarian features, but the alliterative formula at the beginning uses Low German forms; the manuscript also shows a scribal practice which derives from Anglo-Saxon usage. The incomplete poem appears to have been a Christian account of the Creation; any pagan material used was drawn on only to be controverted.

The other text, *Muspilli*, is more decidedly Bavarian in language; it is written in chaotic spelling in a missal known to have been presented before 843 to Ludwig the German. If the original poem consisted exclusively of alliterating long lines, some of them must have been badly mutilated in transmission; but the great length of the lines, by comparison with alliterative verse in English, suggests that this is no early composition. None the less, the poem makes some allusion, if slight, to pagan accounts of the end of the world, for the word *muspilli* suggests reference to the attack by fire on the world by the sons of Muspell, again recounted in *Völuspá*. The word also occurs, however, twice in the Old Saxon *Heliand*, i.e. in an indisputably Christian context; since both pagan Germanic and Christian belief had dire accounts of the destruction of the world by fire, it is not surprising that there should be some contamination between the vocabularies of the two systems. In any case, there can be no doubting the fundamentally Christian, edifying, and even didactic nature of the work as a whole. For while the Last Judgment is a theme which merits epic treatment, the poem contains elements other than the narration, dialogue and perhaps elegiac reflection expected in an epic tradition. There is narration here, but no dialogue, and the reflection is ratiocinative. The poem also gives more than one version of its matter. It starts with a call to repentance based on the judgment of the soul after death; the Last Judgment, or Doomsday, forms the theme of the latter part of the poem. There also appears to be a certain confusion about the outcome of the duel between Elijah and Antichrist to decide the fate of mankind, an episode which is inserted into the account of Doomsday. A group designated the *weroltrehtwison* (perhaps 'righteous') assert that the duel takes place, and appear to suggest defeat for Antichrist; yet 'many godly men' report that it is Elijah who loses, and that it is when his blood pours to the ground that the world burst into flame. If there is an antithesis between two views here, it is the propagators of error who are the authority for the fact of the conflict. Narrative confusion does not, however, destroy the rhetoric of the descriptions, which make the poem an effective call to repentance.

Biblical Narrative in Prose and Verse

The more immediate influence of the missionaries began to make itself felt with Biblical translation. Latin Bibles were of course accessible to the learned, but missionary work, then as now, placed the greatest emphasis on the Gospel narrative. The synoptic narrative of the *Diatessaron*, a compilation of the second-century Syrian monk Tatian, would obviously commend itself to a missionary. As the name implies, the original was put together from the four Gospels in the Greek Testament, omitting nothing that was in any of them, but giving one account only of each event. Thus it starts with the opening verses of St John's Gospel, and continues with St Luke's very full account of the annunciation, nativity, etc. The work found its way to Italy, and a Latin version was prepared in the fourth century from the relevant verses of St Jerome's translation of the Bible. St Boniface is known to have acquired a copy of the Latin text and to have taken it to Fulda, where the earliest Latin manuscript of Tatian is still preserved. It was in Fulda that Tatian was translated into German in the ninth century. The dialect varies somewhat from scribe to scribe, but the basic language is East Franconian, i.e. approximately that of the region. The bulk of the text is such that Tatian is cited as a norm for Old High German, but its phonological status is the only claim that this text has for consideration. A translation of the Bible like Luther's or the Authorized Version, even, is not original literature, but apart from its doctrinal importance it uses language powerful enough to influence subsequent writing and speech in the same vernacular. The translator of the Old High German *Tatian* shows no such linguistic creativity; his language has none of the immediacy of a spoken language and none of the persuasive force of oratory.

The 'Heliand'

The Old Saxon verse epic on the life of Christ, the *Heliand*, and the fragmentary epic derived from Genesis, are datable to the second or third decade of the ninth century, if a Latin text identified as a preface to the work is accepted as authentic; according to this the epic was written at the command of Charlemagne's son Ludwig the Pious (814–40) by an acknowledged poet. Exactly where the work was written is not known, though as Old Saxon seems to have been less productive of written texts than the other dialects of early Germany one may wonder that the work, designed to make the Gospel available to the illiterate as well as the literate, came to be composed in this form. A vernacular prose version, no matter how unidiomatic, would at least help a preacher with the vocabulary, but the verse epic is a specifically literary form. The poet went out of his way to acclimatize his story to the Germanic heroic background; indeed the term *thegan* ('thane') is frequently used for the disciples; the ship in which they sail on Galilee becomes a *hurnidscip*. Modification in this direction is often associated with Peter's access of heroic spirit after the betrayal by Judas, though it may be noted that the text makes him less active than it might have done; in the following passage only the first very general statement is made in terms of actions by Peter:

> Then in wrath he went, the very confident warrior, and stood before his lord, close in front of his master. He was not hesitant

> in his mind or afraid in his heart, and he took up his sword, the blade at his side, and struck at the first opponent in his way with the strength of his hand so that Malchus was marked with the edge of the steel, on his right side by the sword; his ear was cut off; he was wounded in the ear so that his cheek and his ear, made bloody by the sword, were parted by the dire wound. The blood poured forth, flowed from the wound.

Given the expansion, which is common to the whole of the text, there is nothing much here to suggest a quickening of the pulse at the description of swordplay. Expansion is carried out by the known Germanic methods of variation; e.g. the words rendered successively as 'sword', 'blade', 'steel' and 'sword' again are three words, two of them poetic, for an edged weapon. A third poetic word is the first element in the compound translated as 'made bloody by the sword'. The stately process of variation makes every point twice. But if the diction is Germanic, much of the text is also dependent on known Latin Biblical commentaries, so that a large element in the composition and content of the book epic must be accredited to a foreign model.

Apart from the adoption of the technique of variation, the use of Germanic alliterative verse in the *Heliand* does not appear to be particularly happy. The basic structure is there, but its firm rhythm is overgrown with a number of unstressed syllables even greater than those in High German poems, notably at the beginnings of lines. Some of these might be 'rescued' if a greater measure of freedom than is usually allowed is assumed for the placing of the alliterating syllable, and some contamination with the rhymed octosyllable may be suspected.

It was the peculiarity of Old Saxon verse that led to one of the most spectacular discoveries in nineteenth-century German studies. Old English fragments of a Genesis epic showed peculiarities of metre and diction unparalleled in English but similar to those of the *Heliand*. It was therefore conjectured that there must have been an Old Saxon original of which the Old English was a translation. The purely linguistic evidence made such a supposition probable, but its boldness lay in the improbability of a continental influence on English letters at a time when all influence was in the other direction. But the supposition was justified by the discovery in the Vatican library of Old Saxon Genesis fragments.

The extent to which elaborate composition rather than spontaneous inspiration contributed to Old Saxon verse appears to be borne out by recent studies on the subject, which show an astonishingly complex formal relationship between the numbers of lines allotted to the cantos (Fitts) dealing with various episodes in the life of Christ. The figures revealed seem to be too well founded to be dismissed as mere hallucination, but they tell us little about the relative importance of the various parts of the text which could not be deduced by more conventional methods of investigation. Medieval interest in acrostics and numerical problems is, however, well attested, and numerical interpretations of medieval texts will have to be seriously considered unless and until the calculations involved can be demonstrated to rest purely and simply on the properties of numbers.

Otfrid von Weissenburg

It is not only in the adoption of a different kind of verse that the differences between Otfrid's rhymed *Evangelien-harmonie* and the Old Saxon Heliand become apparent. The material on which the narration is based is bound, in the nature of things, to be similar, but the immediate source was not in this case the *Diatessaron*, but the pericopes, i.e. passages of the gospels specified for daily reading. Again, while the *Heliand* is not uninfluenced by commentaries it keeps narration to the forefront, whereas Otfrid reflects and interprets. There seems to be little doubt that Otfrid's audience was primarily monastic, and he makes no more attempt to come to terms with Germanic attitudes than with Germanic verse.

The new form of verse adopted here has affinities on the one hand with the Ambrosian hymn and on the other hand with what was to become the medieval German octosyllable —the classical measure for narration in Middle High German—and later to decline into the doggerel (*Knittelvers*) of the sixteenth century.

Introducing rhyming verse into German single-handed does not make Otfrid into a great poet. Some of the shortcomings of his text may be accounted for by his obvious struggle with his medium; but beyond all linguistic clumsiness there is a want of the imaginative quality which is the obvious requirement of poetry. Otfrid is earnest and well-meaning but unoriginal and dull. In the purely narrative parts of the work little is added in the way of imaginative detail to the bare narrative of the New Testament: there are occasional variants, but these are introduced in many cases for the sake of establishing a rhyme; indeed, the search for rhyme frequently leads to the introduction of almost meaningless phrases. Otfrid has considerable importance, however, from the point of view of cultural history, since the way he presents his material provides an example in the vernacular of methods of thought which dominate medieval writing. This is the technique of threefold interpretation, by which an event is first narrated in its own right (the 'historical' sense), and then may be interpreted either as an allegory of the relationship between God and man (sections headed *mystice* and *spiritaliter* in Otfrid), or as a model for human conduct (*moraliter*). For example, the Wise Men, after presenting their gifts to the infant Christ, are told by an angel of the route by which they may reach their homeland. In the two *mystices* which follow this narration Otfrid identifies our *eigan lant* with Paradise, and this world with a place of exile (*elilento*). The Wise Men therefore become an allegory of the faithful; this rather lengthy interpretation moves over imperceptibly (and without acknowledgment) into the mood of *moraliter*, with encouragment to the believer to seek the proper path.

In such remarks Otfrid's dependence on biblical commentaries becomes apparent. His 'historical' account of other events also makes it clear that he was indebted to sources other than the Gospels for some of his information. Thus his account of the Annunciation, much fuller than that in the *Heliand*, and one of the rare places where Otfrid becomes eloquent, describes how the Angel of God

> flew the path of the sun, the road of the stars, the way of the clouds, to the noble woman, to the lady of high birth, to St Mary herself. Her forbears to a man were all kings. He went into the palace, found her sorrowful, with a psalter in her hand: she sang this to an end as she worked her embroidery on fair cloth, a task she always enjoyed. Then he spoke [to her] with great politeness, as one should always address a lady, as a good messenger should speak to the mother of Our Lord.

This brief passage shows the heights and the depths of Otfrid's ability, and it also shows something of his sources. The royal descent of the Virgin Mary has biblical warrant, but the assertion that every one of her ancestors was a king is an exaggeration. That she is to be found in a palace is, of course, a corollary of her birth; but the fact is confirmed by the apocryphal gospel of Pseudo-Matthew, as is the account of her activities—which recur, of course, in pictorial representations of the Annunciation throughout the Middle Ages and after. Gabriel's journey is described with a wealth of variation which would have done credit to a Germanic poet, and indeed *sterrono straza* and *wec wolkono* alliterate in accordance with the strictest principles of native verse. But there are also lapses: the commendation of Gabriel's politeness is a characteristic piece of lameness—one of the numerous phrases meaning 'as was right and proper' in one line, continuing with a barely tolerable mixture of generalization (*any* messenger) and particularization (the mother of Our Lord) in the next.

The object of Otfrid's *Evangelienbuch* is made clear in a German foreword, explaining the author's motives for writing in German, placed after three German dedications and a Latin one addressed to Archbishop Liutpert of Mainz. The Latin passage speaks, perhaps in traditional terms, of the requests of Otfrid's fellow monks and the persuasions of an unidentified patroness who had prompted him to write the work. The way his mind works is shown by his defence of the division of the work into five books, contrasting with the number of four Gospels, on the ground that the errors he wishes to avert enter man by the five senses. It is convention, perhaps, which leads him to deplore and to wish to replace the vernacular poetry (*cantus obscenus*) which assaulted the ears of his brothers. He goes on to say that he wrote in German so that anybody who fought shy of the difficulties of a foreign tongue might know the holy words in his own. Otfrid's motives may, however, emerge more sincerely from the German preface, which expresses national pride in the realization that the Franks have sung of the deeds of their great ancestors, coupled with a sense of injury that they have so far failed to recount the Gospels in the vernacular.

Minor Poems in Rhyming Verse

A salutary contrast with Otfrid's excessively discursive style is provided by the fragmentary *Christus und die Samariterin*, a text composed probably in the early part of the tenth century, in a southern dialect (Alemannic), with rather more northerly (Frankish) features. There are 31 lines before the text breaks off with 'But ye say that prayers are heard in Jerusalem'. To reach this point Otfrid needed twice as much space. After a rather hesitant start the text gives a straightforward account of the situation and continues almost exclusively with dialogue. The woman's naïvely anachronistic remark, 'Christ knows, the Jews do not partake of our fare' contrasts favourably with Otfrid's treatment of the situation: 'St John reveals at this point why she spoke these words truly, why she gave this account and refused to give him to drink: for the two peoples have no foodstuff in common in any way for their eating in one vessel'—four lines for one.

The *Petruslied*, a Bavarian poem of about the same time or slightly earlier, consists of three couplets of accomplished verse each followed by the refrain *Kyrie eleison, Christe eleison.* Such a short poem cannot develop any narrative momentum, and the whole may be regarded as a short hymn expressing a resolve to turn to St Peter for intercession. More interesting as an early and brief example of the Saint's Life is the *Georgslied*. The text (Alemannic, tenth or eleventh century) owes its very corrupt state to the inadequacy of the scribe, who admits his inability to carry on. The text is little more than an elliptical enumeration of miracles, interspersed with refrains, each used more than once, asserting St George's ability to work miracles or his return to life and activity after successive martyrdoms. Perhaps the most accomplished piece of rhyming German verse in this religious group is the Bavarian version of Psalm 138 (late tenth century), which handles the language with complete fluency.

The 'Ludwigslied'

By the end of the ninth century there seems to be little memory of alliterative verse in German, and rhyming verse takes over a function that had been associated with alliteration—the celebration of great events. There is one such poem written in competent rhyming verse which may be dated within a year: this is the *Ludwigslied*, written to commemorate the Battle of Saucourt (881) within the lifetime of the victor, Ludwig—or rather Louis—III of what was to become France. The poem includes the prayer 'Long may he reign!'; but within the year Ludwig was dead. The poem follows so closely upon the events it describes that there can be no question of recasting history into legendary form, as happened with heroic literature. Perhaps because memory of the event was so fresh in the minds of the first listeners, the poem can afford to be vague about the details of the battle: there is certainly no indication of the tactical advantage secured by the Franks by the use of cavalry, an arm which the invading Northmen had not yet encountered. The battle itself is described in very general terms, saying very little more than that in the excitement of battle, blood suffused the cheeks of the Franks, and that none fought so bravely as Ludwig—'some he cut through, some he thrust through'. A sober historical introduction describing the division of the kingdom at the death of Ludwig II between the hero and his brother Karlmann precedes an interpretation of the Danish invasion as the hand of God punishing the sins of the Franks. Thanks for the victory are given to God and the saints. This treatment of divine intervention on the side of the fundamentally good Franks is basically in the spirit of the Old Testament. Perhaps there is a trace of acclimatization to Germanic legend-making in this poem in the presentation of Ludwig as the somewhat pathetic figure of an orphan, though he is compensated by divine adoption. The expression used for the incursion of the Danes—*obar seo lidan*—draws on the Germanic heroic vocabulary, but such features are no more than superficial, and the general tone of the poem remains firmly Christian and patriotic. It is not a poem which shows great insight into a human predicament, as does the *Hildebrandslied* or for that matter the comparably historical Old English *Battle of Maldon*, if only because tragic situations lend themselves most convincingly to literary treatment.

The *Ludwigslied* certainly excels in merit another Old High German poem of historical content, the macaronic *De Heinrico*, probably recording the reconciliation of Otto the Great with his younger brother Heinrich after an act of rebellion (941). Little of the history appears in the poem, which appears to put a very diplomatic light over the whole incident.

Notker der Deutsche

The large volume of prose left by Notker III of St Gall (d. 1022) is less directly concerned with conversion than earlier Old High German prose writings had been. Most of his works are couched in a mixture of Latin and German. In some the phrases alternate in the two languages, so that both Latin and German are necessary to convey the sense of a passage; in one (*De musica*) the German appears to be a gloss of Latin constructions or of unfamiliar words. There are also some works written entirely in Latin, and others entirely in German. The works translated include two of the key books of the Middle Ages, Boethius' *De Consolatione Philosophiae* and Martianus Capella's *De nuptiis Martis et Philologiae*—the neo-Platonic contemplations of Boethius being amenable enough to Christian interpretation for the *Consolatio* to be translated into several European vernaculars during the Middle Ages and afterwards. Capella's work is very different in tone; it is a compendium of the Seven Liberal Arts, the storehouse of knowledge as it was divided up in the Middle Ages, but treated in a style too involved and allegorical for *De nuptiis* to exist as a mere textbook. Notker translated only the first two books. His other work in the same field includes translations from Boethius' Latin of Aristotle's *Categories* and *De Interpretatione*, both textbooks of logic. Some of the Latin works are also devoted to the Liberal Arts. Notker was, however, not solely concerned with making the basis of knowledge more accessible; he was also active with more directly edifying works, such as a commented translation of the Psalms. The method he uses is to translate each Latin phrase first literally, then if necessary more idiomatically, before giving a partly allegorical interpretation of the passage. The procedure is characteristic of medieval thought, particularly of early medieval thought. The interposition of a more idiomatic translation after the literal one may be seen as a concern for the expressive qualities of German, but even Notker's prose hardly qualifies for consideration as original literature.

The remainder of what is preserved in prose is also not to be included even in the most generous classification of original literature: glosses of single words, marginal and interlinear, a translation of the Rule of St Benedict, the record of place-names in Latin texts. One text deserves mention as a curiosity; a phrasebook of the tenth century, designed as a guide to German for speakers of a Romance language, in the form of a series of dialogues, which can on occasion be mildly amusing, once the barbarous form of the spelling has been mastered by reference to the Latin text which accompanies it.

Latin Literature of the Old High German Period

In quantity and competence, Old High German vernacular literature was outstripped by writings in Latin by German authors. There are several short texts (*modi*) which recount a brief anecdote and have a tenuous association with religion in that they were used as mnemonics for the melismata or *modi* which developed on the final *a* of *Alleluja* sung in the course of the Mass. These short texts, however, are of small importance beside three major narrative works, all of them significant as manifestations of trends met in later German literature. *Waltharius*, formerly ascribed to Ekkehard I of St Gall (about 930) with revision by Ekkehard IV about a century later, but now considered on stylistic grounds to be a later work, is of special interest because it preserves a heroic Germanic story otherwise known fragmentarily and by allusion in Middle High German and from a fragment in Old English. The story concerns the exploits of Walther of Acquitaine escaping from exile with Hildegunde, and beset in a defile by Gunther and his vassals, of whom the principal one is called Hagen. Hagen has ties of friendship with Walther, and stays out of the fighting as long as possible. In the final three-cornered fight Gunther, Hagen and Walther are all seriously wounded before they achieve a reconciliation. This happy outcome is taken to be secondary, a weakening from the tragic situation implicit in Hagen's choice of loyalties.

If *Waltharius* is a heroic epic *manqué*, *Ecbasis cuiusdam captivi per tropologiam* has been described as the first beast epic. The fable, ascribed from geographical references to a monk from the Luxembourg region (Toul, perhaps) and formerly dated to the tenth century, has now, with greater stylistic probability, been fitted to events in the thirties of the next century. *Ecbasis captivi* gives an outer story (*Rahmenerzählung*) of the escape of a calf and his reception by a wolf, and an inner narrative where the wolf recounts the story of his antagonism to the fox. In the story the allegory of the animal kingdom is worked out in detail, the ascription of feudal (and sometimes clerical) offices to various beasts being at times rather puzzling. The outer fable is the more original part, being an allegory (the *tropologia* of the subtitle) apparently of the escape of a cloistered monk into the wicked world, and of the prodigal's safe return. But any reference outside the animal world of the ostensible action has to be inferred: the story appears to be told in its own right, and even the telling of it is rather obscure in places.

The third of these texts, *Ruodlieb*, is unfortunately fragmentary, and appears never to have been completed. This is a story of individual adventure, and as such may be seen as an antecedent of the romance. The hero sets out, provided by his patron with good advice; the way this advice is acted upon is the matter of this, as of many other later medieval tales.

With these texts, the sum of Latin narrative in the Old High German period is by no means made up. There were also chronicles and biographies, to some of which we are indebted for knowledge of literary works which have since been lost; and apart from purely narrative works, there are also, in the second half of the tenth century, what are sometimes called the beginnings of dramatic writing by Roswitha von Gandersheim. Her avowed aim was to provide edifying texts to replace the reading of Terence in convents. The plays are very brief, with scant respect for the unities: great distances and long times intervene between successive scenes, but have to be accepted to explain developments in the action. The technique is to choose picturesque episodes in the chain of events which make up the plot rather than to concentrate on the moments of crisis. There is no real development or even portrayal of character—the plays are a direct confrontation of evil and virtue, and present a naïve steadfastness in the face of adversity, torture and death on the part of the heroines. That the same heroines should miraculously be unscathed by torture and yet succumb to execution is the kind of inconsistency which would occur in any saint's legend. What the plays have to offer is a genuine sense of situation, and an astonishing realism and practicality in the counsels of the characters, who are not afraid to temporize in a good cause. It is hard to envisage the circumstances in which these plays could have been staged, and doubtful whether they would be effective, though productions have been undertaken in the twentieth century with some success.

II

EARLY MIDDLE HIGH GERMAN LITERATURE

Didacticism—Allegory—Asceticism

There is still an interval of a hundred years or so between Notker and the beginnings of what is rightly acknowledged to be the great age of medieval German literature; but the early Middle High German age is interesting in that it brings to light characteristic processes of thought which endure in the classical age of Middle High German in the thirteenth century, and often colour works which may seem on first inspection to demand little preliminary adjustment on the part of the modern reader.

The language did not change overnight or uniformly from Old High German to Middle High German; hence there is some measure of overlap in the stage of the language to which certain marginal texts are allotted. A classification according to the temper of the texts is unlikely to be a great deal more successful, yet the literature of the eleventh and twelfth centuries has been most frequently categorized as being the literature of the mortification of the flesh, of other-worldliness, of the mood associated with monastic reforms which emanated from tenth-century Cluny or with the phrase *memento mori*. However, the expression of a sense of doom is not confined to the eleventh and twelfth centuries: comparable phenomena appear in times of natural disaster or national confusion, and by no means all of the texts of the eleventh and twelfth centuries can simply be written off as expressing the mood of *Weltflucht*.

In the eleventh and twelfth centuries there is, in the first place, a continuation of didactic and edifying literature, though there is not the same close reference to classical sources as there had been in, say, Notker. Instead there is reliance on hearsay and traditional knowledge—and it is just such a store of now forgotten beliefs and lore that makes the earlier Middle High German period such a valuable source for knowledge of later medieval times.

A text like *Merigarto* (eleventh–twelfth century) is insignificant as literature. It contains snippets of knowledge from various spheres, mainly geographical, with no apparent effort at arrangement. The text gives, *inter alia*, a tall story about the *lebirmere*, a stretch of water so glutinous that ships stick fast in it, which has some significance later on as the setting for one of the adventures of Herzog Ernst. The text is short; there is no evidence of originality, though the palpably untrue must have been invented at some time.

A more important text, derived from a second-century Hellenistic Greek source, part factual, but largely legendary, is the *Physiologus*, familiar in other languages besides German, and preserved there in three versions, of which the last is in verse. All the German versions, the earliest of them dated to the second half of the eleventh century, are traceable to a single source. The eleventh-century text deals with some twelve of the 27 beasts of whom the Bestiaries report. Information is given about beasts such as lions and panthers, elephants and sawfish, which would be known to a medieval German only through literary reference. The method employed with each animal is the same: first the name is given, then its real (or imagined) qualities are listed; after this comes the specifically medieval element, the allegorical interpretation, which sees for example a prefiguration of Adam in the alleged mating habits of the elephant. Most of the allegories refer to Christ, the soul of the Christian, or the devil. Some of the observation is ingenious, e.g. the brush at the end of the lion's tail used to obliterate his track: 'even so did Our Lord obscure his divine origin by taking on human shape'. Sometimes function and fantasy are inextricably blended, as with the hedgehog (in the later text) loading his spines with ripe grapes, having first climbed into the vines and shaken down the fruit. The allegory may be fragmented: a characteristic is given an *ad hoc* value, e.g. the viper is a prototype of Jewry because of the expression 'generation of vipers', but the author checks himself in time to recall that Christians are enjoined to be as cunning as serpents. Allegory is used both as prefiguration, and by extension, as an edifying example. In this way the bestiaries continue the methods first met in German in Otfrid, and one which persists with greater or less prominence throughout medieval literature.

The biblical text which above all others came in for allegorical treatment was the Song of Songs. The historical books of the Old Testament could clearly be understood historically and allegorically, but the Song of Songs presents great difficulties—where is its 'historical' level? It is a poem of considerable merit, but its literal meaning is largely ignored in medieval discussion of the poem. Allegorical treatment of the Song of Songs was not peculiar to early medieval German; most of what was written in German was copied or adapted from Latin sources, but this again shows the continuity of the allegorical method. Two distinctive types of interpretation may be traced, both similar in method, and both represented in early Middle High German. The earlier of these texts is that of Williram, from internal evidence datable to 1065. The manuscripts give a Vulgate text, with a Latin commentary in leonine hexameters together with a German version in prose. The popularity of the work is attested by numerous early Middle High German manuscripts, but there are also much later ones, and there is even a sixteenth-century print of the Latin text. Basically this interpretation views the Song of Songs as a dialogue between Christ and the Church, in the guise of lover and bride.

While Williram's text of his Latin source enjoyed protracted familiarity in the Middle Ages, there was, a century after his time, another vernacular interpretation, which is more individualized, if not entirely self-consistent. In an early passage the allegory of spiritual marriage is applied to the Virgin Mary:

> We have spoken of a bridegroom who kisses and of a bride who is kissed; but the kissing of the two is Christ who came from the Most High and took on flesh and blood from the most lowly.

Elsewhere, the feelings of the individual believer most characteristically come to the fore:

> This kissing does not press together the lips of the body but the wills of the spirit. This embracing is not that of enfolding arms, but of holy thoughts, with which one embraces God at all times.

The 'individual' interpretation of the Song of Songs as an allegory of the aspiration of the soul to God survived, if anything, more vigorously than the early one. Allegorical method is also used in several smaller verse texts of the time, not necessarily derived from Holy Writ or sacred lore, but finding in such objects as precious stones expressions of the relationship of man to God.

As a further example of the continuity of the technique of prefiguration, a short passage from the *Summa Theologiae* may be cited. This poem, like many others of its time, is preserved in a celebrated manuscript from Vorau. The essentials of religion are the fall of man as recounted in Genesis and his redemption as represented in the Gospels. In the account of the creation we read that 'God intended to adorn mankind with the four elements: he gave him precious sight from fire, from the upper air the ability to hear, from the lower the sense of smell, taste from water: the motions of the hands and feet he assigned to him from the earth'. The accommodation of the four elements to the five senses is an example of the way in which approximations are fitted to the allegory, and may be compared with Otfrid's remarks on the four Gospels and the five senses, not as a derivative of those remarks, but as an instance of continuity of method.

The same selection of basic religion informs *Ezzos Gesang*, datable from the author's reference to Bishop Gunther of

Babenberg to about 1060. Here the contrast between Fall and Redemption is made explicit in a detailed treatment of Jesus as the 'second Adam'. The treatment of the creation is so full that the poem has sometimes been called an *Älteres Anegenge*, anticipating the title of a much lengthier compilation concerned with the creation, the Trinity and the redemption of mankind.

Concern with the fall of Adam and the need for redemption is, of course, to be associated with that other strand of early medieval German culture which is given such prominence in accounts of the literature of the time. The text known as *Memento mori* is of about the same age as *Ezzos Gesang*, and the two works may have been associated. The content of the texts may at some points be compared with that of the allegorical poems already discussed, e.g.:

> That man is by no means wise who makes a journey and sits down to rest under a tree he finds by the wayside. When sleep overcomes him he forgets where he is bound for, and when he leaps up again, how bitterly he regrets. All of you typify that man . . .

The difference here is that the allegory is created for the purpose instead of being derived from Holy Writ, i.e. it is an independent parable; but the method is clearly ingrained. It is, after all, the method of the homily, and there are other respects in which this poem bears the mark of the sermon. It is full of addresses to the reader, exclamations and antitheses; it owes much of its effect to a detailed portrayal of the horrors to come. These are familiar rhetorical devices, not confined to sermons and spoken contexts, and especially characteristic at this time of the call to repentance expressed in poems of this kind. The *Sündenklage*, in the Vorau manuscript, is one of these. It begins with an invocation to the Virgin Mary which exploits many of the images and emblems associated with her in *Mariendichtung*, and continues with expressions of repentance and dejection. The method is not the enumeration of the sins by which the suppliant has offended against God, but a series of appeals to biblical promises and examples of forgiveness. The call to repentance is also expressed in Der arme Hartmann's *Vom Glauben* (early twelfth century), and more expressively in the two extensive poems of Heinrich von Melk (c. 1160), *Von des tôdes gehugede* (or *Die Erinnerung an den Tod*) and *Das Priesterleben*. Here the theme of the transitoriness of life and the inevitable corruption of the flesh is reinforced by a deep consciousness of the sinfulness of human existence. There is only one late manuscript of the poems, which have been dated from the evidence of biographical details at the end of *Von des tôdes gehugede*, the second part of which is associated in content, perhaps also in diction, with the *Memento mori*: successive sections deal with the misery of life in general, insecurity in high places, the horror of physical decomposition conveyed by detailed description, and the horrors of Purgatory suffered by father for son, preceded by further gruesome accounts of the corruption of the flesh. The first part is an attack on the failings of mankind, starting with the clergy, whose offences are lust, venality and gluttony, continuing with monks given over to vanity before going on to the shortcomings of laymen: judges who are unjust; knights extravagant and lewd, boastful of their amorous conquests; women vain and worldly; all are attacked with a puritanical zeal which runs throughout the text. What appears to be an allusion to a fashionable development in the manners and literature of the time is probably one of the safest guides to the date of the poem. This is in the passage where a lady is bidden to open her lover's grave:

> Now see where are his idle words with which he described and praised the vanity (*hôhvart*) of women. Now see how his tongue lies in his mouth, with which he could sing love songs with such assurance. Now he can utter neither words nor melody.

The word for 'love songs' is *troutliet*, incorporating a term for the beloved which would have been impossibly unfashionable in aristocratic circles by the end of the twelfth century, but might be acceptable nearer the middle. Significantly enough, a new movement in lyric poetry, specifically conditioned by the practices and attitudes of courtly love (*minne*) began to emerge at about the early date postulated for Heinrich von Melk, and, perhaps significantly, in Austria. If the text is much later than 1160, the term may perhaps be considered to be an attempt to reduce the importance of a literary vogue by referring to it in terms which its practitioners would deprecate. There is perhaps some support for the early date, too, in the inclusion of fornication in the catalogue of crimes committed by the clergy and the return to this theme in the other poem, *Vom Priesterleben*, for celibacy was a relatively late requirement.

The language of these texts is a little clumsy, but the general arrangement is very accomplished, as is the direct appeal to an audience, the occasional excursion into a near-dramatic style, with successive speeches comprehensible only as interlocution; such passages imply a dependence on a tradition of oral performance which would classify this text as some kind of sermon, though the normal language of pulpit oratory is prose. There are, indeed, a few sermons in the vernacular preserved from the twelfth century, which besides being composed in prose are far less impassioned than the rhetoric of Heinrich von Melk.

The Vorau *Sündenklage* already mentioned might be described as an amalgam of two tendencies in early Middle High German literature—penitence expressed in extreme terms, and the plea for intercession to the Virgin Mary. This plea is associated with imagery derived from the Song of Songs and other sources, which informs a group of poems collectively known as *Mariendichtung*, which are among the most notable products of early Middle High German. The cult of the Virgin Mary had begun in the early years of Christianity: by the middle of the twelfth century she had become the principal intercessor; an extension of the cult was likely in such a sin-conscious age. Growing activity is evidenced in St Peter Damian's writings in the eleventh century, and notably in those of St Bernard of Clairvaux in the twelfth; his writings and views were more likely to be known and spread in Germany as the Cistercians took a very strong hold there.

The earlier German texts might be said to be an expansion of the last lines of the *Ave*, i.e. an enumeration of qualities, followed by the plea for intercession. The so-called *Litanei*, like the Vorau *Sündenklage*, is based on an urgent consciousness of the need for forgiveness:

> O daughter of David, way of eternal life, the end of error, the resurrection from death, living fountain from which flows the stream of all mercy, root of all goodness, from whom blossomed the branch which has spread far and wide and extended boughs from earth through heaven and thence back again through the inner abyss; Lady, bid thy son graciously to release me from the bonds of my sin. For thou canst do both: command as a mother commands her son, and yet thou shalt pray to him and honour him as a sweetly-disposed handmaiden her master [*sam diu suozze diu ir herren*] that he may remember all things which he accomplished through thee for the sake of sinners.

This passage exemplifies the two tendencies—fervent prayer and the accumulation of epithets. Almost all such epithets are derivable from the Old Testament prophets and the Song of Songs, but there is one which recurs very often, and in fact occurs at the beginning of the well-known Latin hymn *Ave maris stella*, familiar enough to be cited without translation as the first line of a sequence from St Lamprecht (1150–60), and which appears to rest on a patristic false etymology of the name *Maria*. The stanzaic poem from Melk (c. 1140), each stanza ending with the refrain 'Sancta Maria' is perhaps the most exhaustive repository of epithets in early *Mariendichtung*. Most of these epithets are explained: there is also detailed explanation of Mary as an anti-Eve, based in part on the kind of reasoning which saw Jesus as an anti-Adam, and partly on the simple reversal of the three letters of *Eva* into *Ave*. The general spirit of this poem and of the others in this genre is one of rapt contemplation; the imagery is at once luxuriant and still familiar. It is clear that as a literary form, this type of poem is thoroughly static and could easily become stereotyped. Once the epithets have been set down there is virtually no scope for variety. For this reason, perhaps, the genre does not develop, but it is important to note that it does not end with the twelfth century. Well into the thirteenth century, for example, Konrad von Würzburg's *Goldene Schmiede* is every bit as static as the Melk *Marienlied*—and much longer. For a further instance of the survival of the tradition, one has to look no further than to Walther von der Vogelweide's *Leich*. In time, Walther is close to the earlier *Marienlieder*; in the seriousness with which he in this and in other poems castigates the shortcomings of his contemporaries he has some kinship with the more austere writers of the twelfth century, and yet he was writing for a different world, and had lived through a literary efflorescence which appeared, on the surface at least, to have thrown off clerical domination for the worldly ideals of chivalry and courtly love. By giving expression as he does to such 'unseasonable' thoughts, Walther demonstrates that the mood of the twelfth century was no passing feature, but rather was a characteristic form of medieval expression.

Religious Narrative in the Twelfth Century

Mariendichtung has its counterpart in narrative poetry in the treatment of biblical and devotional stories. In view of the concern with the creation of mankind and the fall of Adam as a prerequisite for Jesus and redemption, it is not perhaps suprising that the books of the Old Testament came in for poetic paraphrase. The early books were versified, and the vernacular text was worked over more than once; a version in the great Vorau manuscript is dependent in some measure on earlier ones (the so-called *Wiener Genesis*). Other Old Testament subject matter which found its way into German verse is the song in praise of Solomon (*Lob Salomos*), two versions of the story of Judith and that of the three youths in the furnace (all in the Vorau manuscript). The last texts are different in that they have the limited objective of recounting one incident: they correspond to a short story rather than to history in verse, and are representative not only of continued interest in biblical narrative, but also of the large number of legends which were written down at this time. The subject matter of these is not only biblical and apocryphal, but also recounts the lives of saints of post-biblical times, and also of other historical figures.

There were some Latin legends in the Old High German period, including a set of Saint's Lives by Roswitha; but the *Georgslied* is unparalleled, and it is not until the twelfth century that vernacular writings in this genre start. Not all were written by clerics, and there is, e.g., an early work by Heinrich von Veldeke on Servatius. This, like the legends of Aegidius (i.e. St Giles) and Albanus, is an indication that interest was not confined to the most prominent saints; Saints' Lives, indeed, are often the expression of a local cult. 'Legendary' material, in a more familiar meaning of the term, tends to creep in. For an example of this we may look outside the early Middle High German period to Hartmann von Aue's *Gregorius* from the golden age, where the life of a saint has become entangled with the Oedipus myth.

The technique of the legend may be exemplified as well as anywhere in Priester Wernher's *Driu Liet von der Maget*, a set of poems providing a continuous narrative, but interrupted by meditative passages which in spirit recall the more lyrical *Mariendichtung*. The author gives as his source St Matthew as translated by St Jerome, names himself and dates the poem 1172. The Gospel of St Matthew is very concise about the nativity and has nothing about the ancestry of the Virgin Mary; the real source of this work is Pseudo-Matthew, *Liber de ortu Beatae Mariae et Infantia Salvatoris*, i.e. one of the 'infancy gospels' of the Apocryphal New Testament. The German text is in two differing recensions, presumably representing revision by the author, with some lines at the end which appear to be the work of a medieval 'editor'. The differences are enough to make a synoptic edition difficult or even impossible, but are not in fact substantial enough to make the versions seem materially different from one another. The apocryphal gospel traces the Virgin Mary's descent from a line of kings, and recounts her infancy and dedication in the temple, the miracle by which she was betrothed to Joseph, and the Nativity, more or less as in the authentic gospels, continuing afterwards with more details of the flight into Egypt than are given in the canon books. The Latin text is as spare as that of the authentic gospels; the German version seizes upon every opportunity to insert visual detail, movement and motive, expressed either as an explanation of actions or as thoughts preceding actions, the result of which is to give the work a continuity which anticipates the works of the next generation.

In managing the larger units Priester Wernher shows himself to be a man of education; in manipulating his own language he is less adept. To see what could be done in the way of dressing up pseudo-biblical narrative in vernacular medieval dress, a comparison should be made with such a work as Konrad von Fussesbrunnen's *Kindheit Jesu* in the next generation; the humanizing tendency is confirmed and extended—speech ranges from everyday phrases to soliloquy, and motives are fully explained. But that is a text of the *Blütezeit*, and Konrad's German has been shown to owe some of its qualities to Hartmann von Aue. But even Priester Wernher, a generation ahead of this, shows an astonishing feeling for situation, and it is likely that he would have been better known in the next generation if another literary fashion had not intervened. Lives of other saints, including post-biblical ones, are preserved in the so-called 'vision literature'—legends of Paul, Patrick, Brandan, Tnugdal.

The twelfth century treated world history in much the same way as it treated biblical history. As a parallel to the drastic abridgements of *Summa theologiae* and *Ezzos Gesang* one might cite the *Annolied*, which indeed celebrates Archbishop Anno of Cologne, the tutor of the emperor Henry IV.

This is based on a Latin *Vita*, and may be regarded as of a piece with the legend, but it is in one respect different, in that the preface to the biographical part is taken up with the 'legendary' (in the modern sense) history of the German people and their dealings with the Romans. The account of Anno was incorporated also into the *Kaiserchronik*, a compilation which again shows the view of history as a series of legends developed round the persons of the Roman emperors and German kings. Indeed, several secular legends are recounted in this large work which might be considered as independent texts in their own right. Although this is worldly history, even here events are seen from the point of view of the church. The *Kaiserchronik* shows a keen interest in early Christian history—in the destruction and rebuilding of Jerusalem, the conversion of Rome, stories of martyrs; there is also a tone of didacticism running through the work relating it in some way with the religious writings of clerical authors.

III

THE HOHENSTAUFEN ERA AND THE RISE OF SECULAR LITERATURE

Introduction

In the twelfth century, as for long after, the distribution of power in Germany continued to be unstable. The last of the Salians, Heinrich V, had succeeded in reasserting the right of the king to endow bishops with royal grants of land, and ensured a control of these areas which contrasted with the uncertain loyalties of the inherited duchies and greater nobility. The duchies were still separate, and their separation was reinforced by their several codes of law as well as by linguistic differences; and it became a recurrent feature of a royal election that a relatively weak ruler was chosen. On these grounds the Hohenstaufen, with extensive lands in Swabia, were themselves passed over in favour of the duke of Saxony, but Konrad III was elected in 1138 as the relatively weaker candidate. Konrad's successor, Friedrich I (Barbarossa), had Guelph as well as Hohenstaufen blood, and hoped to bring about some kind of settlement in Germany, but did so only by yielding direct rule in Bavaria to a restored duchy, and enhancing the standing of Austria. In the meantime, to the north, the Saxons were gaining in prestige and power, thanks largely to expansion in the east, and the existence there of large unfragmented territories. The Empire, too, had some eastern territories, but the main area of imperial expansion under Barbarossa was in the south, in Italy, where an attempt was made to reestablish rights in the kingdom of Lombardy. In the administration of Italy the imperial *ministeriales* were active, and this originally landless but educated class of dependents became more and more associated with the lower aristocracy, and with the central interests of the king emperor. The hereditary duchies continued to be unreliable; the refusal of Henry the Lion (Saxon) to provide help in Italy brought about setbacks there, but as a result Barbarossa turned against him and in overcoming him, established his authority over the independent territorial nobility. But the stability of the kingdom was not to last for long. Heinrich VI took over the kingdom at a time of strength, but ruled for only seven years before dying on his way to take part in the 1197 Crusade. His son, accepted beforehand as king by the German nobility, was only three years old. Once again dissension broke out; not only was an anti-king set up in rivalry to the regent (later King Philip), but the Pope intervened, as his territorial interests in Italy conflicted with those of the Hohenstaufen. The next fifteen years or so were a time of confusion in Germany, with great expense of resources in civil strife, and extravagant gifts of property and land to gain support on one side and the other. Even after Friedrich II had been accepted as king, there was little internal peace. He was concerned more with his Italian possessions than with Germany, and spent little time there. He sought to gain support from the clergy by making further concessions to the church, including wider powers of jurisdiction, which as one effect enhanced the status of the cities. For much of the time Germany was administered by Engelbert, Archbishop of Cologne, the tutor of Friedrich's son Heinrich, who was himself given charge of Germany as king in 1228. Friedrich's policy of consolidation led him to offer to temporal rulers the same kind of privileges that had already gone to the church; this aroused discontent among the lesser nobility, with whom Heinrich identified himself. The dispute could only be settled by warfare, the immediate result of which was the deposition of Heinrich and the establishment of the *Landfrieden*, which sought to limit feuds. Stability did not last long, however. Further difficulties in Italy made it possible for a northern group of princes, including some of the Rhenish archbishops, to elect an anti-king, who continued to find support until after Friedrich's death and the succession of the last Hohenstaufen, Konrad IV.

Such times hardly seem the most favourable for the development of a great culture or its expression in literature. Yet the two generations from about 1170 to about 1230 saw the production of Germany's great and distinctive contributions to the literature of chivalry. From time to time, notably in the political poems of Walther von der Vogelweide, a glimpse of events in the historical world may be seen, though the method is one of allusion rather than of record. In other respects, what must have been an age of active soldiering for a great deal of the time for many of the likely patrons of the arts succeeded in idealizing the life of the time in an elaborate code of chivalrous conduct. It was probably no accident in the establishment of these ideals that the first chivalrous orders had been religious ones; indeed, they had come into being out of the experiences of the first Crusade; the Crusades had exposed European knights to other ways of life, and opened their eyes to strange objects. Something of the wonder of the east informs the literature which was written immediately before the great age of medieval German. The knight, individually responsible according to the requirements of military service for his own mount and his own arms, becomes the individual hero of fantastic adventures in the later development of the romance. In the practice of arms and in the practice of letters France showed the way, and Barbarossa's court festival at Mainz in 1184 seems to have introduced to Germany the latest refinements of chivalry and the fantasy world of Arthurian adventure which the French had adopted from Celtic sources. The cult of courtly love appears to have entered Germany at the same time and by the same route. While it is possible to see in the heroes of romance a distantly idealized portrayal of the knight of the day, the origin of the pose of abject devotion assumed by the lyric poets is harder to trace, and indeed, the origin of Minnesang is one of the most hotly and inconclusively contended fields of medieval scholarship.

As it is expressed by its most advanced practitioners, *minne* is a source of refinement no less than is chivalry itself, and it is noticeable that in poetry the lady is treated with a deference which corresponded to that accorded otherwise to a liege lord.

The presence or absence of the attitudes of courtly love is often taken as a touchstone of the sophistication of narrative literature of the early Middle High German period. There do appear to be some slight gestures in this direction in two German adaptations from the French well before the true courtly era—the *Alexanderlied* and the *Rolandslied*. It might also be urged that the interest, in the unsophisticated *Spielmannsepos* of the sixties and seventies, in the hero's winning a bride is an attempt to render in German something which had been dimly perceived in a foreign model and misunderstood—service taken as a means to a very obvious end, and this end in itself power rather than affection.

Narrative Literature in Clerical Hands

The longer clerical narrative texts of the twelfth century form a bridge to the more worldly literature which began to gain ground from the middle of the century onwards. The matter of the *Alexanderlied* was international, but the immediate source of the twelfth-century German account was a French text, as good an indication as any that times were changing. There is an incomplete version, rounded off with a makeshift conclusion, in the Vorau manuscript; a fuller version, from a Strassburg manuscript of about 1170 (now lost), completes the story and is more fluent in the passages common to both. The beginning of the early text, by Pfaffe Lamprecht, is marked by an expression of the vanity of the world; to this frame of mind the conclusion of the Strassburg version returns with the failure of Alexander to storm heaven and a parable to illustrate the vanity of human ambition. In between there lies a new world of military exploits in exotic settings. The Strassburg *Alexanderlied*, like *Merigarto*, shows open-eyed admiration for the marvellous, for example, a musical automaton composed of life-sized models of birds sitting on the branches of a naturalistic tree. In the episode given over to the dealings of Alexander with Queen Candacis there is some dawning of a feeling for personal relationships between man and woman—the beginnings of courtly or romantic love. As in the Latin source of the episode, the *Historia*, Candacis is enabled to recognize Alexander from a secretly drawn portrait; but it is left to the vernaculars, German certainly, and probably the immediate French source, not available at this point, to conclude the episode with a few sentences in which 'the good lady bade me comfort her and to come back and to take from her the terrible pain that she would suffer on my account'.

In a way the *Rolandslied* makes fewer concessions to the spirit of a new age than does the *Alexanderslied*. The date of the *Rolandslied* has been disputed, depending on the identification of the Heinrich to whom it is dedicated. The content is related to that of part of the *Kaiserchronik*, and the two texts are attributed to the same author, but recent views tend to accept a late dating (about 1170) with a strangely archaizing style. Although Charlemagne was the founder of the medieval German kingdom and empire, he has never seized the popular German imagination as strongly as Theodoric before him or Barbarossa after him, though to be sure there is a thirteenth-century verse biography by Der Stricker and a fourteenth-century collection of legends under the title of *Karlmeinet*. In the early German version the interest shifts from patriotic war to holy war: the speeches and actions of Turpin owe much to the spirit of the Crusades. The tragic ending is similar to that of the source, and one which commended itself to a clerical author—signs from heaven at the deaths of the heroes. The death from grief of Oliver's sister Alda, betrothed to Roland, has been taken to presage the new sentimentalism which was creeping into literature at about this time, but there is little enough in language, and less in situation than there is in the *Alexanderlied*, to suggest courtly love.

The 'Spielmannsepos'

The twelfth century sees the beginnings of courtly narrative poems, which indeed reached their classical expression in Hartmann von Aue before the turn of the century. Before the growth of a courtly literature, some rather more popular tales were composed, and since these may in some cases be traced back to historical persons of considerably earlier date, it may be assumed that secular stories survived by oral tradition. Several poems of this type, the so-called *Spielmannsepen*, are preserved; mostly of modest quality, but at their best fast moving and rich in situation and incident. One common feature of these texts is their anonymity. The term *Spielmann* used in the designation of these texts is conveniently rendered 'minstrel', so long as it is remembered that it is used as a general term for itinerant entertainers (*mimes* and *joculatores*; pipers, drummers, jugglers and acrobats) of low social status, and not of the aristocratic lyric poet.

Spielmannsepen are commonly characterized by reference to their content, a superficial but reasonably effective criterion. The plot is mostly concerned with the winning of a bride for a potentate by a faithful retainer, who frequently is, or disguises himself as, a *Spielmann*. Ends are achieved by the use of cunning rather than by valour. It frequently happens that a serious situation from which mother wit saves the hero makes such an effective scene that it is allowed to recur. The texts are a product of their time in so far as the Crusades had opened European eyes to an exotic world in the Near East; there is certainly much to-ing and fro-ing across the Mediterranean in these stories, but the background is not exploited for realism or atmosphere; it is a generally fantastic part of the world where anything may happen, just as anything may happen in the more highly sophisticated Arthurian romance in the Forest of Broceliande.

The texts cover a fairly wide range of time, but do not show any firm line of development; indeed, what must be one of the latest is also one of the simplest. This is *Orendel*. The eponymous hero is a son of a king of Trier, who acquires a *grâwer roc*, the handiwork of the Virgin Mary, and the unseamed garment for which the soldiers cast lots; the poem is to be associated with the establishment of the veneration of the relic at Trier in 1197. In subject-matter the text appears at first sight to be more in keeping with Saints' Lives, but much of it is a worldly story: divine intervention is more or less taken for granted, and there is no account, as there is in Saints' Lives, of the miracles wrought by the hero. A rather better text is the *Oswald*, also assimilable to Saints' Lives in that the hero is St Oswald of Northumbria, but the adventures with which he is accredited have nothing to do with fact, and are completely worldly. Some of the irrelevant episodes suggest direct reference to *Orendel*. *Salomon und Markolf* is a longer text, but it seems to have been the earliest of these primitive *Spielmannsepen*. The central character is based on popular anecdotes connected in the Middle Ages with the name of Solomon, who does not live up to his usual reputation for wisdom. The text has no importance as literature, but it is significant as indicating the spread of the medieval reputation of Solomon (along with Virgil and Aristotle) as a *Minnenarr*.

The best of the *Spielmannsepen* is undoubtedly *König Rother*. Beneath the characteristic *Brautwerbung* action of the genre there appears to be a layer of something more valuable, and the narrative is recounted with a spaciousness that bears comparison with the earlier romances. Historical associations of Rother tend these days to be discounted, presumably because the content of the poem is too trivial to have been handed down by a long oral tradition. The popular revivalist religious fervour towards the end of the poem shows little originality, and the general level of conduct is all too much like that in the general run of *Spielmannsepen*, as is the virtual repetition in the second part of incidents from the first. Although Rother wins the affection of the daughter of King Constantine after a rather attractive, though not very passionate love-scene (involving the fitting of shoes), and though he serves her father well, he has to steal her away.

The second part of the text deals with her recapture by a ruse, and a second expedition to Constantinople in which Rother is captured, condemned and rescued. What might be taken to be the invention of a *Spielmann*, the crass scene where the giant Asprian dashes a lion to death against the wall of Constantine's hall for stealing food from him, may in fact have a historical nucleus. There is also a certain spaciousness about this scene, which argues that the *Spielleute* were able to vary the pace by careful description of settings, and to make actions seem more plausible by the insertion of dialogue.

It is perhaps convenient at this point to look at another text which had a considerable popularity in the Middle Ages, which indeed shows in the best preserved version some of the qualities of a later age—*Herzog Ernst*. The hero is a much better-known figure than Rother, and he is brought into contact at several points with medieval lore. It was he, for example, who snatched from the roof of an underground waterway while he was passing through on a raft the stone which was known as the *weise* (*Waise*, 'orphan'), which formed the most notable adornment of the Imperial crown, and comes to our notice again when it is mentioned in Walther von der Vogelweide's political poems. Another adventure brings Ernst's fleet into the *lebirmere*, reinforcing the suggestion that part of the background to this text is the fantastic geography of the Middle Ages. But this is not all; it is above all an adventure story, and the adventures are set among such creatures as the crane-folk and the Arimaspi who populate fantastic travellers' tales from late Greek times to Sir John Mandeville and later still. As is to be expected for the discoverer of a royal jewel, an attempt is made to link Herzog Ernst to a historical personage, and indeed, he appears to be conflation of two, or even three, historical figures. Two of them were rebels with no justification, but the Ernst of the story is sent into exile as the result of a conspiracy against himself—a piece of whitewashing comparable with the reinterpretation of the deeds of Theodoric the Great when he became Dietrich von Bern.

A fragmentary account of the adventures of Herzog Ernst, written in stanzas, dates from the 1180's, but for a complete version of the story we have to wait until the 1220's. Comparison between the two suggests a 30 per cent expansion; not a great deal, but enough perhaps to incorporate some of the advances in story-telling and changes in the assessment of human motives which had taken place in the interval. Latter-day refinements include the emphasis of important passages by means of description and explanation, or the creation of tension by the use of dialogue in an inherently dangerous situation. The original popular tale has acquired a veneer of sophistication on being retold in the *Blütezeit*.

Although the earlier twelfth century was not so exclusively dominated by despair as might have been thought, the *Spielmannsepos* does in a way represent a departure. Worldly situations in the writings of clerical authors had been peripheral; on the other hand, any devotional elements which remain in the *Spielmannsepos* are so overlaid as to be virtually unrecognizable. But this development would have led nowhere if Germany had not been receptive, for the first though not for the last time, to vernacular influences from abroad. At about the same time as Priester Wernher was humanizing the apocryphal gospels and tales of sheer adventure were being written down to please a largely unsophisticated audience, the first moves were being made towards the creation of the courtly literature on which the fame of German letters in the Middle Ages rests.

Early Romances of Chivalry

The practice and technique of chivalry developed rapidly in the second half of the twelfth century as successive crusades were called. Crusading brought German knights into international contact, not only with their European colleagues, but also with their Saracen enemy. Contact with the East left its mark on the popular literature of the twelfth century; it is the manners of Europe, especially of French knights, which have the most marked effect in courtly literature. International contact is generally held to have been at its strongest when the emperor Barbarossa held a court at Mainz in 1184 on the occasion of dubbing his sons knights. There certainly appear to be traces in the literature of the late eighties of an attitude to chivalry as something new which has to be learnt. It is possible that literary contacts were formed at the same time, and that Germany received about then the full impact of Arthurian romances and the art of courtly love. In both, the individual comes to the fore and interest shifts from the movements of large forces and dynastic considerations which had provided the characteristic content of the popular epic. Courtly love as it finds expression in the lyric is not quite the winning of a bride in which a knight's adventures characteristically culminate, but it probably needs less explanation than it normally receives, since the attitude of helpless devotion has remained one of the clichés of the love-lyric down to the present day; though it should, perhaps, be emphasized that this attitude was new in the twelfth century, and that the knight as lover expresses his feelings in the terminology and with the characteristic gestures of courtly society.

Indeed, it is the expression of the relationships between the sexes rather than the details of the chivalrous code which marks the beginnings of a new direction in German narrative. The earliest German romances are the *Tristrant* of Eilhart von Oberg of about 1160 and the anonymous *Graf Rudolf* of perhaps a decade later. The latter text is preserved only in fragmentary form, and we may perhaps assume that the name of the author was recorded at the missing beginning or end. It cannot have been a well known text in the Middle Ages, since the manuscript tradition is so slender and there is no known parallel or source. The content of the story has to be reconstructed from the fragments, and at first sight the setting and perhaps the action suggest the *Spielmannsepos*, for the story is set in the Middle East, and the battle scenes are general melées, rather than the duels which form the staple of chivalrous encounter. However, the setting is little more than a backdrop; Rudolf finds he has taken service with an Eastern potentate, which involves him on one occasion in fighting against Christians: he is able to salve his conscience and keep up appearances by striking with the flat of his sword. In the conflict of loyalties involved here may be seen the prototype of the conflict between friends which features largely in the fully developed Arthurian romance; service with a non-Christian ruler has a parallel in Book I of Wolfram von Eschenbach's *Parzival*, where Gahmuret enters the service of the Baruc of Baldac.

Eilhart's version of the story of Tristan and Isolde is the only complete medieval German version, and although it is derivative, it is also the earliest complete text in any language. The nearest parallel to this text, the French version of Béroul, has lost beginning and end, and runs parallel to Eilhart for only about half of its 4,000 lines; where the two texts are comparable their resemblance is close, notably in descriptions and in the allocation of speeches, but either Eilhart or Béroul was eclectic. It is probably only chance that we have the complete text of Eilhart; the two manuscripts are considerably later than the date of the poem, and there are in fact only fragments from the twelfth century. Some features of the completed text, for which there is no early fragment and no parallel in Béroul, have been taken as later interpolations; and it must be borne in mind that what is for convenience called Eilhart's work may contain an element of working over. The most curious factor in the creation of this poem is that Eilhart came from a court and a region—Saxony—remote from romance influences; but the language he uses is not that of his homeland, nor is it the southern German which predominates in the literature of the next generation.

It is no accident that the Tristan story is one of the most frequently retold tales of the Middle Ages. It is, after all, the archetypal 'eternal triangle', though as such it would lend itself to greater popularity in an age when the cult of courtly or romantic love had reached its zenith. By a careful comparison of all extant versions an original story has been postulated in which Tristan was the innocent victim of Isolde's affections; but all the completed versions of the text show her in some way dying for love, and all identify her as the niece of the giant Morhold, whom Tristan has killed. All extant versions agree in making one lover as guilty as the other, but pass the blame on to a magic drink which produces irresistible love in the couple who take it in one another's presence; all versions have some account of the lovers living away from society, hiding in the forest; all accounts have something to say about a sword in the bed. The details of these incidents vary from one text to another, but the last two, in particular, enable us to form a fair picture of Eilhart's treatment of his subject. His Tristrant and Isalde lead a wretched life in the forest; they have been caught, for the second time, almost *in flagrante delictu.* Mark determines to kill them both; they are captured and separated, but Tristrant escapes in time to save Isalde from being handed over as a paramour to a band of lepers—then they flee into the forest, where they live a fugitive existence for six months, living on vegetation and such game as Tristrant is able to catch. The account of the sword in the bed is as follows:

> Then Tristrant had one custom, in which the lady concurred with him: whenever they lay down and conversed with one another, he saw fit to draw his sword from its sheath and placed it between himself and her. The hero would in no circumstance fail to do this, and they would not go to sleep unless the sword lay between them. That was a strange idea for a man, and yet it worked out to their advantage afterwards, for it chanced one day that one of the king's huntsmen came secretly to their hut early in the morning . . . .

King Mark sees them but does not wake them, but by an exchange of swords makes it clear that he has been there. At this the lovers take fright and retreat further into the forest. However, they have to be brought back to the court somehow for the sake of the story, if only to undergo a further series of adventures, and this is achieved by the simple device of allowing the potion to lose its effect after a stated period (four years), after which the lovers can voluntarily return. This does not prevent further intrigues once they are back again.

In general this text falls a long way short of the works of the *Blütezeit*, in technique and in spirit. Much incident derives from chance encounter, and the motivation is sometimes crude enough to reduce the characters to automata, yet the work does in some ways anticipate what is to come. The duel of Tristrant with the giant Morhold is an individual encounter in keeping with later practice; Tristrant wins one bride (for King Mark) by a fight with a dragon, and another (for himself) by defending her father's land in general battle, and the various magic poisonings and cures all suggest the external trappings of romances of chivalry. In the rather sordid scenes where Tristrant helps his brother-in-law by means of a forged key to gain access to his lady-love in the absence of her husband, there may be seen, on the one hand, something of a caricature of Tristrant's own situation and on the other a presentation of the extreme position implicit in courtly love. Gottfried von Strassburg expunged the incident in his more highly sophisticated version of the story. In view of such crudities, it is not surprising that a *Minnemonolog* by Isalde is sometimes ascribed to an interpolator; but speech as a retarding device, and dialogue in particular, is well handled at some places in this story, and at times is highly stylized into stichomythia. Eilhart even shows originality of a kind in inventing some kind of permanent abode for the lovers in the forest. In general the faults are those of the story—it is hard to maintain a conventional morality when your hero offends flagrantly against any known code of behaviour. Everything Tristrant does is narrated with approval, even his assistance to his brother-in-law, and though he does come to a bad end, this is not explained as the outcome of his wickedness. In this limited acceptance of a world of make-believe in which the ordinary rules of conduct do not apply, Eilhart is in striking contrast to other writers of about the same time, and may in this respect at least be called a precursor.

Like Gottfried von Strassburg's later working of the same story, Eilhart's romance gives his hero parents, Rivalin and Blankeflur, who are in some measure a prefiguration of the Tristan figure in making a runaway and highly romantic match. The name of Blanscheflur is also that of one of the lovers in anonymous fragments of a romance of *Floyris* datable to about 1170 preserved at Trier.

In subject-matter, Heinrich von Veldeke's *Eneide* is remote from the usual run of chivalrous narrative poems. The story is in fact a retelling of the *Aeneid*, which might be thought too weighty to provide the material for a romance. Virgil's poem was known to the educated in the Middle Ages, but it had been adapted in French in the twelfth century, and it is on this text, the *Roman d'Énéas*, that Veldeke's German version is based. He tells us something in his epilogue about the way his version was nearly finished when he lost the manuscript of his exemplar, and he was kept waiting for nine years before he retrieved it. The work was completed under the patronage of Hermann of Thuringia, who at one time and another also supported Walther von der Vogelweide and Wolfram von Eschenbach, and who became a legendary figure as a patron of the arts. This may have some bearing on the text of the poem: Heinrich's native tongue was virtually Dutch, and there are traces in the rhymes of the most dependable manuscript of the text of a vocabulary and of forms of words which are more recognizably Dutch than German. The manuscript represents an attempt to accommodate this language to the Central German dialect of Hermann's court. As the work was begun in Veldeke's homeland, there is a strong case for restoring the *Eneide* to the language in which Veldeke may be presumed to have written it. The text is also datable by direct reference to the Mainz gathering of 1184, and there was an occasion in 1174 when the source might have been purloined in the way Heinrich suggests. The text was therefore in all probability completed in the mid-eighties, considerably later than Eilhart's work, but again not in an area most obviously open to foreign influences. But Veldeke's birthplace, to judge from the adaptation in Middle High German of some words of fashion from the Low Countries, was in the direct path of cultural borrowing, and this is also evidenced by Veldeke's lyrics which, again rather before their time, show the influence of Romance models.

Book IV of Virgil's *Aeneid*—the story of Dido's love for Aeneas—is one which is perennially effective, as Aeneas' predicament can be presented as the choice between two courses of action, neither of which can be adopted without disaster. In the Middle Ages the content of this book receives even more prominence; but it is noticeable that both the *Roman* and Veldeke show differences in emphasis from Virgil, and that in the course of this narration Veldeke makes one of his few independent modifications. Probably the most obvious change made in the narration of the whole work, however, occurs at the very beginning, which relates the escape of Aeneas and his men from Troy, matter which Virgil saves up for the third book. Virgil, in fact, as often noted in the Middle Ages, starts his narrative *in medias res*, with the storm at sea. There is no doubt that such a scene is an effective beginning for any work; and in adopting it, Virgil had the additional advantage of being able to portray Aeneas as the innocent victim of enmity among the gods, the cause of which might be assumed to be known to a Roman audience. Veldeke's Aeneas, once he is on the high seas, is, indeed, beset by a storm sent by Juno, but Juno's direct appeal to Aeolus and Neptune's intervention on behalf of Aeneas are omitted; the latter is replaced as follows: 'They had to ride out the storm until the fourth day, when the wind dropped and the mighty waves began to grow calm'—a natural hazard of seamanship in place of the implacable hostility of the gods. Rather similarly, Venus does not in the vernaculars create a wraith of Aeneas for Turnus to pursue, and he is led on to the ship in pursuit of a stray bowman who strikes him with his arrow. The result is that he is no longer able to imagine himself to be pursuing a fleeing opponent, while Aeneas still has the same vision of Turnus running from him. Such reduction of divine participation has an important bearing on our judgment of Aeneas' relationship with Dido; for his actions no longer seem to be dictated by the decrees of heaven, but rather by a casualness which is discreditable to him, particularly when he leaves her. To be sure, the gods tell him to go, and this grieves his heart, but the matter is passed over with the minimum of attention; there is no account of an apparition, no words and no dire threats of the evils which will befall him if he dares to thwart the will of the gods. Aeneas' excuses to Dido when she comes to hear of his intended departure are extremely lame. They are not, indeed, very convincing in Virgil, but there they are at least backed up by an appeal to the divine will. Aeneas is no longer 'pius Aeneas' but something like *der maere helt*, the hero of 'another' romance.

Strangely enough, there is one point in the medieval texts where interest in the doings of the gods is rather greater than in the Latin. This is where Venus, seeing Aeneas in a difficult plight, begs Vulcan for help in making armour and weapons. The fact of her plea is a token of reconciliation, but Virgil does not need to recount, as the medieval authors do, the story of Mars and Venus. Is this a concession to an audience that does not know its classical mythology, or is it a sign of an interest in *minne*? Certainly there are other opportunities for retelling the story in the terms of the universal motive of medieval romances, not least in the way young Lavinia falls in love with Aeneas. She has to be told what *minne* is, and her mother's only explanation is an account of the symptoms. When she sees Aeneas riding past the very medieval castle in which she lives, she suffers these symptoms, and writes a letter which is shot by an arrow to Aeneas' feet. The whole episode is tricked out with all the means available to an author to prolong a situation: descriptions of states of mind and physical effects, speeches and soliloquies and the more purely linguistic devices of antithesis, repetition, etc. Both Lavinia and Aeneas give vent to their sorrows in passages which extend over several hundreds of lines. Lavinia's *Minnemonolog* is particularly famous: its affinities with that of Isalde in Eilhart's romance have suggested that this passage was a post-Veldekan interpolation in Eilhart's text. The artificialities of *minne* were undoubtedly very suitable for the young Lavinia, but they seem rather out of place in the Dido episode. The sufferings of Dido's sleepless night come in for considerable expansion in both the medieval texts, but it is Veldeke who recasts the scene in what can only be called, well before its time, a rococo spirit by having Dido, the mature widow, shyly spell out Aeneas' name to her sister.

Some of the minor features of narration are also characteristic of medieval procedures. In particular, descriptions have taken on their characteristic medieval static guise, not always to their disadvantage. For example, Virgil's Carthage is certainly a bustling place, but everything is allowed to happen at once, from the laying of foundations to the election of an assembly. Veldeke visualizes Carthage as a medieval city with seven gateways and a hundred towers (*bürge*), set, like so many cities in romances, on the coast and defended to the landward by a deep river. The well-being of its inhabitants is briefly touched on with the superlatives which are to become characteristic of descriptions in romances. Two architectural descriptions, of the tombs of Camilla and of Pallas, are fantastic and extremely hard to visualize, in spite of the great amount of visual detail which is given, though they suggest a fascination with the construction of arch and dome. Fantasy also extends towards the grotesque in Veldeke's description of the Sybil, a description which to some extent anticipates Wolfram's Kundrie. The gap between the beautiful and the ugly is immense, and in the extremes of contrast between them may be seen another characteristic which is to become very important in the next generation.

The Thuringian School

In adapting classical matter to German Veldeke was not quite alone, and it may not be altogether coincidence that two other large-scale works on classical themes were composed under the patronage of Hermann of Thuringia. Herbort von Fritzlar produced an abridged German version, variously dated 1190 or 1210, of Benoît de Saint-Maur's *Histoire de Troye*. There is here little of the refinement of narrative technique observed in Veldeke, for instance speech is not extensively introduced in order to vary the pace, and the battle scenes have little enough to do with knight-errantry. Still, the *Trojanerkrieg* is a characteristic product of its age in its treatment of three romantic episodes, the stories of Jason and Medea, Troilus and Cressida (a medieval invention), and Achilles and Polixena. In one respect Herbort is original, in the creation of little vignettes like the medievalized vision of dawn at Troy:

> The watchman (*wahtære*) sat upon the battlements and sang his song of daybreak, his voice sounding resonantly. He sang, 'Dawn has already broken. Daylight is shining into the hall. Wake up knights, everywhere, wake up, it is day.' As he sang his heart was greatly and terribly afraid: he saw in readiness, gleaming against the great sea hauberks, shields, helmets, swords and banners of many a hue. . . .

The other comparable text is Albrecht von Halberstadt's *Metamorphosen*, almost certainly a product of the thirteenth century. There were great difficulties in the way of adapting Ovid's brief disparate adventures—there is certainly no overriding central theme which would naturally lend itself to treatment as a romance. There are also difficulties in approaching Albrecht's texts, for they are known in a complete form only from a sixteenth-century edition published by Jörg Wickram. As Albrecht's name implies, his native dialect was that of Hermann's court, but he seems, on the evidence of the small early fragments of his work which are preserved to have adjusted himself to writing in what must have been an acquired language. The prologues of the text (approximately coeval with Herbort von Fritzlar) would, in its treatment of the beliefs of the pagans, have done credit to the more austere traditions of the twelfth century, but in the stories nereids, naiads, dryads and nymphs are treated without such heavy-handed disapproval, and they are in fact acclimatized as *waltfrawen, feien, elbinne* (naiads), *mer-frawen, feien, wassermaget* (nymphs); *waldmenlin, gezwerge, elbin* (fauns and satyrs), etc. They are not treated as false deities, but as magic creatures rather like the more exotic beings in romances. One respect in which Albrecht differs from other medieval German writers on classical subjects is that he appears to go straight back to his Latin source without a French intermediary.

The setting of Meister Otte's *Eraclius* (written about 1210) provides some point of contact with the 'Roman' stories, but the text is in fact a curious amalgam, containing episodes which might otherwise be expected in a *Spielmannsepos*, a romantic intrigue of a rather novel kind and a legendary adventure reminiscent of Saints' Lives. The crass episodes are a chain of scenes which begin with the hero persuading his mother to sell him into slavery, where, to be sure, he will be able to live by his wits. The manifestations of his wisdom involve his choosing a wife for his king. It seems to be conveniently forgotten a little later, when the king is summoned away to a war, that Eraclius' choice was supposed to be infallible, and Eraclius connives at her unfaithfulness by a complicated manœuvre by which she deliberately falls from her horse into the mire in front of the house where her lover is concealed, and dries herself at a providently lit fire. The story is treated with every appearance of seriousness, but it can be read as a parody of the mystique of *hôhe minne*. The aspirations are omitted, and all that is left is the sordid intrigue which must have underlain any adventure that was not fictional. But the discrimination which parody involves can perhaps hardly be expected in a text which goes on to allow the same Eraclius to succeed the emperor Focas and undertake an expedition which leads to the retrieval of the True Cross from the hands of the Persians; for all its date in the thirteenth century, this is a text of great naïveté.

IV

THE ROMANCE IN THE MEDIEVAL GERMAN GOLDEN AGE

Hartmann von Aue

The achievement of Hartmann von Aue appears all the greater against the background of the pre-courtly and early courtly romance. At the level of content he must be held responsible for the introduction into Germany of Arthurian romance. The court of King Arthur is conceived as a body of excellent knights, whose qualities are codified in German as *zuht*, *triuwe*, *mâze* and *milte*. *Zuht* is the proper way of carrying on the profession of arms and conduct in general according to the principles of chivalry; *milte*, the virtue of generosity, had always been admired, but begins to acquire something of the meaning of magnanimity in the classical sense; *triuwe* is taken to fantastic lengths; the knight's word is his bond, and can be exploited as the opportunity for practising a trick on him. Hartmann's two romances of chivalry (*Erec* and *Iwein*) are concerned with *mâze* in a particular way, but the quality is otherwise the classical one of the golden mean. The laudable possession of these qualities gives *êre*, which is initially the public recognition given to a man who fulfils his obligations, good reputation, but which comes to have some of the overtones of the modern meaning of 'honour'. A working knowledge of the principles of chivalry may be deduced from the actions of the heroes of the romances themselves, though two famous first-person accounts of the ways of knighthood, one in Hartmann's *Iwein*, and the other in Wolfram's *Parzival*, suggest a caricature in which chivalry is presented as little more than the bellicosity of Tweedledum and Tweedledee, for nothing appears to be at stake but the reputation of the combatants.

It has to be remembered, however, that the speaker is in each case a practised knight addressing a simpleton, and we may assume that a knowledgeable audience was highly amused by such *reductiones ad absurdum* of the chivalrous code; but tournaments, at least, seem at first sight to have no more purpose than sporting fixtures, and are considerably more dangerous. They are, of course, an institutionalized form of the training a mounted knight would have to undergo to fit him to take part in serious and purposeful fighting. In the course of the romances, a knight's valour is directed to a purpose, though this purpose is represented often in a somewhat stereotyped way as a fight against overwhelming odds, such as a giant or a monster, in order to redeem a kingdom from a curse or to relieve a city beleaguered by opponents who have taken advantage of the succession of a woman to power, the classical reward for the successful accomplishment of this task being the hand of the woman for her defender. The knight's actions result in the triumph of right and the restoration of *mâze*. Marriage should be the outcome of the most exacting and the concluding adventure of a knight's career, for marriage clearly involves, or should involve, fresh responsibilities. Grail knights explicitly, and Round Table knights by implication, are in a literal sense knights bachelor. In each of these communities the ruler is married, and perhaps as a result is less mobile than his retinue. The knight who marries stays at home as the ruler of his own province.

Some such highly idealized picture of chivalry may emerge from the romance in the hands of the medieval German classical authors. The picture is, however, incomplete; even in literature, even in the golden age, knights do at times fall below the ideals they claim for themselves. The German Lanzelet, and even once in no less a text than Wolfram's *Parzival* the incomparable Gawan, fall into sordid amorous adventures. Medieval German literature at its best, however, appears to take the ideals seriously. Hartmann does not translate the *Lancelot* of Chrétien de Troyes, though it was available, and he chooses for his adaptations instead the stories of Erec and of Iwein, two complementary studies of the incompatibility of knight-errantry and marriage.

Credit for the themes belongs, however, not to him but to Chrétien de Troyes, who wrote in addition romances on Cligés and Lancelot, and an incomplete Perceval story, in addition to the two complementary romances on Erec and Iwein. Hartmann may be credited perhaps with very discriminating powers of selection in adapting these very two stories, but he did not adapt Chrétien's romances in their first flush of literary novelty, for they were written a good generation before. It seems feasible that the stories of chivalrous adventure reached Germany at a relatively early date, possibly in what might be called 'pirated' versions recounted orally but not committed to writing, and that the work of the reputable poets was precisely to give classical form to a tale that was already well known. This would account for the anxiety with which a source was sought and the jealousy with which the authenticity of a version was proclaimed.

Hartmann's narrative works are generally held to show consistent advances in technique from *Erec* onwards: marks of the beginner appear in *Erec*, notably the frequent recapitulations in the form of *als ich iu gesaget hân*, and a certain disjointedness in narration; events tend to rush by, and then prominence is given by large passages of static description—or rather events hastily narrated tend to follow detailed scene-setting. The beginning of *Erec* is lost, including presumably the passage in which Hartmann named himself, as he does in his other long poems, for which there is a complete manuscript tradition. Erec rights a wrong to Queen Guenevere and himself, and by doing so wins himself a wife. The action moves swiftly to marriage, whereupon Erec falls into uxorious ways and becomes a laughing-stock. He reacts at once to his wife's complaints about this, bids her dress and arms himself; as they set out he forbids her companionship of bed, board or speech. Erec's adventures after this point may be classed as his rehabilitation, a series of adventures with apparently no more than random sequence, save that each exploit in turn is described as the most hazardous so far undertaken.

An attempt has been made to see in the places where Hartmann expands a clue to the form of the work. The most obvious piece of expansion is the description of Enite's horse (lines 7264–7766), but this is in fact the second one given her, and horses are prominent elsewhere in the text: Enite curries Erec's horse in her father's humble home, and on her later travels she is given charge of horses captured by Erec from his defeated opponents. In these scenes there is perhaps a kind of poetic injustice; it is the fact of servility that counts, rather than any specific symbolic value of the horse. Alternatively, if the horse is a symbol, it is more than anything a status symbol, as the fastest means of locomotion available to medieval man, and the mark of the knight. The fact of description, not its subject-matter, is the important factor when Enite's second horse is described. There are other descriptions as well, most notably of tournaments and passages of arms which, while less obviously static than those of objects or persons, do not greatly contribute to the momentum of the story. Single combat can almost be reduced to a formula: a charge on horseback, symmetrical unhorsing of the two opponents, not always at the first attempt; swordplay in which the hero is wounded; fresh inspiration from thoughts of the beloved which enable him to fight like a new man until he receives an acknowledgment of submission (*sicherheit*) from the defeated opponent. The loser has to name himself, as is made explicit in Erec's encounter with Sir Kay, King Arthur's seneschal and a figure of fun in all Arthurian romances. For this reason, the account of this fight itself reads like a parody of one with a worthy opponent—Kay has borrowed Gawein's horse by agreement, but is not dressed for fighting:

> When Erec perceived that he was unarmed, how well Kay enjoyed Erec's virtues. With great speed he reversed his spear so that he should not harm him. He turned the shaft against

> him and lunged with such force that Kay lay beneath his horse like a sack—as he deserved, but not like a good warrior. Erec took away the horse. Kay, the cunning man, ran swiftly after him and called out aloud: 'No, good knight, as you are valiant, let me keep the horse, or I shall always be despised and ridiculed. Dash it all, it isn't mine!'

This passage seems to suggest that the practice of chivalry was sufficiently well-known to be a subject for humour, but other passages in *Erec* show Hartmann at pains to impress upon his audience the one and only correct way of doing things. This is not a prime function, and is explicable perhaps most readily as delight in the arcana of the New Chivalry.

Hartmann's straightforwardness leads him to recount every event in chronological order, even if his technique in this early text is not quite able to eliminate redundancies and cross-references. Yet there is one point, towards the end of the text, where Hartmann does keep an ace up his sleeve: only after admitting defeat does Mabonagrin reveal the nature of his rash promise to his wife, to remain at home and kill all challengers until he himself was defeated, when he would be released from the vow. His conduct is an extreme example of *triuwe*, but Mabonagrin's main significance is as an embodiment of all that Erec has ceased to be; Erec's victory is a victory over himself. Devotion to a woman was the undoing of both of them, even if devotion took a different form in the two instances. But if this is the meaning of *Erec*, it is a bogus one, for while Erec is reformed he returns to different circumstances. His father 'providentially' dies, and he inherits a throne; as kings appear to be allowed wives, the problem of how to resolve the claims of *minne* and chivalry is shelved.

Iwein, Hartmann's later Arthurian romance and probably his last work, is first and foremost an anti-*Erec*. Iwein wins his wife, is persuaded at the tournament in honour of the occasion by Gawein to ask for leave of absence, overstays his leave, is cursed, runs mad in the forest, is cured in part by chance, befriends a lion, which subsequently accompanies him and helps him in moments of crisis; and then rehabilitates himself in two series of interlocking adventures, in each of which the promise to appear and help is deferred by an intervening challenge. In the earlier series, Lunete, imprisoned for having brought about Iwein's disastrous marriage, is vindicated; in the second, we are kept in suspense about Iwein's ability to arrive in time to keep his appointment to fight Gawein, whose honour we must regard as having been engaged on the wrong side; but neither of these series of episodes brings Iwein any nearer to regaining his wife, and in the end he has to reactivate the magic by which he had won her.

The vindication of Lunete is recounted very spaciously, not only by the insertion of episodes—an account of the abduction of Guenevere in addition to Iwein's own fight with a giant—but also by Hartmann's prolonging the initial failure of Lunete and Iwein to recognize one another beyond credibility, enabling himself in the process to recapitulate much more effectively than he had done in *Erec*. Added sophistication may be seen, too, in the treatment of the duel with Gawein. This is in fact not described: just as it is about to start Hartmann avoids the issue by going into hyperboles of the prowess of the contestants, using elaborate word-play before the charge, and more word-play before the knights dismount; such details of blows as are given turn out to be generalities. But all these words take time and space, give prominence to the situation and an illusion of activity. Individual incidents in the text are, if anything, more implausible than those in *Erec*, most clearly so Iwein's bride-winning. By pouring water from a magic spring on to a stone he has produced a most remarkable storm and actuated the defender of the spring to come out and fight. Having killed his opponent, Iwein marries the widow. This takes some time to bring about, but implausibly little. As in Chrétien, it happens largely on the advocacy of Lunete; comparison of the Hartmann and his source at this point is one of the best trodden fields of medieval German scholarship. It is very difficult to discern anything but reasons of state—the defence of the spring—as decisive in either text; if anything these are urged rather more diplomatically in Chrétien than in Hartmann, since Chrétien makes his Lunete introduce at an early stage the unthinkable suggestion that her mistress might have a husband even better than the one she had lost.

There are some other discrepancies: Gawein's enlistment on the 'wrong' side, the abduction of Guenevere, and the misadventure of Kalogreant at the spring have all been taken to show that all was not well with King Arthur's court, and that the work is in fact a critique of the pretences of chivalrous society—and Iwein's lion then becomes the symbol of the natural forces to which the hero must ally himself if he is to be more than a sham. There is, indeed, some gentle mockery of Arthur in Chrétien for taking a siesta, where Hartmann is at pains to deny any suggestion of sloth. It seems that Hartmann goes out of his way to explain everything in a favourable light, and if his sympathies are not taken at their face value, he is involved in a vast game of double bluff. Criticism of the hero has long been attributed to Hartmann, and it still is, though it is virtually confined to one passage, where Iwein pursued his opponent *âne zuht*, and lunged at him from behind. Apart from this, and even before this, Iwein's actions are accompanied by expressions of evident approval; he seems to be regarded as the perfect knight, too keen on the profession of arms to pay heed to his wife. The import of the text seems in this case to be that there can be excess in chivalry, just as there can be excess in marriage. The extravagances of Hartmann's two Arthurian heroes add up to a plea for *diu mâze*. This may seem a rather disappointing conclusion from two works of classical status, and it represents a reversion to a rather old-fashioned view of Hartmann, one which is, none the less, fully in accord with his utterance in the lyric. Erec's fault was carrying over into marriage the attitudes of *hôhe minne*; Iwein's the failure to accept responsibility in the pursuit of chivalrous pleasure. It should not be forgotten that courtly love and chivalry were the twin innovations of the culture and literature of the medieval golden age, and the balance which Hartmann draws between the two is a mark of a basically sober and practical approach to life. But realism of this kind cannot make the adventures less fantastic or more serious. Iwein is often in danger, and the size of the danger is built up by the device of interlocking episodes and the strength of his opponents, but he is bound to win; the intelligent lion will always be allowed to intervene in a real crisis, tacitly giving the hero an advantage over his opponents. The reader's sympathies and concern become actively engaged on behalf of the hero, but from the time he recovers his reason there is no doubt in his mind about the right course of action. It is true that there are killings, though with the exception of Laudine's first husband, who seems to be harmless enough, the victims are dragons, giants and evil men. In this context Hartmann's efforts to build up Kay as a more worthy character are strangely out of place—but they are in keeping with Hartmann's unwillingness to reproach Arthur and Guenevere at the beginning of the text. This suggests a fantastic story with no especially profound implications, told to delight a courtly and chivalrous audience, whose courtliness and chivalry were not, however, so strongly confirmed as to permit jesting at these codes.

Erec and *Iwein* are inevitably complementary texts, but between writing them Hartmann left an interval of ten years or so. He may be expected to have developed in skill in this time, especially as he had in these years written two other narrative works. The later work gives the impression of continuous movement, where *Erec* was frequently static. Minor points in the plot are made still firmly, but less obtrusively. Speech in general is much more important than in *Erec*, though there is less of a tendency to set pieces; even Iwein's suicide monologue is overheard, and becomes the means of starting fresh action.

Descriptions are much more discreet than in the earlier text, but if they no longer interrupt the narrative flow, they also lack the detail and vigour of Chrétien's. There are other differences between Hartmann and his source: the slow pace of mutual identification between Iwein and Lunete suggests a determination to use technical devices to enhance the inherent tension of a situation. The means used by Hartmann to vary the pace of his narration and give emphasis to the most important points are of several kinds; it is within the manner of telling the story that Hartmann's modifications are to be found.

Hartmann's Legends

Hartmann's two other narrative works, *Gregorius* and *Der arme Heinrich*, are distinguished in their subject-matter from the romances. He is not now concerned with social problems, but with moral ones, sin and redemption in *Gregorius* and the nature of sacrifice in *Der arme Heinrich*. Within this framework *Gregorius* can be distinguished as an early work in much the same way as *Erec*. Indeed, the same recapitulatory phrases recur. There is a real difficulty in dealing with parallel accounts first of Gregorius, the offspring of incest, and then of his mother, after he has been put to sea to chance his fortune. It is not surprising that when he in turn sets out again as a young man and reaches the shores of his mother's land there is need for a recapitulation, but it could have been handled less baldly—perhaps he could have heard a report from the inhabitants after his arrival: there is even a cue for this, 'One of the most eminent amongst them instructed him—as I have told you before—about their troubles.' Not enough was told, of course, for Gregorius to be able to identify his mother. *Der arme Heinrich* manages the presentation of information much more subtly. Stricken with leprosy, Heinrich goes to Montpellier for a cure and is thwarted in his hopes (four lines), he then goes on to Salerno, and is told that he has no hopes of a cure, save in the cryptic terms 'that he was curable and yet would ever be without a cure'. This is then explained in a speech which leads up gently to details of the operation which has to be performed. The process of gradually leading up to a point is carried to an extreme—a hint in the text, a medium-long speech working up to the point, followed by a long speech by a different person leading up to the same point by different stages—i.e. the greatest prominence is given where the greatest effect is required.

The opening invocation of *Gregorius* is longer than the introduction of any of the other works, and it sets the tone. It starts with a renunciation of worldly writing, which is attributed to foolish youth, and continues with a call to repentance, ending with the assurance that any truly repentant sinner is certain of redemption, providing that he does not relapse, and casts aside doubt or despair (*zwîvel*).

The narration builds up the offence of Gregorius' father and mother in agonizing detail: first temptation by the devil, then particularization of the causes of the sin of Gregorius' father. Gregorius' parents are conscious of the act of incest; when Gregorius' turn comes to enter into a marriage with his mother, neither is aware until it is too late of their relationship. It is perhaps a strain on credulity that they did not attempt to find out rather more about one another before marriage, especially after the mother recognized Gregorius' clothes. But the point is made that the offence was committed unwittingly, and this means that the offence was not culpable in the eyes of the church. Gregorius is also not to be blamed for his birth. In what, then, does his offence lie? It has been suggested that his offence was pride in seeking worldly honour and abandoning his vocation as a monk to become a knight. It seems possible, however, that Hartmann was drawing on traditional revulsion from incest, and it is certainly true that after Gregorius' unwitting offence Hartmann emphasizes the penitence of both mother and son, and most significantly allows Gregorius to point out to his mother the inadmissibility of doubt. The narrative concludes with the superhuman endurance of Gregorius' seventeen years chained to a rock and nourished only by dew, of the miracles by which Gregorius became Pope; features belonging to the tradition of the Saint's Life. Yet *Gregorius* is also firmly rooted in the courtly world of the thirteenth century; in particular the deeds by which Gregorius liberates his mother's land and becomes in the eyes of its inhabitants an eligible husband reflect a recurrent situation of romances—a concession, in a text which had specifically renounced the way of the world, to the taste of the times.

Der arme Heinrich has fewer of the externals of the romance of adventure. This text shares with *Iwein* fluency of language and convincing speeches, most noticeably in the words of the girl who manages to convince first her parents, then Heinrich, then the surgeon at Salerno of her unshakable will to die for the sake of her lord. Her longest speech, indeed, is one to her parents about the transitoriness of life, and her words carry conviction by a fluency held to be divinely inspired. Hartmann builds up the tension by making the surgeon describe his operation in detail and allowing Heinrich to hear the knife being whetted; at which Heinrich interrupts proceedings, but is not thanked by the girl, who expresses frustration at the loss of a martyr's crown. On the way home, Heinrich's devotion is rewarded by a miracle, and he is cured; he marries the girl, and they live thereafter in great prosperity.

This should be something of an anticlimax in a story concerned with self-sacrifice. It is, in its way; but the miraculous cure happens to Heinrich, who must be seen in refusing to accept the girl's sacrifice to be accepting his own disability, and by doing so repudiating his former worldliness in spirit, as he has already done socially; and there is no suggestion at the end that the girl has to put up with marriage as a poor second best as a reward for her presumption.

The legends of Hartmann von Aue stand apart from other narrations of the *Blütezeit*. They are sometimes called 'courtly legends' to distinguish them for the Saints' Lives which were a prominent feature of the literary output of the previous generation. They are edifying stories with one foot in the courtly world, aware of the civilization that is contemporary with them.

Hartmann's place as a narrative poet is at the threshold of the *Blütezeit*. In his two last works, *Der arme Heinrich* and *Iwein*, he attained a fluency of expression unexampled before his time which served as a model for his successors. He is fundamentally a serious writer in that his romances represent more than meaningless adventures, but he was overshadowed before very long by Wolfram, perhaps the most medieval and the most German writer of the *Blütezeit*.

Ulrich von Zatzikhoven

Nevertheless, there was a modest 'school' of Hartmann. Ulrich von Zatizikhoven's *Lanzelet* is a romance which is stylistically derivative from him; in view of the date which can be attributed to the work (1194), there was, indeed, no strictly Arthurian romance in German available as a model apart from *Erec*. Ulrich's model was not Chrétien's *Lancelot du lac*, though there are some features and adventures shared by the heroes of both. On the whole, the contrast with a work like this points out the essential seriousness of Hartmann von Aue: it is hard to see in Lanzelet's adventures much more than a series of tall stories. The hero is 'unproblematic' in the sense that he appears to be unaware of any conflict between duty and inclination, or love and chivalry, or love and religion. He staggers from one adventure to another, more of these between the sheets than is quite creditable. Ulrich's text introduces the heroes of other Arthurian romances as background figures: this is not unique, for Gawein and Kay at least recur many a time, but reference is here so rich that it suggests the attempt to follow a successful pattern, which would imply that the content of romances of chivalry was known before the stories found classical expression.

Wirnt von Gravenberg

Wirnt's *Wigalois* was presumably written considerably later than *Lanzelet*; there is an even wider range of allusion, including some reference to the early books of *Parzival*. The style of the early part of the work is held to derive from Hartmann, that of the later part from Wolfram, and the influence of Wolfram is particularly apparent in the description of armed combat. *Wigalois* is primarily a series of adventures. There is growing seriousness in the latter part of the text: the castle where Wigalois meets Roas is more genuinely ominous than the setting of most romances. The earlier part of the text is less portentous. Much is made of a magic belt which ensures Wigalois of invincibility, but its loss makes no difference to the hero's career. His father had left it at home and thereby lost the means of returning; as Wigalois' father is none other than Gawein, who in other texts is the bachelor *par excellence*, one might doubt whether this oversight was completely unpremeditated; but of course there is nothing of this in the text.

'*Moriz von Craûn*'

This text is unusual in several ways; in length it is more of a short story than a novel, and its content, while acknowledging the practices of chivalry and courtly love, does not refer to the make-believe Arthurian world. It purports to be derived from events in the life of a twelfth-century French knight, and the story found its way into German about 1210. Although short, the text is rather unevenly constructed: there is a long introduction on the origins of chivalry which is worthy of the pseudo-histories of the time, and would certainly not be out of place in a full-length romance. The central anecdote is that of the hero obtaining the favours of his mistress on condition of arranging a splendid tournament, and exerting himself so strenuously that he is too tired to claim his reward. This plot is one of those which most strongly confirm the impression of courtly love as elegant adultery, but the story goes beyond the recital of incidents to show Moriz receiving his reward, and then with a fine show of ambivalent emotions leaving his mistress. The text is otherwise notable as a source of information on medieval tournaments and pageantry, and it gives far more visual detail than the majority of German texts of its time.

Wolfram von Eschenbach

It was left to Wolfram to give high moral purpose to the romance. Wolfram's main work, *Parzival*, in 16 books and some 25,000 lines, may be considered to be a life's work; there is evidence that the work was taken up and laid down several times, and that the first two books, dealing with the adventures of Parzival's father Gahmuret, were composed after some of the books about Parzival himself. For this part of the text there appears to be no source at all, and as the source for the Parzival narration, Chrétien de Troyes' *Contes del Graal*, was incomplete, Wolfram must be credited with a great use of the imagination in drawing on hints in his source to complete his narration—not that the conclusion was undisputed in the Middle Ages. Where there is a source, Wolfram's treatment of it is in any case incomparably freer than Hartmann's; and he fills in innumerable details from a seemingly inexhaustible imagination, keeping the involved threads of personal relationships in mind throughout a long text which must have taken years to write, and delighting, apparently, in covering his tracks and making an important episode depend on the slightest hint, something mentioned perhaps in passing. It is the organizing capacity which Wolfram shows in *Parzival* which makes one regard his other lengthy work, *Willehalm*, as involuntarily rather than deliberately incomplete. Wolfram's third narrative work, the so-called *Titurel*, survives only in two fragments, probably all that Wolfram wrote, and distinctive from other romances of chivalry in being composed in an elaborate stanzaic form, which may have militated against its completion. The content conspires with the stanzaic form of this work to give it an elegiac quality not otherwise found in Middle High German romances.

Mention of the two figures of Sigune and Schionatulander,

the heroine and hero of *Titurel*, in Wolfram's complete and justly more famous work suggests that their story would not be a typical romance. When Sigune first appears in *Parzival*, her lover is already dead; she is still with his body on the subsequent occasions when Parzival sees her. She is important for Parzival in being the first person to name him by his proper name, in giving him the first intimation of the seriousness of his lapse in the Grail castle, in being herself a link in the intricate chain of personal relationships which holds together the characters of an extraordinarily long narration.

Parzival is not only the flower of chivalry, he is also something of an Everyman. Part of his greatness lies in his weaknesses and his faults; he attains his objective, yet his greatness lies not in his mastery of the Grail, but in his mastery of himself. Arthurian heroes leave the court of King Arthur to find their own adventures, but the main result of their quest seems as often as not to be acceptability within the code of martial prowess and social good form. Most heroes leave the court of King Arthur with some celebration as they go off to take up their own rightful kingdoms, but Parzival sneaks away, virtually in a symbolic realization of the inadequacy of mere good form.

Yet the knight who was to excel all others in humanity starts off as a simpleton; the boy Parzival's simplicity is recounted in detail so embarrassing as to be scarcely credible. The effect is to cause his attainment of normal human discretion and the specific skills of chivalry, taken for granted with the average hero of romances, to appear as an immense and painful process; by implication his progress from the Arthurian to the Grail circle takes him as far above the common run of chivalry as the boy Parzival was below it. It is in response to naïve questioning that Parzival receives from Karnahkarnanz a most unsatisfactory account of the nature of chivalry, and it is this meeting which first sets him off in his determination to seek knighthood. It is not, however, quite the beginning of his questions; nor is he altogether to blame for knowing nothing about knighthood, for his widowed mother has had him brought up in isolation in the hope that he will thereby know nothing of the ways of chivalry, and not go out to his death as his father had done. Perhaps the isolation was too severe; at an age when he would be ready to bear arms he is still capable of questions and misunderstandings worthy of a five-year-old. It is appropriate that when his mother sends him out in search of knighthood she dresses him in fool's garb in the hope that he will soon be laughed out of his ambitions. His simplicity manifests itself in his literal interpretation of four pieces of advice which she gives him, which in two cases have comic but insignificant results, and in the other two a direct bearing on his conduct as a knight and an indirect bearing on his conduct at the Grail castle. In literal and clumsy obedience to the injunction to seek the greeting and the kiss of women he succeeds in estranging Jeschute from her husband Orilus, a slight which he puts right long after he has met conventional success as a knight, and, perhaps significantly, immediately after his failure to satisfy the more exacting demands of the Grail has been brought home to him. The instruction to follow the advice of an 'old grey man' brings him to Gurnemanz and more instruction. Among the rather longer list of precepts with which Parzival leaves Gurnemanz is the one 'not to ask too many questions'. As a mark of his increased sophistication, Parzival does not interpret this instruction literally, but in accordance with medieval idiom understands it as an embargo on all questions. The result of this is the débacle in the Grail castle, where his failure to ask a question denies relief to the wounded Amfortas, and brings about his own ejection from society and rebellion against God. It is in accordance with the spirit of romance that he should eventually succeed in his quest, but not until he has passed years in seemingly hopeless wandering—a passage of time marked as much by Gawan's as by Parzival's adventures—and only after an acknowledgment of contrition is he allowed to enter the Grail castle again and rise to its challenge.

The incidents mentioned in the last few lines are the essential ones of the text, but they are only a fraction of its content: nothing is said here about Parzival's father, whose adventures in the first two books are a prefiguration in some measure of Parzival's career; nothing about Parzival's half-brother by Gahmuret's previous marriage, the piebald Feirefiz; nothing about the hostility of Orilus and his kinsmen to Parzival's family; nothing of the details of Gawan's adventures; nothing about Parzival's marriage to Condwiramurs (Book IV); nothing about the attendant circumstances of the Grail ceremony or about the Grail itself; and only the slightest of hints about the Grail family, to which Parzival himself belongs.

Indeed, one of the most cogent reasons why Parzival is allowed finally to succeed in his quest is that he is born to possession of the Grail kingdom by descent on his mother's side, every bit as much as he inherits chivalry on his father's side. At one point Parzival is told specifically that there is no second chance to ask the question which he failed to ask on his first visit; yet Parzival succeeds at a second attempt. He fulfils an implicit condition for success in being the nearest eligible male member of the Grail family. But he still has to prove himself worthy; and his early actions show little enough promise of what is to come. The successive stages in his growth to awareness and maturity are marked by successive encounters with his kinswoman Sigune; but these encounters do not mark the points where Parzival makes decisive changes of direction—these rest on successive impact of the advice of his mother, of Gurnemanz and of Trevrizent.

It is unfortunate for Parzival that none of his advisors tells him straightforwardly what he has to do; for much of his life Parzival is unsure of his objective, and for the rest of the time he is unaware of how to reach it. It is one of Wolfram's great achievements to allow the reader to participate very intimately in the development of his hero by presenting information fragmentarily, just as it is presented to Parzival. This technique is one of the factors, even if it is a superficial one, in the mystery surrounding the Grail. It is possible, even, to wonder whether Wolfram himself was quite clear in his mind about its nature at the outset of the story, and the scene in which it is first presented shows Wolfram not to be fully at ease with his source. This cannot, however, be the only reason for Wolfram's idiosyncratic view of the Grail; one must assume on the one hand a strong oral tradition, and on the other a most vivid imagination at work. For Wolfram the Grail is no longer the chalice of the Last Supper, but a solid stone. Its first manifestation is the feeding of the Grail company. This has been likened to the feeding of the five thousand, which would raise the Grail *ipso facto* into a venerable cult object, but it should be pointed out that the details of the food it dispenses suggest the worldly luxury of the court in medieval romances. Further details, revealed to Parzival—and the reader—only later, suggest a further ambivalence: Trevrizent states that it was brought down to earth by angels who did not take sides when Lucifer rebelled. The penalty for their neutrality was to guard the Grail on earth. There then remains the problem of whether it was forgivable to be neutral when God was attacked; and a later passage states categorically that the neutral angels were finally cast out. This may in itself be considered a sidelight on the problem of *zwîvel*, a key-word in the whole of *Parzival*, occurring in the very first line and characterizing the hero's lost years after he has been told that he has forgone for ever the possibility of becoming Grail king. Parzival is, of course, forgiven. The association of the Grail with the neutral angels is not in itself the best augury, but all the other accompanying features relate it to the most solemn elements of the Christian faith; a dove descends from heaven each Good Friday to replenish its powers, and the dove is the emblem, too, of the Grail community. The Grail has life-preserving powers, and the ceremony which accompanies its first appearance suggests that it is a reliquary. Immediately before the Grail ceremony Parzival is the witness of a scene in which a lance figures prominently, and which causes distress to the whole assembly. The incident is not explained, and although later hints suggest that the blood on the lance could have been that of Amfortas, the scene bears overtones of the holy lance. The name of the Grail castle—Munsalvaetsche—may be interpreted as *mons silvaticus*, *Wildenberg*, but the second element carries also a suggestion of 'salvation'. The function of the Grail company, however, appears to be entirely compatible with the selfless acts of Arthurian knights; and the vow of anonymity imposed on the Grail knights seems to be little more than a triviality, as in the case of Parzival's son Lohengrin (called Loherangrin by Wolfram), a trait which is in any case paralleled in Arthurian tales. Parzival himself takes the tradition as far as it can go by being unaware, until he is told, of his identity; here the convention has become a symbol, in the sense that Parzival's progress may be seen as a series of steps towards knowing himself. In part the very simplicity of Parzival's beginnings contributes to the impression of unassailable maturity at the end. He achieves some kind of a synthesis, in which his natural reactions, after first being suppressed as he learns the external code of chivalrous conduct, are allowed to regain their full expression in the context of chivalrous maturity; but there is no way of expressing this maturity so as to make it as readily apparent as the naïveté of Parzival's infancy had been.

The place of Gawan's adventures as a kind of allegorical analogue to the development of Parzival is another factor in heightening the significance of Parzival's spiritual growth. Gawan is an accomplished knight at the outset; his adventures do not produce any development in his human qualities—on one occasion (Book VII) his adventures appear to be a conspicuous parody of the excesses of *Frauendienst*, his next adventure shows a lapse from the high standards of conduct of an Arthurian knight, and well on in his career he is exposed to ridicule. The contrast between his purely worldly and at times unedifying adventures throws Parzival's despair and his conviction of sinfulness into sharper relief, yet Parzival's development is not in fact so closely argued as might appear to be the case.

The crucial book is Book IX. That Parzival meets Sigune for a third time is some indication that he is near the Grail castle again, and it is his good fortune to have arrived on a Friday, after Kundrie has brought Sigune her provisions for the coming week, so that he is able to follow the tracks of her horse. But the track peters out, and Parzival is on his own again; a passage of arms in which he captures the horse of a Grail knight guarding the perimeters of the castle comes to nothing. A third meeting, with an elderly knight and his family in penitent dress on a Good Friday pilgrimage, is decisive in that Parzival is overcome by shame at desecrating the day by riding fully equipped for battle, but in fact no argument is offered to deter him from his deliberately chosen godless ways. It must be assumed that the devotion of this knight suddenly recalls Parzival to his vows, for at the end of this brief meeting, he releases his hold of the reins and leaves it to his horse to find the way as God directs. There is a presumption that the horse will find its way back to the Grail castle, but the way goes more shortly than this to the hermitage of Trevrizent, where Parzival's first words are a confession of sin. We are not presented with a gradual conversion, but rather with the workings of chance—or divine providence. Parzival is qualified by penitence to receive Trevrizent's absolution at the beginning of his stay at the cell, but this absolution is not given until Parzival has been told more details than he ever knew before of the depths of his guilt, and a full account of his membership of the Grail family, together with some hope that he may succeed in his quest. Parzival's ultimate success must be seen as a single act of grace rather than as a process of maturation or persuasion, and the actual moment of conversion is passed over extremely rapidly without any comment on its nature. This is characteristic of Wolfram's manner of proceeding, which uses the lightest of links to associate remote parts of the text with one another, and prefers on the whole not to elaborate the motives or dwell on the scene.

Allusiveness is characteristic of Wolfram's presentation of details about the Grail and its defenders. Parzival apparently learns the details piece by piece in a random order. He is even told by Trevrizent at the end that some of his earlier information was deliberately misleading, in a passage which may be variously interpreted as a palinode by Wolfram for heterodox opinions he had allowed the same speaker to present in Book IX, or at their face value as a true explanation of something which had previously had to be concealed; but neither explanation is fully convincing or even fully self-consistent. Wolfram's appeals to his source, the Provençal Kyot, are also tantalizing: as Kyot has not yet been finally identified, the name is now generally taken to be a cover by Wolfram to excuse his more elaborate flights of fancy and most blatant divergences from the story as it may have been commonly known; but this interpretation has been challenged of late. Part of the fascination of *Parzival*, but only part, lies in the unsolved and perhaps insoluble questions which present themselves to the reader, perhaps even more insistently, even, to the attentive and knowledgeable reader. But its qualities lie above all in its presentation of a fascinating character and a whole age, with a vigour and vividness which was never surpassed.

For the next generation Wolfram was to become the model *par excellence* for writers of chivalrous romances. There is something in the richness of his invention, something, too, in his exuberant but only apparently undisciplined language which appealed to his followers, and which make him the most characteristically German of the authors of the *Blütezeit*. His imitators adopt some of the superficial features of his language, but no one after him succeeded in matching a theme of universal significance to a highly personal style.

Indeed, the task proved to be too much for Wolfram himself; hints are given in *Parzival* of a romance involving Sigune and her lover Schionatulander, who is not otherwise a live character. The hints are worked out a little further in the two fragments known as *Titurel*, erroneously so from mention of Titurel's name in the first stanza. Perhaps it was the elaborate nature of the metrical form which inhibited the completion of this text, or perhaps the story, which started, at least, from an apparently trivial incident:

> Thanks, and all that a maiden should ever grant her worthy noble friend I promise, and no one shall deter me from it if your purpose regains the cord which the hound you had brought me for my pleasure took away as he went.

On the face of it this appears to be no more than a childish whim, and certainly no just cause in which to send a man to his death; yet the fact that Schionatulander's unsuccessful exploit led to such a melancholy end gives him an elegiac quality denied to other heroes of romances, and Wolfram might have been able to make something of this work comparable with *Parzival* if he had continued with it. The fragments became a challenge to his imitators, who spun them out into a voluminous romance, but it is generally held that Wolfram abandoned work on the project, and turned to another subject for another work, also incomplete.

Willehalm is again different in spirit. It reverts to the verse technique of *Parzival*—rhyming couplets arranged in groups of thirty lines; in other respects it marks a return to themes, and to some extent to motives, which had been current before Wolfram's time. That the hero is a saint, and that Wolfram turns in his introduction to his hero with a plea for intercession is not, of course, unprecedented, and there are parallels to the adaptation of Saints' Lives to a courtly milieu; but the tradition of the 'legend' does not account for all of *Willehalm*, for this is less a victorious struggle with the dangers of the world on the road to beatification than a physical struggle against the enemies of Christendom. If crusading spirit relates *Willehalm* to Saints' Lives, the fighting itself suggests a return to the *volcwîg*, or general battle, of popular twelfth-century narrative. Some of the differences between *Willehalm* and the other tales of the time are accounted for by its different source; not this time a romance of chivalry, but a *chanson de geste*, a more primitive type of work, and one with a historical nucleus. The closest parallel should be the *Chanson de Roland* and its German derivative, but both the French source (*La Bataille d'Aliscans*) and *Willehalm* contain a secondary action involving a giant child of nature called Rennewart, who like others of his kind in the literature of the time is armed with a club instead of a gentleman's weapons, and whose conduct gives rise to incidents which recall the *Spielmannsepos* as much as anything. But besides drastically comic episodes, there are tender and touching ones as well. In the first and unsuccessful battle, Willehalm's young and brilliant nephew Vivianz is killed, and the event, sad enough in its own right, is given great emphasis and profundity by the presence of the hero who receives confession and gives absolution, bringing back, at an even more serious juncture, the spirit of Book IX of *Parzival*. Tenderness and devotion are expressed in the relationship between Willehalm and his wife Gyburg, a princess of heathen origin baptized on her marriage. Her origin, indeed, is the cause of the conflict, and personal and religious motives are invoked side by side. But while a holy war is being fought, human values on both sides are respected. The most direct expression of tolerance comes, appropriately enough, from Gyburg on the eve of the second battle, when she pleads with Willehalm's men to bear in mind that their opponents are 'God's handiwork' and to spare them. Nothing could be in more striking contrast with the attitudes expressed in the *Rolandslied*. Gyburg herself was, of course, a very special case, but there seems to be in the development of Rennewart in Wolfram's hands a presentation of what may be called the 'noble savage'; for Rennewart, too, is of heathen origin, and it is hinted that he is the kinsman of Gyburg. In his simplicity and directness there is something of the spontaneity of the young Parzival; his budding romance with Alize is some indication perhaps that his more superficial roughness was to be lost, but we do not know in fact what happened to him. He shows great valour on the field of battle, not least in preventing some of Willehalm's followers from deserting, but when the story breaks off he is nowhere to be found. As there is no kind of a peroration, and as the narration ends in the middle of a group of thirty lines, it is hardly likely that the text was deliberately left as a fragment: surviving medieval texts show a predilection for tying up loose ends. It is unlikely that the whereabouts of Rennewart would have been left inexplicit, or the full revelation of his identity and the outcome of his concern with Alize left undisclosed. The kind of calculation which has been applied to completed works might be applied here to give some idea of how much is missing, and it has been suggested that we have the bulk of *Willehalm*. Like *Titurel*, it found its continuators, but the only completed narrative work by Wolfram himself is *Parzival*; this alone is enough to raise him to pre-eminence in the literature of his time.

Gottfried von Strassburg

There could hardly be a greater contrast than that between Wolfram and Gottfried, who represent coexistent literary tendencies, both in the treatment of large expanses of material and in the structure of sentences and phrases, in subject-matter, of course, and in the attitude expressed towards the subject-matter. Linguistic form may be accounted for in some measure by geography: Gottfried was likely to be exposed more effectively to the literary fashions of France than were some of his contemporaries; if Hartmann had been conscious of his scholarship, Gottfried was conscious of the aptness and propriety of his diction. He is very much the conscious artist in words, and at a point significantly chosen in his romance of Tristan, a digression gives what is the first critical survey of German literature. According to Gottfried, Veldeke had been responsible for 'grafting the first scion' in the German language. His words are well chosen, for Veldeke was an innovator precisely in the art of the Middle High German efflorescence of adapting French tales to a German audience. Whether Gottfried knew of pre-courtly authors or not, he does not mention any author earlier than Veldeke. It is likely that he or his audience knew of Eilhart's version of the story he was telling, for one of his purposes is to tell the 'true' version, received from the Anglo-Norman Thomas; and Gottfried's silence about his German predecessor is an eloquent one. Gottfried suppresses the name of the one later author whom he criticizes adversely, but from allusion and counter-allusion in the two authors it is clear that Wolfram is meant. For Hartmann von Aue, Gottfried reserves the highest praise, for the clarity of his diction and the apt adornment of his narrative work. The literary digression continues with a discussion of the lyric.

The occasion of Gottfried's literary digression is interesting in its own right as an example of deliberate stylistic evasion, of a type provided for in the handbooks of rhetoric. He has reached the point where his hero is to be dubbed a knight. This could easily become the occasion for a descriptive set piece, with accounts of the great number of young men who were similarly honoured on the same occasion, descriptions of their luxurious dress, of the banquet and ceremonial tournament which followed the accolade. There was an audience for this essentially retardative element in a narrative poem, but Gottfried declines to appease it, and makes a self-deprecatory feint, saying that others were better equipped, and discussing their merits at length; by the time this is done, Tristan is a knight, and we are spared a lengthy cliché-ridden passage.

Chivalry is less prominent in *Tristan* than in other romances, not necessarily because Gottfried as a burgher was uninterested in the deeds of knights, but because Tristan  is predominantly a lover. His deeds of valour are relatively few in number, but when it comes to showing his mettle Tristan acquits himself every bit as well as the titular hero of other romances. Certainly his fights with the giants Morholt and Urgans show a comparably reckless attitude to superior odds, as does the killing of the dragon. There remain a few doubts—whether for example Tristan was acting fairly in fighting the dismounted Urgans from horseback, but it surely would have been quixotic for Tristan to dismount when his assailant's first blow was on the way. Similarly, the impetuous killing of Morgan by a blow with the sword in the course of a parley which had no prospect of a friendly issue has been invoked to show Tristan to be wanting in chivalrous spirit, but this was no more than sudden revenge for an unwarrantable imputation of bastardy; and since his opponent had on that ground refused to allow Tristan to fight according to chivalrous rules, the unchivalrous blow was the only way out of deadlock. The recovery of Isolde from Gandin does, however, appear to be rather discreditable: surely a knight worth his salt would have fought and killed his opponent, and not abducted the lady like a *Spielmann*! But even here it is at least trick for trick. In general, the epithets applied to Tristan are favourable, and he can be seen to be criticized only if all the indices of overt approval and disapproval are reversed.

Gottfried tells the main story of Tristan in such a way as to appeal to a discriminating audience whom he calls *edeliu herzen*, a term about which there has been a considerable amount of debate. It has been set as low as the 'gentle reader'; Gottfried's preface, however, emphasizes the power of discrimination possessed by a 'noble heart', which does not crave for easily won and superficial pleasures, but a deeper satisfaction derived from self-identification with the lot of his titular figures. Gottfried is very conscious of the suffering of his hero and heroine, and interprets the satisfaction to be gained from vicarious participation in it in a symbolism which includes the words for 'death' and 'bread'. The associations of the terms, stronger in German than in English, even, by virtue of their rhyme, ensure that Gottfried's *Tristan* is an extreme statement of the force of love, and of the way it involves characters and readers alike in ambivalent emotions which efface any elements of elegant trifling there may be in the more usual manifestations of courtly love. This emphasis removes the story from the merely anecdotal level of the ruses the lovers have to employ in order to evade detection or divert suspicion. If such superficial details are relatively unimportant for Gottfried, they formed, none the less, the basis of the story his audience expected to hear. Some ambivalence lies, of course, in the material itself: ties of family loyalty no less than of marriage should keep Isolde from Tristan and Tristan from Isolde, but these are overruled by the administration of the potion, which allows them to offend in all innocence. These are the elements which are seized on and developed by Gottfried. When the potion is drunk in his poem, Brangaene, through whose oversight it was taken, is making more than a hyperbolic statement when she declares that it will be their death, and the separate monologues of Tristan and of Isolde, as the effects of the draught become apparent, reveal a personal awareness of conflict within themselves, and not only between social obligation and individual inclination. For them, love becomes an overriding force, a force for which the constraints of society and the artificiality of the courtly code are alike irrelevant. At one time, indeed, Gottfried seems expressly to indicate divine approval of the lovers, at the point where Isolde swears an oath before undertaking an ordeal which is ostensibly to prove her faithfulness to King Mark. Gottfried describes the oath as 'envenomed' (*gelüppet*), and comments on the outcome that it demonstrated how Christ the courtly was as pliant as a sleeve blown by the wind, an observation which at face-value is directly blasphemous, but which is conventionally explained as a reference to the disrepute into which trial by ordeal had fallen. It is in any case unlikely that a medieval author would expect such a statement to be understood literally; we have to assume an inflection of the voice which made it clear that mockery was directed here, as elsewhere, at the fabric of the story that the audience expected—a piece of detachment that marks out Gottfried as the conscious artist distanced from his material.

Some detachment from his source may even be seen in his

account of the Cave of Love—the *Minnegrotte*, for he introduces it by saying that he knew it well, and concludes by saying that he had never set foot in Cornwall. At the most superficial level this seems to disclaim any excesses that there may be in the scene by casting a doubt on its reality. Yet in the course of the episode itself there can be no doubting Gottfried's enthusiastic presentation of the lovers' idyllic life, prefaced as it is, after Thomas, by King Mark's act of voluntary renunciation in sending them away. The opening statement would suggest, then, that Gottfried's sympathies for the lovers were strong enough to transport him there in spirit, without ever having seen the actual place. The setting is itself an idealized landscape; the cave is circular within, and the basis of the description is a splendid dome-like structure comparable with the elaborate tomb-structures described by Veldeke. But there are no arches here; the walls are perfectly round, showing no corner where deceit may hide; the floor is of green marble, signifying constancy, and the bed is crystalline for utmost purity. Apart from its obvious perfection, the building has allegorical meaning, and it has been pointed out that the allegories used correspond to those which are used in descriptions of churches, so that what we have here is a description of a temple of Love. Possibly the allegories were, indeed, so familiar that Gottfried felt prompted at the end of the passage to set in doubt the existence of the *Minnegrotte*; but it should be remembered even here that allegory was not necessarily systematic, and that the properties of each item are little more than unusually striking metaphors of perfection. That there is perfection is certain, and it is a perfection attained only by the initiated and worthy, and at the cost of exclusion from the real world. At the most superficial level, the lovers are presented favourably in contrast with society; interpreted more subtly, life in the cave proceeds according to a higher principle, according to which the lovers—almost 'hermits'—live for themselves conjointly attuned into an existence which transcends even the luxury of a royal court. This elevates *Minne* to a principle of higher value than the claims of society; a religion which has its initiates and its mystics.

This unreal world, in which the constraints of the real world do not apply, cannot be entered except by those of the right disposition; it includes Tristan and Isolde, but excludes Mark. This fact leads Gottfried to one of his boldest pieces of reinterpretation. It was in the tradition that the lovers should be discovered with Tristan's sword lying between them, and that Mark should be so touched by this sight that he refrained from killing them or even waking them, contenting himself merely with exchanging his own sword for Tristan's and placing his glove on Isolde's cheek to protect her from the sun's rays. The effect of these actions is to bring the lovers ultimately back to the court. The two romantic gestures are denied Mark by Gottfried by the very romantic setting of the Cave. The fugitives must know by some means, however, that King Mark has been there, so he is allowed to cover one of the three windows set high in the wall of the cave through which he has seen the lovers. The object, here as elsewhere, is to protect Isolde's tender cheek from the sun. This confirms that they have been seen—but why was Tristan's sword unsheathed between them? Earlier explanations are not enough for the subtle Gottfried; he allows the lovers to have heard the calls of King Mark's hunting expedition on the previous day, and states that Tristan deliberately placed the sword between himself and Isolde as a deceptive symbol of their innocence. Tristan's action at this stage is of a piece with the recovery of Isolde from Gandin; the incompatibility of the inner world of the Cave and the outer world of the court could hardly be better expressed. In order to accommodate himself to the outer world, Tristan has to stoop to deceit.

There can, however, be no doubt of Gottfried's sympathetic attitude towards the lovers, no matter how 'practical' his treatment of the story may at times be. At times he even seems to come close to transforming the philtre from an agency of magic to a symbol of a pre-existent state of affairs;

but the hints of such a development remain no more than hints, and even appear to be overlaid by more 'realistic' considerations. Something of this is shown by Isolde's treatment of Tristan before the philtre has been drunk. She has regretted his (tactically) assumed lowly birth, which would make him ineligible to receive her hand even though he has fulfilled the condition of killing a dragon; but on discovering his true identity as the killer of her uncle, her immediate thought is for vengeance. She would, indeed, have killed Tristan, had not her mother intervened and invoked the laws of hospitality. Afterwards Gottfried asserts that she would have spared him in any case, out of womanly good nature. This afterthought may be enough to awaken in the reader who knows the story the expectation that Isolde has already fallen in love before drinking the potion. Yet such a deduction seems to be ruled out by her conduct after the couple have embarked on the voyage to Cornwall, but before the draught is taken. Here Gottfried allows Isolde to restate, rather unseasonably in view of the binding oaths that have been sworn all round, her hostility to Tristan. How convincing are these protestations? Gottfried, to be sure, is at pains to assure us that the beginning of love in Isolde was unexpected and even unwelcome to her, but is he here again revealing his detachment from his source—or playing with his reader? If so, his play is of a kind radically different from Wolfram's, for Wolfram's way was to pass over material facts with the lightest possible touch. In Gottfried's work the facts are known, but their interpretation opens up at times unending vistas of fresh implications.

Gottfried's language builds on Hartmann's lucid model, but develops it with conscious use of the devices of linguistic ornament as they were known in his day. His visual sense is much sharper, and he has also a keen ear for the precise term, nowhere more so than in his account of Tristan's dissection of a hunted stag, which is precise enough to be offensive to squeamish modern taste. Such inhibitions seem, however, not to have applied in Gottfried's time, yet he is nevertheless able to deplore Wolfram's use of medical terminology (*rede diu niht des hoves sî*), because it is socially unacceptable. In the literary excursus, the appeal to the Muses and other (not altogether accurately recorded) beings of classical mythology gives Gottfried's text a renaissance air not completely unprecedented in the writings of Hartmann, but strikingly different from the idiosyncrasy of Wolfram.

Gottfried's mastery of his material did not allow him to complete his work; the loss is the more tantalizing since his immediate source, the text of the Anglo-Norman Thomas, is preserved only in a mutilated form, with the beginning lost, and an overlap of only some 150 lines with the German version. Gottfried's text was certainly unfinished at his death, for two thirteenth-century authors wrote completions, strangely enough reverting for their source to more primitive versions of the story. Why Gottfried should have left only some 18,000 lines is unknown: medieval poetic output seems in general to have been small in compass compared with the amount that modern authors write, a fact attendant in some measure on the circumstances of recitation and listening rather than silent reading, of committing to memory, of the laborious and costly process of writing a text by hand on parchment. But allowing for this, 18,000 lines does not amount to a life's work: obviously Gottfried had to earn his keep by other means than by writing fiction, but even so there may be other reasons for his leaving the work unfinished. Given Gottfried's critical and detached attitude towards his material, the conclusion of no known version could have been satisfactory to him. In the crudest versions the lovers returned to the court because the effect of the philtre wore off; yet once their life in society had restarted they found it impossible to keep apart. The somewhat discreditable and unsavoury adventures which had led up to Tristan's marriage, for the sake of her name, to Isolde of the White Hands, had been eliminated in Gottfried's most immediate source, but the fact of this marriage and of Tristan's long absence from Cornwall was in turn inconsistent with the properties of the potion as given by Gottfried; this, indeed, was a difficulty which had already been ignored when Tristan had been absent for some time at the court of Duke Gilan. There remains the problem of the nature of the episodes, which were essentially repetitive, with Tristan returning first in one disguise and then in another to Tintagel, and with variations on the theme of discovery and flight. The conclusion itself need have presented no difficulty—the fable of the black and white sails was inevitable, and Isolde's death of a broken heart was recounted even by such an unimpassioned interpreter as Eilhart—but the intervening episodes were no more than a series of anecdotes of no great value. They could not all be abandoned when the story was recounted to a knowledgeable audience, and Thomas had shown commendable restraint in reducing their number; but they add nothing essential to the relationship between the lovers and King Mark, and very little scope for reorganization and reinterpretation. In a sense Gottfried's incomplete work says all that need be said: it is the fullest statement of the incompatibility of the claims of the newly discovered romantic love and society. Gottfried's decision in favour of love entitles *Tristan* to be called a 'Hohes Lied der Minne', even if the mystical associations of such an epithet may, perhaps, give a rather one-sided view of Gottfried's genius.

V

THE MEDIEVAL GERMAN LYRIC

Courtly Love

The lyric of the Middle High German efflorescence is characterized by the expression of the newly-codified courtly love. The poets of the chivalrous age are *Minnesinger* or poets of courtly love. It is as well to remember, however, before looking in some detail at their work, that there were other subjects for lyrical verse available at the same time. There was a strong and continuing stream of religious poetry, particularly *Mariendichtung*, which may, indeed, have supplied some of the diction of the poetry of courtly love; there was a well-developed crusading lyric, associated with the love lyric in so far as one of the readiest themes was the reluctance of the knight to go abroad; there was also homespun gnomic verse which might by courtesy be called lyric, and which has, by the same kind of courtesy, been included in the collection of Minnesang; there is verse drawing on nascent national feeling, which finds its first and highest expression in Walther von der Vogelweide. What comes off very short in medieval German is nature poetry; nature is seen only in passing as a reflection of or a contrast with the mood induced in the poet by his current situation, or rather by the situation in which he purports to be.

The appreciation of lyric poetry as confessional dies hard, and hardest in medieval poetry, where a rearguard action is fought against consigning fresh and intimate verse to 'mere' poetic convention; but such criticism surely accords ill with a type of poetry which expresses a highly stylized relationship set in a society governed by rigid conventions, and the fact that named poets who mostly sing of the obduracy of their mistress are identified as the authors of other poems in which a widow laments a lost husband should be sufficient warning against assuming that every event recorded in Minnesang is literally true. At times, indeed, especially in the more involved polystrophic poems of the later Minnesingers, successive stanzas in the same measure are mutually contradictory, and we have to assume that not all stanzas in the same measure were necessarily performed together on any one occasion, that juxtaposition arises from the medieval collector's zeal for order, that a poet was capable of revising his work, or adding a fresh stanza when a poem was brought out again before a new audience, or even that he was capable of self-commentary. In extreme cases a poet may write a pastiche of another's work in the same metrical form; but this is unusual, for the metrical form was the one place where originality was shown, and this was associated with a melody which was jealously protected by its originator. The decipherment of the melodies which have been preserved, for the most part, unfortunately, in rather late manuscripts, is not absolutely certain, but there has been great activity in this field in recent years, and no full-scale study of Minnesang can now afford to leave the music out of consideration.

The corpus of Minnesang is arbitrarily divided owing to the accidents of publication. When a collected edition of early lyrics was planned, the works of Wolfram and Walther had already appeared elsewhere; works which appeared to antedate them provided a collection of manageable proportions, and this was published under the somewhat romantic title of *Des Minnesangs Frühling*. This gives a good picture of the growth and establishment of the code of courtly love in the twelfth century, but lyric poetry continued to be written in the same forms, and with variations of the same themes throughout the thirteenth century, even though (as Walther must have felt) the code of courtly love gave little scope for lyrical originality.

The immediate source of the content as of the characteristic stanza form of Minnesang was the Provençal troubadour lyric; about the ultimate source much has been written. There are four major possibilities: a native tradition, classical Latin poetry, medieval Latin poetry, Arabic poetry. Of these sources only the last showed the appropriate attitudes of subjection on the part of the poet; the others contributed in the sense of supplying the subject-matter of sexual love, which might be thought to have been one of the perennial themes of verse, but seems to be so only because courtly love is an early expression of attitudes which have remained familiar in the language of romantic love down to the present day. The highest and the most debased form of its practice may be seen in the various uses of the one English word 'mistress'. Medieval courtly love was a fictive transference to a woman of the fealty and respect owed to a feudal lord. Respect and worship of womenfolk, on the evidence of the romances, certainly did not survive marriage. From the fact that the expression of the Minnesingers is confined almost exclusively to recounting the obduracy of a *frouwe*, it has frequently been assumed that the lady was inaccessible for one or both of two reasons, that she was a social superior and that she was already married. Colour is given to this supposition by the adventures the troubadours recount of themselves, and by Andreas Capellanus' textbook on courtly love; whether or not the excesses of the troubadours were true, and whether or not Andreas Capellanus' work was a *jeu d'esprit*, the German courtly lyric of the twelfth century, at any rate, is much more 'respectable' than one might be led to believe.

The Beginnings of the Courtly Lyric in Germany

The earliest German practitioners of the courtly lyric, however, form a self-contained group about as far removed as possible from direct Romance influence, the Danube valley; and in fact their poems show few traces of the fully-developed cult of courtly love. The first identifiable poet of *Des Minnesangs Frühling*, Der von Kürenberg, is still so remote that we have not even a personal name to attach to his poems, and there are several places called Kürenberg from which he might have come. The long lines of his verse look like an inheritance from Old High German, but the rhymes, such as they are, are no longer at the caesura, but at the end of the line, and his quatrains look as much as anything like the stanzas of the *Nibelungenlied*. In most cases his poems are no longer than a single stanza, though two, and perhaps three, on a related theme may be grouped together into a single poem of rather greater compass. Related stanzas are not even necessarily adjacent in the one manuscript that records them, e.g. the two-stanza poem which is held together by the use in both stanzas of the phrase 'rûmen diu lant'. It is clear that the speaker is not the same person in the two stanzas. The poem is a kind of dialogue *in absentia*, rumination separately by two people about a situation which affects them both, to which scholars have given the name *Wechsel*. The speaker of the first stanza is to be presumed a woman, in the second a man. The situation is a curious reversal of what might be expected in a male tradition of romantic love, in that the woman expresses affection and the man seeks escape. What appears to be expressed is an urgent desire not to submit to thraldom; almost as if it were a protest on behalf of the old social order against new conditions. If this were so, the fiction or fact of servitude would have been known in German-speaking lands before it found direct expression in poetry. The most famous poem of Kürenberg is without doubt the *Falkenlied*. Controversy arises over the interpretation of the falcon literally as a bird trained by a knight, or symbolically of the knight himself, 'tamed' by the lady who has to be regarded, in this case, as the speaker of the whole poem. The former interpretation is elliptical, in that it has to be inferred that the falcon is used in some way to signal the presence of the lover, but it accords well with the distribution of masculine and feminine rhymes, which should suggest another *Wechsel*. The second interpretation, generally held until comparatively recently, accords well with the attitude expressed in the other dialogue poem.

A number of poems are attributed in three codices to the second of the early lyric poets, Dietmar von Aist: scholars have divided these into an early and a late group, composed perhaps by two Dietmars. The later poet is credited with stanzas of short lines, the earlier one with stanzas with the same essential form as Kürenberg's. Some of the features of Kürenberg may still be traced, but there are signs of the coming acceptance of the values of courtly love, as for instance in such lines as:

> How could my heart ever be really content that a noble lady does so much to grieve me!—one whom I have served faithfully, as her inclination took her. Now she will take no account of my many sorrows. Ah, welladay, I must be absent for a long while. . . .

This is far removed from the elliptical manner of a Kürenberg. The stanza is the first of three, knit into a whole (exceptionally) by the refrain 'welladay'. The second stanza is explicitly spoken by a woman; in the first and third it is a man who speaks, but in these cases there are no inquits. In his stanzas the man accepts subjection. The woman is not obdurate; emotion is shared, and the cause of sorrow is forced parting. This, and the dialogue form mark the poem out as being of the earlier Austrian school of Minnesang. Two other dialogue poems of Dietmar are significant in the development of Minnesang: in one a bird in a linden-tree and flowering roses prompt a male speaker to give his recollections; nature is not observed for its own sake, nor is it the source or the recipient of the poet's feelings; it is present as an exemplary or contrastive background to the present. Dietmar is credited with the introduction of nature into the medieval German lyric: it is present, also, in the form of a bird, in Dietmar's other innovation in the German lyric, the *Tagelied* or dawn song. The situation, the parting of a pair of lovers at dawn, is conveyed in dialogue, without attribution of speakers, but stating at one point that 'the lady began to weep'. Although written in short lines, the poem is now attributed to the earlier or 'genuine' Dietmar. Another short-line poem deals with a falcon, and has been described as 'primitive', but in Dietmar's treatment there is little of the mystery that characterized Kürenberg's. There is no question of the falcon symbolizing the knight; the female speaker of the lines likens its actions to her own, and if it is a symbol at all, it is a symbol of freedom, contrasted with the speaker's plight.

A third poet of the 'primitive' stage of Minnesang, Meinloh von Sevelingen (Söflingen, near Ulm), is geographically remote from Kürenberg and Dietmar. His poems, based on the long line, show a relative smoothness comparable with Dietmar's rather than with Kürenberg's work. Also like Dietmar's, they invoke some of the stock in trade of the more highly developed system of courtly love, notably the *merkære*. There are also some textual resemblances between his work and Dietmar's, which appear to amount to rather more than the common use of idiomatic phrase, though it is probably impossible to determine the direction of influence.

These poets between them give an impression of the earliest stages of Minnesang; beside their increasing delicacy the simplicity of early *Spruchdichtung* becomes all the more apparent. The medieval *Spruch* is no epigram; it is rather a piece of worldly wisdom, formulated, sometimes neatly, in a single stanza of the form otherwise associated with the lyric. Among the poets of the early part of *Des Minnesangs Frühling*, the name Spervogel is given to the works of two writers of gnomic verse, distinguished in part by their use of different stanza forms; the later of them may, indeed, have been writing in the next century. Their verses offer generally simple advice, though it is sometimes couched in telling terms, and give also some idea of the precarious life of the professional poet of the Middle Ages.

The Adoption of Romance Attitudes

Credit for the introduction of the Romance stanza into Germany is generally given to Friedrich von Hausen, who came from another region—the upper Rhine; for purely geographical reasons he was likely to be more exposed than the Austrians to foreign models. He is known to have been a fighting knight, to have taken part in Barbarossa's Crusade of 1189, and to have died abroad a few weeks before his emperor. The experience of distance and absence is an important factor in his poems; in some, absence is directly attributed to the call of the crusade, but this does not account completely for the attitudes and relationships expressed in others. For Hausen develops fully for the first time the convention of servitude to an inexorable lady, coupled with a consciousness that something outside the writer has taken charge, as when he complains in a jaunty triple (or dactyllic) measure that *minne* has failed him. The poem treats love as an external force, but is less concerned than some others with the immediate relationship to a person. Where the personal relationship comes to the foreground there is a kind of dialectical play with the situation which is also unprecedented in German. One four-stanza poem, for example, plays with the idea of *huote* (surveillance), where the advantage of *merkære* in keeping undesirables away from his mistress is weighed against the inconvenience to himself of being unable to approach her—but the two theoretical stanzas are succeeded by another pair which present the chagrin of the poet at the fact of surveillance. Even the serious business of crusading is discussed in dialectical terms. His heart and his body, he declares, wish to part company. It is the body which will go out and fight the heathen; the heart, as seat of the affections, must remain behind in Germany. This gives rise, in turn, to reflections about the 'lifeless' man. In other poems the contrast is expressed with rather less *pointe*, and for modern tastes with much greater sincerity and effectiveness: the seriousness of the thought finds expression in a prayer to God for forgiveness for allowing thoughts of the beloved when matters of greater moment are on hand; and the next stanza expresses the bleak realization that 'no man knows how near death is to him'. Hausen is perhaps one of the most difficult of the poets of *Des Minnesangs Frühling* to represent by means of extracts or translation: he has no striking imagery, and even the invocation of nature has receded from its modest beginnings; the language is that of polite society, with a strong element of convention. Even the outward form of his stanzas is undemonstrative: the tripartite form of the Romance stanza is less clearly marked than it it is in later writers, and rhyme-schemes are still simple; there is a frequent economical use of two rhymes throughout a whole stanza.

It is perhaps convenient at this point to consider the last of the poets in *Des Minnesangs Frühling*, Hartmann von Aue. As well as being an exemplary writer of narrative works, he also produced a modest number of lyrics, and these poems, like Hausen's, may be divided into love poems and Crusading poems. Allusion to Saladin in one of Hartmann's crusading poems has been taken variously to indicate that they refer to the campaigns of 1189 or of 1197, though the earlier date, based on a textual emendation, has found favour of late. His other lyrics, some of them at any rate, would in that case also have been written in the eighties. Although Hartmann's lyrics are not generally as highly regarded as his narrative works, comparison with Friedrich von Hausen reveals a great development in technique which can only be explained by an assumption that while Hausen had written his Crusading lyrics as an old man, using the techniques he had acquired some years before, Hartmann's lyrics are the work of a younger man, exposed to more highly developed influences. Hartmann's lyrics are most frequently criticized for being 'impersonal'—which may mean no more than that they do not lend themselves to biographical interpretation. Yet a surprisingly wide range of feeling is, in fact, expressed; resignation, delight, resentment and even rebellion, though Hartmann decides finally in favour of quietism, a middle condition between longing and satisfaction known only to him who has not ventured. It is the consciousness of 'too high an aim' which leads Hartmann also to make what may be the first expression in German of *niedere Minne*—the rejection of the distant high-born mistress in favour of an affectionate companion of a station in life appropriate to the poet's own.

The crusading poems are by common consent Hartmann's best achievement in the lyric, though it is interesting to note that the techniques used are comparable to those of the generally rather harshly criticized love poems. The 'Saladin' poem is, however, unusual in beginning with a statement of personal resolve. If the crusading poems were connected with the death of a feudal lord, the poem known as the *Witwenklage* (widow's lament) may be occasioned by the same event. The poem is often held, even by those who otherwise favour an early dating for Hartmann's poems, to be modelled on a similar poem by Reinmar von Hagenau, which can be dated to 1195. The restraint of Hartmann's language and the greater eminence of Reinmar as a lyric poet have led to an unnecessarily unfavourable criticism of this poem; in spite of the artificiality of the rhetorical devices used here as elsewhere in Hartmann's lyrics, the writing is by no means pallid. There is not even any reason for assuming that it is Hartmann's poem which is derivative; and if this poem is given an early date, Hartmann's contribution to the courtly lyric may be held to have been equally effective in establishing a norm, as his contribution to the romance.

Heinrich von Veldeke, like Hartmann, had a relatively small but interesting output as a Minnesinger. There is considerable variety in the length of his poems, some of which consist of single stanzas and conform to the type of gnomic verse; mostly there are two or three stanzas, but there are occasionally poems of five or six stanzas, which by the complexity of the thought they enshrine appear to anticipate subsequent developments in the genre. The form of the stanzas is still relatively simple.

As he is so far removed geographically from Dietmar, his invocation of nature may probably be considered independent, and in any case his view of nature is at once more visual and more specific:

> In April, when the flowers burst forth, the linden comes to life and the beech turns green, when the birds start up their song with a will, since they find love where they seek it among their kind. . . .

This is a far more active nature, and one which comes near to existence in its own right rather than as a prefiguration of a state of mind. Consciousness of change taking place in the outside world is not isolated in this one poem, but the invocation of nature is, of course, only a small part of the art of Minnesang. The social conventions of courtly love appear to be well established in Veldeke's poems; the need to preserve secrecy before jealous and hostile bystanders is asserted, there is play from one poem to another with the notion of a favour asked and refused, and later—by inference from a tone of triumph—granted. Indeed, the conventions are so well established that they can become the object of word-play, or even parody. What are we to make of such lines as 'Since I saw that she could elude her guards as easily as the hare eludes the hound, since then I've had no qualms about my grandsire's granddaughters'? It might seem that Veldeke comes rather early in the tradition of Minnesang to mark a deliberate break away from it, but he is already capable of looking back to a golden age that is past. An appeal to past perfection—part of the poet's stock in trade from the earliest times—and a light-hearted treatment of existing conventions do not make profound poetry; the essential quality of Veldeke's lyrics lies in his strong visual sense and the vigour of his attitude and expression, which contrasts sharply with the expected languor.

There is playfulness, too, in some of the poems of Heinrich von Morungen, though the abiding impression made by his lyrics is one of visionary imagery and high seriousness. One or two minor dialectal features in his poems suggest that he was of central German origin, and there is a suitable

Thuringian family whose arms as recorded in the sixteenth century accord with those attributed to Heinrich in MS. C. A persistent legend makes a traveller and Crusader of 'Der edle Moringer', but there is no trace of crusading in his poems, which are devoted exclusively to courtly love. The near-anacreontic nature of some of them should remind us that court poets were among other things the entertainers of an elegant society. There is an unexpectedly light touch in other Minnesingers, but none blends playfulness with such compelling imagery or with such a vivid interplay of the real and the imaginary as Heinrich von Morungen. As an example of a poem which has elements at least of superficiality, one might consider the following:

> She has wounded me right through the soul into the mortal spot, when I told her how I raved and suffered on account of her kindly mouth. On one occasion I begged it to commend me to her service, for if I might steal from her a tender kiss, I should be saved. Alas, why have I become hateful to her rosy mouth, which I have never forgotten! But still it gives me great sorrow, because it so forcibly refused to do my bidding on one occasion. This has tired me so much that I would as soon burn alive in the abyss of hell as serve her for an uncertain reward.

The anacreontic elements: rosy mouth, kisses, especially stolen kisses, are in fact embedded in language of great portentousness. The wound suggests the darts of Venus, and the 'mortal spot' suggests, in a more or less conventional way, that the heart has been struck; but is the mention of the soul and the pains of hell, at the beginning and the end of the poem respectively, mere hyperbole, or a more serious strain in the thought of the poem? It is not quite certain here, but another poem which also starts with anacreontic attention to the lips changes the image in a disquieting way: [in a vision] 'I saw her noble virtues and her resplendent form, beautiful and exalted above all women, save that her red mouth, so generous of joy, was slightly withered.' Elsewhere Morungen combines the dialectical notion that his lady has only to grant him favours in order to be rid of his importunity, since he will promptly die for joy, with the idea of being put under a spell; the light of her eyes inflames him as fire inflames dry tinder. And here we are in the central range of Morungen's imagery—fire and light. He has chosen his beloved in preference to or as a substitute for the sun; the lady is his day star; this thought is developed and combined with the thought of her rising beyond his reach and a wish for evening, when she may come down again and console him. Put in so many words, this extension of the image appears to be a concetto like so many others, but there is about Morungen's language an element which defies such facile categorization. Morungen comments on the tradition of secrecy—treated partly with witty superficiality by the promise to open his heart and reveal her image inside, and more seriously by contrasting the activity of singing with the sad content of his songs, where singing is represented as a social duty; he had given the public little pleasure when he stood before them dejected. But there are few poems in which Morungen represents himself as dejected; his emotions are the energetic ones of enthusiasm, triumph and anger. Apart from the 'ich' poems, we have a *Tagelied* couched in the form of a third-person *Wechsel*, in which it is highly characteristic that the scene should have been envisaged in terms of light and seeing—and waking and dreaming states merge.

If Heinrich von Morungen is the Minnesinger who has the most immediate appeal to the untutored modern reader, it seems likely that Reinmar von Hagenau (Reinmar der Alte) was held by his contemporaries in the highest regard. Gottfried praised Walther as the one most likely to succeed Reinmar as the most eminent lyric poet, but Reinmar is incomparably more difficult to approach, because all his poems are written within the strict code of *hohe Minne*, and his output, larger than that of previous Minnesingers, concentrates on the expression of relatively few situations; one thinks of him as permanently lamenting his misfortune, and the distinguishing feature of his poems is the elegance of his diction, which was obviously more approachable to his contemporaries than it is to us. Evidence that Reinmar was a court poet in Vienna is provided by a widow's lament laid in the mouth of the consort of Duke Leopold V of Austria, who died on the last day of 1194; a crusading poem has presumably to be associated with the 1197 campaign, but this is the sum of external reference in Reinmar's poems. It is true that he sometimes speaks of other people watching him, and indeed he sometimes speaks to them, but his relation to them is primarily that of artist to public rather than of lover to rivals. He characteristically boasts of his eminence as a practitioner and a singer of courtly love—no one, he claims, could bear his sorrows so elegantly (*schône*). Nature hardly enters into his poems; only once is there a *vogellîn*. There are no *Tagelieder*, properly so called. There are not even *merkære*; the misfortunes of the lover are laid fairly and squarely at the lady's door. Circumstances are not to blame—or rather, the circumstances which are to blame are taken for granted, and expressions of regret are made at the unwitting or unwilling instrument of the pressures of society, the lady herself. Not that Reinmar invariably addresses complaints to her; he is much too polite. In fact, only four of the poems preserved in Reinmar's name are addressed directly to the beloved, and the authenticity of all of these has been impugned. The range of Reinmar's poems is rigorously restricted and demands a knowledge of Middle High German idiom, for among his other acts of self-denial is a very sparing use of imagery; he relies for his effect on the careful and precise use of the language of polite discourse of his time, and especially of the socially acceptable forms of irony and understatement. Pride in his craftsmanship, and some measure of its nature, is evinced by stanzas like the following—as large in compass as whole poems by his predecessors, but here only three of a longer set of stanzas in the same measure.

They say that constancy is a virtue, mistress of all others. It is well for him who has it. It has broken off my joy in my youth with its pleasing discipline, so that I shall never praise it again until my death. I can see very well that women these days love rather him who goes about raving like madman than a man who cannot act like this. I never spoke so harshly to them before!

I have long know the way which leads from joy to sorrow. The other one, which will lead me from sorrow to joy, that is not yet made for me. That my thoughts cause me such grief I hear, and pretend not to understand. If love gives nothing but distress, then love must be accursed, for I never saw her look pale!

For my life's days I will be master of one thing and nothing more. I wish the praise may be accorded me, and the world in general may acknowledge my skill, that no man can bear his grief so elegantly. If a woman does to me what I cannot conceal by day or night, I have such a gentle heart that I take her hatred as a joy: but ah, how unhappy it makes me!

Each of the three stanzas is in fact capable of being treated as a separate entity. The first protests against uncourtly behaviour; suffering and dignified resignation are things to be proud of, and the epithet 'pleasing' is a hint of the ennobling influence of grief. In the next stanza it is love which takes the blame, or rather the courtly system which condemns the poet to misery. In the third, Reinmar seizes from the wreck of his private happiness pride in the superlative skill of his expression. The stanzas resemble one another in ending with an aside which to some extent removes the mask assumed in the preceding lines. But the content of the poems is in other respects purely 'social', in that personal feelings towards the beloved are given limited expression by comparison with the influence which society has on the relationship.

Reinmar appears to be conscious of tradition in his art; not surprisingly, since he had precursors who all had considerable individuality. A falcon-poem must surely contain an element of pastiche of the genre represented, significantly enough, in the earliest Danubians, especially the single stanza by Dietmar. Reinmar echoes Dietmar in the use of octosyllables; but here we have not the alternation of masculine and feminine rhymes, and there is in fact a tripartite rhyme-scheme, marking the modern dress of an old theme. There is perhaps further allusion to Dietmar in a poem which turns the situation of the dawn-song inside out: 'Whenever dawn draws nigh I dare not ask, "Is it day?" . . . Happy is he who can say he left his love longing and grieving . . . Alas, dawn seldom comes to me as I would have it come.' There are allusions to, or echoes of, other Minnesingers in others of Reinmar's poems; perhaps to Hausen in the crusading song, to Morungen in a reference to the 'sweet word called yes', to Hartmann. It is not clear whether resemblance amounts to dependence, or whether all the poets derive their content from a limited set of situations, and above all write their poems in a stylized diction which permits of little innovation. It is in keeping with regional tradition that he writes *Frauenlieder* attributing to a woman the samc frustrations caused by the requirements of society as those usually represented as experienced by a man. In lighter poems, a woman is presented as addressing the messenger who will convey her commands to her admirer, and on one occasion she reveals her affection unashamedly before recanting in the last stanza. Elsewhere, anacreontic spirit emerges again, notably in a poem which speaks of stealing a kiss. Poems like this seem to suggest a Reinmar much more light-hearted than would be assumed from a general reading of his works.

When Walther wrote an obituary poem for Reinmar he singled out one poem of Reinmar's for particular praise—*so wol dir wîp, wie rein ein nam*, a poem which from the allusion appears to initiate some kind of aesthetic appreciation of womankind as a beneficent social influence. This is not altogether borne out by other stanzas in the same measure, but *wîp* or womankind are praised for giving the world *hôher muot*, a virtually untranslateable quality, but among other things a serene happiness consistent with the calm exterior of court life; to this quality Reinmar's poems are also a contribution. A threat to sing no more therefore gives greater force to a poem which, in printed editions, at least, opens with the words:

What will long continue to raise my spirits is raising them now: that I never harmed a woman with my words. If anyone else spoke of them otherwise than kindly that was an offence which I never forgave. No man stood so low in their esteem who would more gladly receive their praise, and who would more dearly receive their favour. Yet they have my service; for all my solace and my life, that must belong to a woman (*wîp*).

The idea of collectivity is here—in the indefinite article there is both a reference to a specific woman and a wider reference to womankind in general. And if this stanza, with its use of key words of the vocabulary of *minne*, stresses the exemplary nature of Reinmar as a poet, a subsequent one speaking of *leit mit zühten tragen*, 'bearing grief graciously', shows the same pride in courtly perfection as a lover.

The lyrical output of Wolfram von Eschenbach is ascribed to his youth on account of a specific renunciation of the ways of *minne* in one of the poems. The eight fairly long lyrical poems preserved under Wolfram's name are for the most part *Tagelieder*, among the most powerful of their kind. Even in these poems Wolfram is to a high degree a narrator. The scene is carefully set, and dialogue is specifically introduced, with each participant named. More than once a third character, the watchman (*wahtære*) is added to the participants and becomes emotionally involved in the situation. Officially he announces the arrival of dawn, and by implication he is responsible for warning the castle and its inmates of approaching danger; yet the sympathies he expresses are with the lovers. The stress he gives here to the dangers of the situation represents the intrusion of the real world into a make-believe situation. The realization of the implications of this situation makes a final renunciation of the genre necessary for the serious-minded Wolfram. It is characterstic that the watchman should be addressed in the opening lines of Wolfram's anti-*Tagelied*; the main burden of the poem, however, is the contrast between the perils of illicit amours and the security of marital bliss. The language of Wolfram's lyrics is as individual as that of his narrative works; he gives one of his watchmen the most graphic description of dawn in medieval German literature, in which dawn is shown tearing away darkness with 'his' talons—the first words are *sîne klâwen*, and it is some time before the referent of the pronoun is identified as 'day'. The situation gradually becomes clear, as it were, as the light steals on the lovers. Even more striking than this opening, perhaps, is the description of the lovers' final embraces before parting. Earlier German dawn songs had been much more reticent, contenting themselves with the exploration of mental distress. Wolfram paints the scene in almost embarrassing detail.

Walther von der Vogelweide

By far the most eminent lyric poet of medieval Germany, and the one poet of his time who is immediately comprehensible to the modern reader with no need for detailed explanations of esoteric literary conventions, is Walther von der Vogelweide. The poems by which he is most widely remembered are not, however, those which follow most directly in the tradition of Minnesang. Anthologies of German verse most generally include his 'Elegy' (in which an old man looks back to a golden age in his youth and compares the decadence of the present), his *pastourelle* 'Under der linden' (a love poem in all conscience, but one which appeals directly by the vigour and freshness of its language, and anti-Minnesang rather than Minnesang in the attitudes it expresses) or the poem whose opening line provides the content of the well-known portrait of Walther sitting with his chin cupped in his hand, pondering the shortcomings of the world. This poem, like the elegy, belongs to the tradition of edifying and gnomic verse rather than to what might be called the lyric proper, but unlike the elegy it is referable to a known historical occasion.

Not only are these poems probably the best known of Walther's entire output, they may be held to be representative of his highest achievement. Perhaps for this reason, the large number of poems by Walther which adhere to the convention of courtly love, and which justify his inclusion at the head of the lyric poets in the literary survey of his near-contemporary Gottfried von Strassburg, reveal themselves only on closer acquaintance with his works. It has long been the practice to account to Walther's early years a respectable number of poems in the manner of Reinmar, but the establishment of a list of such poems is not the simple matter it may seem to be, for there is nearly always some slight departure from the strict code which Reinmar had adopted. Conventional attitudes beneath an appearance of unconventionality may be seen in a poem like the following:

> They ask and ask me again too often about my lady, who she is. That annoys me so much that I will name her to them all: perhaps they'll let me alone then. Graciousness and ungraciousness: my lady has both these two names. They are unequal; one is poor, the other rich. If any one deprives me of the rich one, he must be ashamed of the poor. . . .
>
> Fair as the meadows (*heide*) are decked out in manifold colours, yet I will assert that the woodland holds more marvels, and the farmland (*velde*) has received even greater favours. Praise to you summer for such courtesy. Summer, if I am to praise you all your days, come consolation, console my complaint. I'll tell you what is wrong—I am repugnant to her who is dear to me.

The second stanza translated is the last of a set of four; it contains the only reference in the poem to external nature, but even so this nature is much livelier than in most earlier Minnesingers. Summer is not visualized, but personified to such an extent that 'he' can be addressed. The first stanza establishes a situation which is part of the stock of Minnesang, and plays with the code of anonymity, threatening to break it, but only as a piece of bluff. The vocabulary is refreshingly simple. 'Graciousness' (*gnâde*), contrasted with its negation, is probably the nearest the stanza comes to using an esoteric code word.

Walther's imitation or development of the manner of

Reinmar apparently won him a following, and this may underlie the literary rivalry which finds expression in allusion and counter-allusion in their poems. Walther's words in places give an appearance of considerable acrimony, and it was he who took the initiative in the feud by taking up suggestions in two of Reinmar's poems, one which called his mistress his Easter Day and claimed by implication that she surpassed all others, since to praise her as one would praise others would not be enough. This may have caused some comment, for the second Reinmar poem asserts that the lady is one who never stepped a foot from womanly virtue. That, he asserts, is checkmate to 'them'. ('They' are assumed to be his critics.) The last stanza, however, goes on in anacreontic fashion to toy with the idea of stealing—and replacing—a kiss. Walther's riposte is blatantly announced as a parody by the adoption of the same rather striking metrical structure as Reinmar's poem. The first stanza of Walther's parody is so full of allusion to Easter Day and checkmate that the syntax is highly involved and the transmission corrupt. A second stanza is attributed to a female speaker, objecting to the notion of the stolen kiss and disclaiming any intention of letting it be returned. There has been a certain amount of idle speculation whether the speaker is Walther's or Reinmar's mistress, but this surely is the *reductio ad absurdum* of biographical interpretation. Reinmar took up the challenge with a textual allusion to Walther, and animosity continued. One of Reinmar's best-known poems begins: 'Let no one ask what tidings I bring: I am unhappy . . .' He rebuts an accusation of showing too little devotion to his lady, and continues with the line, 'Hail to thee, woman, how fair a name!' (*so wol dir wîp, wie rein ein name!*), where discretion is so great that it is hard to tell whether a specific individual is meant, or womankind in general, as Walther apparently took it to be. The first reaction by Walther to this poem seems to have been to seize on the one word *mære* ('tidings') in its first line in addressing a general encomium to German women, assuming as he does so the rôle of one who has just arrived from a distance. Indeed this assumption might account for the whole poem, were it not for further allusions to Reinmar's words. Cross references between the two poets become slighter and slighter after this, until Walther after Reinmar's death cites this same poem as the one above all others on which Reinmar's claim to fame—especially with women—should rest. After textual allusions in the first stanza, Walther concludes the memorial poem with lines which, superficially at least, suggest strained personal relationships accompanied by a genuine admiration for literary achievements; perhaps also a poet's realization that the work is greater than the man, or even an admission that Walther's achievement was in fact still relatively slight at this time.

Walther's output by this time was, however, considerable and varied. The poem which adopts the pose of the returning traveller has been connected with Walther's reappearance at the Court of Vienna in 1203 after an absence of some four or five years. His departure is ascribed to his failure to find patronage there after the death of Duke Friedrich I in 1198. Walther's moves after this time are not altogether clear; he had to find patronage where he could, and in 1203 he seems to have been in the entourage of Bishop Wolfger of Passau; before that he had been attached to the court of Philip of Swabia, the regent and for a time successful contender for the German throne. It was in this environment that Walther first emerged as a political poet, an environment that he found congenial, but not one, apparently, in which he found an established position. Walther's poems of this time are full of the need to restore stability and legitimacy in Germany by the coronation of Philip ('Ich saz ûf eime steine' and 'Ich hôrte ein wazzer diezen'). The former of these poems dwells on the current state of disruption and goes on to represent a medieval triad of values—*guot, êre, gotes hulde*—wealth which fitted one to take part in the civilized life of the court, good repute among one's contemporaries, and the blessing God gives to faithful servants. In the unsettled circumstances of the day, Walther doubts whether any one person will ever again possess all three.

Walther's enthusiasm for the cause of Philip survived intervention by the Pope in favour of the Guelph Otto, and hostility to the Pope became a recurrent feature of Walther's political poems. Walther's return to Austria in 1203 seems not to have found him patronage at the court of Vienna, and in the next few years he seems to have been in the protection of Hermann of Thuringia and Dietrich von Meissen, two noble patrons of the arts, whose political allegiances were equivocal. At the death of Philip, Otto became the person most likely to achieve national unity. No poem of Walther's expressing support for Otto can be dated to Philip's lifetime, but there is a series of stanzas beginning *Her keiser* and *Her bâbest* datable to early in 1212, when Walther, in the company of Dietrich von Meissen, was present to greet Otto's return to Germany, having been crowned by the Pope in 1209 and subsequently excommunicated for an attempt to conquer Sicily. Walther's poems at this time are studiously unenthusiastic, and perhaps even double-edged, presenting a case for a patron whose loyalty was still undetermined, at a time when Otto's foreign support was weakened and the cause of Friedrich II, by now some sixteen years old, was finding increasing favour. Indeed, Walther attached himself within a year or so to Friedrich, and under him found at last the steady patronage he had so far lacked.

The poems Walther wrote as comments on the events of the time are among the most vigorous of his writings, and they are also amongst the best known. Walther may have found a model in the Latin poems of the *vagantes*, the wandering scholars with whom he had probably consorted in his unsettled years, and from the same quarter, too, he may have derived some of the carefree attitudes expressed rather later in the Latin and macaronic poems of the *Carmina Burana*, which had none of the inhibitions of earlier vernacular courtly poems. This type of poetry finds its reflection in Walther's poems of *niedere Minne*. This was not 'lower' in any moral sense, but socially 'lower', being addressed, apparently, to women of low degree. A contrast between the distant reception accorded to a poet by a *frowe* and the complaisance of a *wîp* had already been made schematically by Hartmann von Aue, but in Walther it finds full expression. In one notable *Spruch*, which may also contain some allusion to Reinmar's abstract encomia of womankind as *wîp*, he draws on the contrast in extreme terms, classifying some *frowen* as unwomanly (*unwîp*), a contrast all the more effective because all *frowen* in another sense are *wîp*, and there is no term *unfrowe*.

Another poem gives a lively account of a meeting at a rustic open-air dance, and most famous of all, the *pastourelle*, laid in the mouth of a girl, gives expression at once vivid and coy to carefree love. In this poem nature is interwoven with the human content in a way which eluded most of the Minnesingers, evidenced as clearly as anything by the voice of the nightingale interrupting the flow of the language. Spontaneous as Walther's *pastourelle* appears to be, it should, however, be pointed out that this, too, belongs to a highly developed literary convention—not least in the assumption of a rôle which could never have been the poet's own. But Walther the singer of nature and of natural human relationships is not the only Walther, and it is convenient perhaps to associate some staider poems with Walther's assured position as a court poet. The beginnings may perhaps be seen in the general encomium of German women of 1203, but a fuller expression is found in 'So die bluomen ûz dem grase dringent', which reveals Walther's awareness of womankind as a generalized and somewhat impersonal aesthetic phenomenon. There is something here of the abstractness of Reinmar's work, but Walther's poem is marked out by a feeling for nature and an informality of language which is the fruit of Walther's contacts in his unsettled years. Many of the poems of this phase of Walther's career stress the value of such qualities as *mâze*, the golden mean, recalling the classic calm of Reinmar; and at least once Walther launches into a diatribe against writers of unseemly verse, which by an allusion in the text is identified as non-courtly verse. What is commonly called his elegy, his last poem, shows all the concern of an old man for the decline in decorum and morals currently going on; it includes a call to higher things, to participation in a Crusade, which is the means of dating the poem to 1227 and regarding it as Walther's swansong. Walther is here not only a critic of society, but an advisor: the advice he gives is conventional enough in content, with its promise of eternal reward to the crusader, but it reveals Walther as an enthusiast and a partisan to the last. It is probably the vigour of his partisanship in his public poems as much as the directness of the speech in the private ones which endears him above all other medieval poets to the modern reader. His changes of allegiance in public utterance may seem at first sight to mark him as something of a time-server. There is, however, a consistent thread of patriotism throughout his public utterance; if the precarious position of a court poet is not enough to absolve all his vacillations, his brief association with the Guelph cause may be regarded as an unfortunate episode, when none was more keenly aware of the false position he was placed in than Walther himself, as witness the double edge of his greetings to Otto.

With Walther, the peak of the medieval German lyric is reached, but the form was to continue for another century or more. The outward form of the stanza lasts longest, and survives in the didactic poems of the Meistersinger of the fifteenth and sixteenth centuries; in the thirteenth there are still poems reflecting the full panoply of the *minne* system, but there is also a development of the new line which Walther began, of reference and appeal to non-courtly circles.

VI

THE *NIBELUNGENLIED* AND OTHER MIDDLE HIGH GERMAN HEROIC TEXTS

The 'Nibelungenlied' and the 'Klage'

The matter of the *Nibelungenlied*, unlike that of the fashionable romances of chivalry, has a native origin. The *Nibelungenlied* is notoriously a combination of legends deriving from different localities, and differences between the closing scenes of the *Nibelungenlied* and their parallels in other literatures suggest alteration in the interests of a view of history that could not have been held by the originators of the legend. It is important to remember, too, that the extant version of the *Nibelungenlied* was written down at a time when the major narrative authors of Germany were busy writing tales of courtly and chivalrous adventure, and that many of the social attitudes and some of the diction of the *Nibelungenlied* belong to the courtly world of the turn of the twelfth–thirteenth century, though the long lines and the stanza form, like the anonymity of the author, are a reflection of the past.

It is perhaps the result of prior acquaintance with later treatments of the material that one expects the central figures of the text to be Siegfried and Brünhild; but Siegfried is killed halfway through the story and Brünhild, having incited Siegfried's murderer to the deed, fades out and is hardly mentioned again. The figure generally singled out as providing continuity of narration is Kriemhild, Siegfried's bride and widow, who is introduced almost as a romance heroine, but becomes progressively sterner, until her husband's death turns her into an avenging fury, a 'she-devil' (*vâlandinne*).

This term is a comment on her last actions which would have appealed to a civilized courtly audience when the text was written, but it sits very loosely on the text as a whole; and the young princess of the first part, for all her forebodings and second sight, hardly prepares the reader for the harpy of the second. But this reading fits Kriemhild better than it fits one other major figure of the *Nibelungenlied* who is present from beginning to end—Hagen. He, too, grows in stature, and his decisive intervention in affairs in the first part, the assassination of Siegfried, is the event from which the second part springs. No epithet is too harsh for him before the deed, and for some time after, yet towards the end of the poem he is presented as the embodiment of valour and resourcefulness, and of defiance when all is lost. The engagement of the narrator swings so sharply in his favour that the reconciliation of the attitudes of the two parts is problematic.

The solution to the problems raised which found favour throughout the nineteenth century and for much of the twentieth was a genetico-historical one. The matter of the *Nibelungenlied*, or something like it, is conveyed in so many sources that the reconstruction of the stages by which it may have reached its present form is a fascinating pursuit. The carnage at the end is a reflection of the destruction of the Burgundians under Gundicarius by the Huns (not under Attila, the Etzel of the *Nibelungenlied*) in A.D. 437. A further piece of history, the sudden death of Attila at the side of his concubine Hildiko, of conquered Germanic stock, became the nucleus of a tale of vengeance—vengeance exacted upon Attila by a Burgundian wife for the slaughter of her brothers. From this garbled and personalized history there arose the legend that Attila coveted the wealth of the Burgundians, that they were warned by their sister against coming, but came nevertheless with resignation or bravado, were killed by Attila and avenged. The switch in the second part from revenge on Attila for killing the brothers to revenge on the brothers for killing a husband appears to have been effected relatively early on, probably by the Bavarians, among whom the legend was cultivated, since they did not share the otherwise general view of the barbarism of Attila. As a husband and as a source for the treasure, the mythical figure who is the Siegfried of the *Nibelungenlied* was introduced. There are legendary parallels for his murder, instigated by Brünhild, but their motives are obscured in the *Nibelungenlied*, though there is an inescapable minimum of such matter present, which can only with difficulty be accommodated to the fabric of the work as a whole. The addition of the story of Siegfried to that of the Burgundians was the last of a series of alterations and adaptations which had befallen the material, and the blending of the two traditions has not been fully accomplished.

The two parts of the *Nibelungenlied* are compatible so far as Kriemhild's motives are concerned, though it remains problematic that vengeance which is approved in prospect should in its execution meet with such summary punishment from Hildebrand. The change in sympathies towards Kriemhild is slight in comparison with that towards Hagen. It should be noted that while Kriemhild's vengeance involves the deaths of all her brothers, Hagen is no brother, but a vassal of Gunther, the oldest brother; Hagen is, however, the murderer of Siegfried, and as such the principal victim of Kriemhild, yet no words are good enough for his stubborn and reckless courage at the end. The *Nibelungenlied* is not, of course, the only literary text which reports the fall of the Burgundians and the death of Siegfried, but no two versions of either event tally fully, and it is differences between Eddic poems, the *Prose Edda*, the *Völsungasaga* and the *Thidrekssaga* which have made it possible to establish a scheme for the genesis of the *Nibelungenlied*. But even when the major shifts of sympathy and interest are genetically explained, there remain a number of small inconsistencies in the narration of the *Nibelungenlied* as it stands. Most of these concern the youth of Siegfried as it is represented in the text and as it must have been known orally at the time. Siegfried assumes a symbolic vassalage to Gunther in order to persuade Brünhild of Gunther's might and prowess—but this demonstration could mean little enough unless Brünhild and Siegfried had been previously acquainted, and this is denied elsewhere. Hagen gives an account of Siegfried's youth which is at variance with what emerges about it from the text of the *Nibelungenlied.* Siegfried's second conquest of Brünhild for Gunther is specifically stated to be innocent, yet he takes from her tokens which ought to indicate the reverse—and presents them to his wife. He is prepared to swear an oath which ought to establish his innocence before Gunther, yet Gunther is implicated in the plot against Siegfried. One would think that, by the murder of Siegfried, Hagen had offended enough against Kriemhild to enjoy her undying hatred, yet he is made in addition to steal her treasure, with or without the connivance of her brothers. The aggressive manner of Siegfried's first appearance at Worms, in which he demands the hand of Kriemhild as a price for keeping the peace, accords ill both with the account given of his upbringing as a knight in the tradition of the romances and with the warnings he has been given of the danger which awaits him at the court of Gunther. This last episode is the more problematic, since it could have been eradicated without affecting anything else; there has been a latter-day genetic explanation as a result of which Siegfried becomes an antagonist driven away from the court of Worms by the loyal Hagen! But this interpretation, like all other interpretations which proceed from reconstructed earlier stages, relies for its conviction on discrepancies, and a tacit implication that the work is flawed.

This is not to say that attempts to interpret the *Nibelungenlied* as if it had no prehistory, and as if it might be assumed to be a perfect unity, are necessarily any more convincing. In recent years various attempts have been made to treat the text as a whole, to penetrate the contradictions of the surface content to deeper levels of meaning, seeing for example Siegfried as a representation of strength, Kriemhild of beauty, Gunther of the kingly, Brünhild of the queenly principle. This is in fact an abstraction at the level of appearances which does not take account of the incompatibility of the pairs. A rearrangement, with Gunther and Kriemhild on the one hand as the representatives of courtly society and Siegfried and Brünhild on the other as the representatives of natural forces, comes much closer to the underlying theme at the outset of the text; though the two who might be thought to represent the stronger force are for one reason or another inactive for the second and more important part of the work, while one of the other two reveals at best how thin the veneer of civilization is, and the other, although allowed to make the conventional gestures of valour, is a relatively unimportant figure. A more promising suggestion is that the text presents disaster inevitably overwhelming those who for one reason or another try to break the bounds of natural order—a social order in the case of Hagen, a moral one in the case of Kriemhild.

Such unitary interpretations rest on the assumption that the poet of the *Nibelungenlied* was entirely successful in recasting his material to suit his purpose. Yet the persistence of stories of the boyhood of Siegfried long after the poet's time in a form substantially similar to the account given by Hagen suggests at least a concession to the expectations of an audience, if not a direct oversight. Much the same may be said for some of the other discrepancies. If such a view is accepted, we are forced back to the position that any unity in the work is imposed on it from outside, that it is imperfect. But an admission of inconsistency, even of such a diametrical change of sympathies as that shown in the *Nibelungenlied*, need not detract from the qualities of its greatest moments. Whatever its origins, the story of Siegfried is effective, and in spite of the boorishness of his irruption into Worms, in spite of the account given of his acquisition of the treasure, it is difficult to see his death as anything but a tragic waste; the reader has great sympathy for Brünhild, who is, to say the very least of it, the victim of a misunderstanding; but—in the first part at least—none at all for Hagen, although both are involved in the killing of Siegfried. This, at least, is the disposition of affections induced by the comments interspersed through the text at the ends of stanzas; on the whole it seems to be reasonable to take these comments at their face value until they are controverted by fact. Between the first part and the end of the second, a change takes places in the sympathies expressed by the author, and in general he carries his readers with him. The romantically minded may be unable to be wholeheartedly in support of Hagen even at the end, but his gestures in the closing scenes have the magnanimous disregard for safety which is the stuff of the heroic.

There is an air of doom about the end of the *Nibelungenlied* which marks it out from other works of the Middle High German *Blütezeit*. The mood in which Hagen meets his death derives from a Germanic fatalism; his death is heroic, but the tragic choice which makes it inevitable has been taken long before. The strength and size of the catastrophe was great enough to resist any unconvincing application of a happy ending; great enough to generate, against the grain of the literature of the time, a new tragic figure in Rüedeger, who befriended the Nibelungs on their way to Etzel and remained aloof from the fighting until his liege lord Etzel called him in against them. The chivalrous gesture by which he hands his shield to Hagen is a denial of self-interest and personal welfare which to cold calculation can only seem excessive, but is in keeping with the older heroic spirit, and a fine symbol of the way his loyalties are torn between his friends and his lord.

The narration of the *Nibelungenlied* is much less fluent than that of the romances. This comes in part from the end-stopped stanza form, which involves frequent recourse to a half line, or even a whole line, with very little meaning—perhaps a comment expressing approval or disapproval, or else a prophecy of dire events to come. This latter type of interpolation may, indeed, contribute to a sense of foreboding in the reader, but it does not help the narrative flow, any more than do the standing epithets which are applied elsewhere to the characters. The first and more courtly part of the *Nibelungenlied* otherwise shows considerable affinity to the romances of the same time: the same kinds of scenes are included, e.g. the accolade of Siegfried; there is the same air of luxury and pomp, and some of the excessive descriptions of dress are described by the derogatory term *Schneiderstrophen*. Resemblance to romance at this stage is more than skin deep. Siegfried, in spite of his turbulent arrival at Worms, puts on the languishing attitudes of a courtly lover; he is even prepared to fall in love with Kriemhild before first sight. Siegfried's exploits in the Saxon wars should justify his claim to her hand, but he undertakes the additional task of winning Brünhild for Gunther before making good his claim. Even the formal celebration of the Burgundians' arrival in Etzel's kingdom in the second part has the stamp of public functions at King Arthur's court—there is a *bûhurt*, a kind of simulated cavalry charge performed as a sport. It is a sport which can, and on this occasion does, cost lives, but the death of a Hun in this recreational skirmish is not the signal for the outbreak of general hostilities; and, tense as the situation is, nothing comes of the incident. Apart from this, the quality of events in the second part is clearly different from that in romances. It shares with them perhaps the quality of exaggeration, as for example the numbers ferried single-handed across the Danube by Hagen or the numbers involved in the battle in the burning hall at the end of the work—nameless numbers who have to be eliminated before the major figures come into conflict one by one. In the two parts the progression is stately: it is usual for the reasons for a fresh initiative first to be narrated, then related as the thoughts or the words of the initiator, then presented as happenings; though this explicitness does, in fact, break down at key points in the narrative. The language itself shows some characteristic differences from that of the romances. Most obvious perhaps is the use of old-fashioned words for persons, like *recke* and *degen*—the latter occasionally used elsewhere for 'knight', the former belonging to the heroic vocabulary, though watered down from its historical meaning of 'exile' into something resembling a doublet of *degen* itself. Some of the adjectives also recall an earlier stage of the language, and the use of standard epithets, and more especially their frequent position after the noun to which they apply, seem to be almost an antiquarian pastiche—though such practices recur in later ballad style, and may represent a type of verse orally current. Certainly earlier texts than the *Nibelungenlied* written in rhyming couplets do not display such apparently archaic features. The verse, like some of the content, may lend support to the postulation of an earlier version of the second half or the *Nibelungenlied*, the so-called *Ältere Not* of about 1170, and also account for an old-established but unsubstantiated tradition that the author of the earlier version was Der von Kürenberg, the time and place of whose activity appear to coincide remarkably well with those postulated for the *Ältere Not*; though one may still assume earlier sources based on oral poetry, perhaps of a type approximating to the ballad. Whatever its history, and whatever its faults and inconsistencies, the *Nibelungenlied* remains a text of great inherent significance—a twin peak with Wolfram in the achievements of the Middle High German golden age. Its view of life differs from Wolfram's and that of other writers of his time in being fundamentally tragic, not simply because it ends in a bloodbath, but because, in spite of its scale, it gives a fundamentally pessimistic view of the individual human lot. This by itself is enough to give some profundity to the *Nibelungenlied*, but the heroes are more than life-size—not so much in the sense of being superhuman, but of being essentially more significant than the heroes of romances as part of an interpretation of a half-forgotten past.

The stanza of the *Nibelungenlied* is stately at its best, even if it is clumsy at times. Whether a similar verse form could have saved the *Klage* is questionable. This text is a recital in rhyming couplets of the lamentations by the survivors for the victims of the Nibelungen catastrophe. Its content is essentially static, and it draws on material provided by the major work, on which it is a kind of parasite.

Kudrun

Structurally, the way in which the *Nibelungenlied* falls into distinctive parts is somewhat reminiscent of the *Spielmanns-epos*. The resemblance is carried further by the exaggeration of numbers, particularly in the closing scenes. But the *Nibelungenlied* material was strong enough to resist the grafting of a happy ending on to an intrinsically tragic story. The other great Middle High German narrative poem of Germanic origin, *Kudrun*, was less fortunate, and the resultant text is far less compelling than the *Nibelungenlied*. Nevertheless it has qualities of its own, including a strongly-developed sense of personal rivalries and of individual courage in situations of great adversity. Like the *Nibelungenlied*, it is anonymous and composed in stanzas. The stanzas themselves have a less assertive rhythm than those of the *Nibelungenlied*, and the greater length of the lines, coupled with feminine rhymes, matches the rather more conciliatory content of the poem.

The text of *Kudrun* survives by the slenderest of chances—a single sixteenth-century manuscript—and it is calculated that the source of this can be dated no further back than the middle of the thirteenth century. The name of Kudrun, the heroine, has a form which could not have existed naturally in the Bavarian milieu in which the story was told, and the setting, on the North Sea and other coasts, suggests an origin remote from the area where the tale was last told. The name of the heroine belongs, in northern treatments of the Nibelungen material, to the Kriemhild figure; and other names in *Kudrun* echo those of heroic literature, though the figures themselves have nothing to do with their namesakes. The adoption of names from better-known heroic cycles might seem to be an attempt to gain for the text some kind of borrowed authority, and there are incidents in *Kudrun* which suggest late compilation from a wide range of disparate sources. All this looks at first sight most unpromising;

the general structure of the poem is hardly less so. There is what might be called a prologue recounting the adventures of the boy Hagen (a reflection in some way of the very different boyhoods of Parzival and Tristan?), who is plucked away from a court festivity in his native Ireland and carried away to a forest by a griffin. He manages to kill a whole family of griffins (reminiscence of *Herzog Ernst*?) and escapes with three princesses who have been held in a similar captivity. The next section of the text takes place in the next generation. Hagen has married one of the princesses, and has a daughter called Hilde after her mother. Hetel, king of Denmark, sends his faithful retainers on a wooing expedition to Ireland. There are one or two incidents, including the sweet singing of Horant, at the Irish court, before the daughter is abducted by a ruse not unlike one used in *König Rother*. After pursuit and battle, Hagen consents to the marriage of Hetel and Hilde. For the third stage of the story, we again move on a generation: Kudrun is the daughter of this marriage, and is as jealously guarded as ever her mother was. A rejected suitor abducts Kudrun, is pursued and overtaken, but in the course of a battle on the Wülpensand, Hetel is killed, and his quarry makes good his escape with Kudrun. Her life in exile in Normandy is wretched in the extreme, and as a culminating humiliation she is forced by Queen Herlint, as a price for her refusal to consent to the marriage, to wash the royal linen unshod on the seashore in all weathers. She is eventually rescued by her faithful suitor Herwig; and the text ends on a conciliatory note, with weddings between all eligible couples, including erstwhile enemies, though not until the oppressor Queen Herlint is put to the sword. There is clearly a resemblance between the second and third parts of this story and the construction of the *Spielmannsepos*, and resemblance continues into small details, most notably perhaps in repetition of incident, e.g. fighting is stopped once by Hilde, twice by Kudrun, between two people for both of whom she feels affection. The good quality of the construction lies largely in the ingenious way in which the actions of Kudrun's three suitors become interlocked; and the most original part of the text is the development of the character of the ogress Herlint, both by her words and by her deeds, into one of the most convincing portraits of malice and cruelty in Middle High German literature. On the whole, the depiction of villainy is more successful than that of faithful affection; little enough attention is given to the touching constancy of Kudrun's love for Herwig over fourteen years. So far we have a text which is attractive, but not what one might expect to call a heroic poem. More akin to the heroic spirit is the fight in an enclosed space when Kudrun's deliverers come to Normandy. There is bloodshed, but the outcome is in no sense tragic; the casualties are the representatives of evil, and the defenders of the right are confronted by no fateful choice, yet the setting is right. We come a little closer to the essential heroic spirit in the fight on the Wülpensand, where Kudrun's father is killed, an incident which might be called melancholy rather than strictly tragic, but one which is out of keeping with the happiness and success which marks by far the greatest part of medieval German literature. The incident is in fact a clue; and a further one is found in Lamprecht's *Alexander*, a century or so earlier than *Kudrun* itself, which speaks of a battle which took place on the Wolfenwerde (Wülpensand: *werde* = 'island') between Hagen and Wate, in which Hilde's father is killed. The names belong to the story, but, except for Wate, a timeless Hildebrand-figure, to the previous generation. Essentially the same incident is recounted in the *Prose Edda*, with earlier support from the ninth-century Norwegian skald Bragi, in which versions the battle lasts all day, representing a stage in the growth of the story of Kudrun which involved the annihilation of large forces. This at last seems to give a clue to the source of the Middle High German text. Attempts have been made to draw up a genealogy of *Kudrun* on the lines of that of the *Nibelungenlied*, but if anything they are less convincing, because the parallels are so much fewer. None of the figures has the significance of the characters of the *Nibelungenlied*, but the text is interesting as a latter-day reworking of very ancient material, and has been very aptly described as 'ein sentimentaler Heldenroman' —a unique blend of genres and attitudes.

As an appendix to *Kudrun*, mention might be made of a text that has only comparatively recently become available. This is *Dukus Horant*, a work which survived even more precariously than *Kudrun*. There is only one manuscript, written in Hebrew characters, which found its way to a synagogue at Cairo before being rediscovered and acquired for Cambridge. The manuscript is dated with some confidence to 1382, i.e. well before the unique manuscript of *Kudrun* itself, though the text as it stands must be considerably more recent than that from which *Kudrun* was transcribed. The text is written in stanzas which move lightly and easily, in keeping with the ballad-like nature of much of the diction. There is one mark of antiquity, in the name of Heten for a figure who corresponds to Hetel, a form closer to those preserved in the very early Norse parallels. Der wilde Hagene and Hilde occupy the expected places in the story; Heten has vassals called Horant and Wate. Horant distinguishes himself as a singer, here as in *Kudrun*: this, and the prominence of the wooing expedition, suggest affinity to the *Spielmannsepos*; but *Dukus Horant* goes further in this direction than *Kudrun* by taking over the name and the character of the grotesque figures of Asprian and Widolt from *König Rother*.

Fictional Exploits of Dietrich von Bern

The prominence of Dietrich von Bern in later medieval German literature may appear to be unjustified in the light of the remarks made so far about twelfth- and thirteenth-century texts. He does, indeed, survive the carnage at the end of the *Nibelungenlied*, but there is little there to raise his stature above that of the Burgundians. It is not insignificant that Dietrich's army is on that occasion annihilated, with the exception of Hildebrand, as this explains why Dietrich spent thirty years in exile: after the disaster at Etzel's court, he had to wait for a whole generation of warriors to reach fighting age; though this 'fact' need be no more than opportunistic exploitation by a relatively late redactor of a pre-existent legend, once the place of Dietrich's exile was determined.

It must also be conceded that the texts which celebrate Dietrich as their central figure are distinguished more by their bulk than their merit. This is, no doubt, one reason why they are comparatively little read; another is that while the name and the memory of Dietrich persists into early modern literature, there is nothing in medieval German that can be regarded as a complete biography, even a fictional one, of the hero. The 'events' of his life have to be pieced together from several accounts which to some extent overlap. Dietrich, the lord of Verona ('Bern') is the nephew of Ermrich (Ermanaric). The latter comes under the influence of an evil counsellor (Sibeche), who induces him to have two other nephews—the Harlungen—killed. He finally attacks Dietrich, who is unable to defend himself successfully and goes into exile in the land of Etzel. Later, Etzel provides an army with which Dietrich is to reconquer his inheritance. There is a battle with Ermrich's army, in which the two sons of Etzel and Helche (Etzel's wife before he married Kriemhild) and Dietrich's brother die at the hands of Witege. Dietrich is victorious, but returns to Etzel's land, where all his warriors, except Hildebrand, are killed in the events of the *Nibelungenlied*. Finally Dietrich goes back with his wife and Hildebrand, and regains the land after the death of Ermrich. Such an outline is a very bare one; in fact it leaves out a first exploratory trip back to Italy, which is successful but made useless because Dietrich, for no good reason apart from a desire for good company, leaves his land in what he thinks are the safe hands of Witege, who, however, proves to be a traitor. The themes are those inherited from an earlier warrior society: loss of rightful possessions and lands, and their recovery; conflicts of loyalty, betrayals. There is none of the despair which characterizes the end of the *Nibelungenlied*, though there are incidents which are grievous enough in themselves: the loss of a generation of warriors in Etzel's castle is potentially tragic; the killing of the young princes touching, perhaps, rather than tragic. The part of the Dietrich legend which derives from a long tradition shows, however, rather less dependence on fashionable courtly literature than does the *Nibelungenlied*; these stories remain vigorous tales of adventure with little, if any, concern for romantic love.

The earlier part of the career of Dietrich is narrated in the text called *Dietrichs Flucht*. This gives a long list of Dietrich's predecessors as kings of Bern, and goes on to an account of the intrigues between Ermrich and his wicked counsellor. The text is unusual in this type of literature in that the author names himself: he is Heinrich der Vogler, a man of substance who lived in Austria in the late thirteenth century. The text is written in continuous rhyming verse. The writing suggests affinities with the *Spielmannsepos* rather than the romance; there is a similar use of set phrases and easy rhymes, which may seem rather surprising a century after *König Rother*. Dilation upon such scenes as banquets and embassies show some acquaintance with later literature. The 'life' of Dietrich is continued with *Die Rabenschlacht*, written in stanzas of six short lines. Allusions by other authors show that details of the content were known by the end of the twelfth century, though the work as we have it was probably composed at about the same time as *Dietrichs Flucht*. The most memorable episode of this work is the story of the deaths of the sons of Etzel, who accompany Dietrich on his expedition to Ravenna, and prevail upon their guardian to bring them from the rear for a closer view of the city; by chance they meet Witege, who, as an experienced warrior, kills them. This incident is the most attractively-told part of the whole lengthy work; indeed, it is the only part which may claim to have any narrative shape. But, as the title implies, the text goes on to recount the Battle of Ravenna

—after which Dietrich looks for the princes; on learning the truth he sets out in fruitless pursuit of Witege's companion, Heime, before returning chagrined to Etzel. The most memorable part of this text is that which is likely to have the least possible root in fact; but, after all, the *Hildebrandslied* also is part of the marginalia of Dietrich's career. It cannot be claimed that the story of youthful folly, however sad its consequences, is any match for the tragic intensity of the story of Hildebrand and Hadubrand. The nucleus of the tale may well lie, however, in a pre-courtly age; at least it seems to perpetuate the loyalties of an earlier warrior society. Legendary traits in the figure of Witege also suggest great antiquity. The spirit of the thirteenth century is, however, present in detail, most notably perhaps in the duel between Diether and Witege, which is almost a copybook example of fighting according to the rules of chivalry.

The central incident of *Alpharts Tod*, an incomplete text written in the measure of the *Nibelungenlied*, is held to be a late accretion to the story of Dietrich, since there are no literary allusions to it before the end of the thirteenth century, and these may well derive from this text. It is concerned with one incident before Ravenna, where Alphart is on the lookout and falls foul of Witege and Heime. The narration shows concern for the ethics of chivalrous conduct. Heime and Witege are differentiated, Heime being reluctant to join his companion in attacking Alphart; eventually Witege ensures his death by attacking from behind while Alphart is engaged in front with Heime. The chivalrous concern with fair play shown here belongs also the heroic age; certainly the *Jüngeres Hildebrandslied* suggests concern for the proper conduct of armed combat, obscured in the interest of providing a happy ending. This late text is relevant here, for although it reaches us only as a sixteenth-century ballad, there is evidence in the rhymes of an earlier text underlying the extant version, and the form of the stanza has an affinity with the measure of *Nibelungenlied*. There is also a melody attached to the *Jüngeres Hildebrandslied*, which may mark it out from the lengthier texts, though it has been postulated that the performance even of such a text as the *Nibelungenlied* was a matter of melodic declamation.

More about the quasi-historical figure of Dietrich is recounted in the *Nibelungenlied* and the *Klage*, but most of the other texts about him must be considered apocryphal, even by the relaxed standards of medieval historicity. It is often only the names of the characters which mark out these texts from Arthurian romances; from these they derive the outward forms of chivalry and the quality of their adventures. They share with romances the use of description as a means of expansion; descriptions are usually confined to the static enumeration of physical details, and since in fact each item is merely listed as the best of its kind, very little information is given. A case in point is the tent of Queen Virginal, in the poem named after her, which has all the 'Arthurian' qualities of exaggeration and perfection, and calls to mind some of the elaborate description of an *Erec* or, even more, of a *Wigalois*. Much the same may be said of the palace of Laurin.

Perhaps the extreme example of embroidery is seen in the latter-day invention of a duel between Dietrich and Siegfried. The encounter takes place on chivalrous terms; the only essential acknowledgment of heroic legend implicit in this fabrication is that the scene is set at Worms, and the time is specifically attuned to the 'biographies' of Siegfried, Brünhild and the rest. The version of these events which reaches the *Thidrekssaga* is not to Dietrich's credit: he is armed with Witege's sword Miminc (the incident takes place before Witege's defection), and Siegfried refuses to fight with him on these terms; thereupon Dietrich swears the sword is not in his hand, which he substantiates by thrusting the point in the ground behind him. In the German *Rosengarten* texts, all is fair play. Dietrich is justly getting the worst of it, when Hildebrand recommends a trick; this suggestion so enrages Dietrich that he fights on with renewed vigour, so that Hildebrand achieves his ends by somewhat unforeseen means.

In addition to legendary tales of Dietrich von Bern, the *Heldenbuch* contains variant accounts of a cycle of events connected with another Dietrich—Wolfdietrich in the title of the texts, a name explained, perhaps after the event, by his being exposed at birth and carried off by wolves. This Dietrich is also a historical figure, but Frankish instead of Ostrogothic. The stories which grew up about him have relatively little to do with the heroic; they are rather a series of stories reflecting popular lore and superstition, which might have been attached equally well to any other figure. The *Wolfdietrich* texts are so remote, indeed, from the heroic, that they are evidence of the themes and techniques of the *Spielmannsepos* rather than the heroic.

Apart from a few names, little that is heroic survives the Middle High German golden age; though the names are invoked often enough in literature which can best be described as 'popular'. The ballad of Hildebrand and Hadubrand is an instance of this; another is the garbled version of the exploits of young Siegfried known as *Der Hürnen Seyfried*, which tells all the incidents which the *Nibelungenlied* had suppressed. But besides such relatively 'specialized' sources names and allusions occur alongside names from romances and names from classical mythology in works like the Shrovetide plays and anecdotes of Hans Sachs and other Meistersingers in the sixteenth century.

VII
THE POST-CLASSICAL AGE

Introduction

The short and troubled reign of Konrad IV (1250–4) brought even nominal Hohenstaufen rule in Germany to an end. The anti-king continued in authority in the Rhineland, and two rival kings were lawfully elected; neither of these was fully accepted, but no moves were made for a fresh election until after the death of Richard of Cornwall in 1272. The period between the last of the Hohenstaufens and the first Habsburg is known as the Interregnum; there was in fact no central authority, and the larger territorial princes asserted autonomy, while the lesser nobility and towns attempted to acquire or assert immediacy—independence of an intervening power between themselves and the king. The tenure of the throne by the first Habsburgs was not unlike that by the first Hohenstaufens; and their authority lasted a mere fifty years before they were succeeded by the Luxemburg house, which again was in insecure possession until the election of Charles IV in 1347, and the Golden Bull of 1356, which was designed to regulate future royal elections. This was a very necessary measure, for until Charles was elected with papal support, there had again been two kings and civil war in Germany.

The age is marked by the growth of urban culture. The towns had often originated as markets set up under the aegis of the church. By now there were also the imperial cities, which had also a great measure of autonomy, ranking corporately with the great princes. The structure of a patrician society had begun to take shape in the thirteenth century with the guilds of merchants; by the end of the century they were well enough established to become patrons of the arts—builders of great churches and civic buildings as well as supporters of literature. The fourteenth century saw the rise of the crafts, and with them the beginnings of a simple but independent culture which finds characteristic expression in the more popular literary works of the fifteenth and sixteenth centuries. But while the towns were growing, changes were taking place in the countryside as well. Within the classical era there are literary references to the ostentation of well-to-do peasants, all the more offensive to the knights, because they, after campaigns at home and abroad for many years, were themselves relatively poor, a galling situation for those who considered themselves the guardians of civilization. By the middle of the thirteenth century peasants were benefiting by a rise in the value of land consequent on the exhaustion of fresh areas to colonize. This was not, however, a permanent situation, and a steady move from country to town may be reckoned with in the fourteenth and fifteenth centuries. Indeed, the countryman appears again in the literature of that time as the butt, not this time of a social superior, but of a quick-thinking townsman—though often enough the tables are turned.

The involved political history and unrest of the second quarter of the fourteenth century were aggravated by the imposition of an Interdict, and on top of this came the Black Death, which must have been regarded as a divine visitation. Its reflection in literature, at least, is a move away from the world to contemplative speculation, which has relatively little to say about the precariousness of life, but all the more about spiritual comfort.

The Post-Classical Romance

Nothing was produced by the generations which followed Hartmann, Wolfram and Gottfried which matches in quality the works of their day. The three names are constantly invoked as models, and in a sense they had between them covered virtually all the ground available for writers of romance. Hartmann had established the genre, and with it a highly-polished and subtle language for straightforward narration; Wolfram had added to the tradition a depth of purpose expressed with lively imagination and virtuoso use of language; Gottfried had explored the implications of *minne* in opposition to the claims of society until he reached an impasse. It remained for the next generation to outbid the masters in the fantasy of their plots, the scale of their action or the exuberance of their diction. Some material lay ready to hand in the unfinished works of Gottfried and Wolfram.

Wolfram's *Willehalm* breaks off virtually at the end of the second battle of Aliscans; hints have already been given of the relationship of Rennewart to Gyburg, and a romantic attachment between him and Alize has been sketched in, yet where the text breaks off he is nowhere to be found. A conclusion was not a difficult thing to supply: in addition to the expected marriage of Rennewart and Alize, however, Ulrich von Türheim's *Rennewart* (the name is supplied by the editor) goes on to give an account of the rest of their lives, and of how Willehalm and Gyburg retired from the world; a conclusion fully consistent with Wolfram's address to his hero as a saint at the beginning of the work and with the spirit of the religious legend, which is one part of the texture of the story. It is unsurprising, perhaps, that the compass of this conclusion is about three times as long as Wolfram's original text, but prolixity was far from a disadvantage when it was written; no fewer than thirty-two manuscripts are known. Another Ulrich, Ulrich von dem Türlin, wrote an extensive prehistory of Willehalm and Gyburg, also known as *Willehalm*, taking up hints from Wolfram's texts about the love of Willehalm and Arabel, her conversion and renaming, together with such conventional matters as Willehalm's accolade as a young man. The work does not come from the same region as *Rennewart*; it was dedicated to King Ottokar II of Bohemia. The two *Willehalms* and *Rennewart* enjoyed joint circulation in several collected manuscripts.

Perhaps even more remarkable is the fate which befell

Wolfram's editorially misnamed *Titurel*. A connected narrative, giving the life of Sigune and Schionatulander, was built round Wolfram's two fragments, basically in the same complex metre, but with identifiable features of its own. There are three major episodes: the quest for the *Brackenseil*, developed from hints in Wolfram; a journey to the East to avenge Gahmuret, appropriate in associating Schionatulander the more closely with Parzival; then an account of Schionatulander's last fight with Orilus, which takes place, so to speak, off stage in *Parzival*, just before the first meeting between Sigune and Parzival. There are also further episodes devoted to Parzival, Feirefiz and Parzival's son Loherangrin. Throughout the Middle Ages, and until nineteenth-century textual scholarship disentangled fact from fiction, the text was attributed to Wolfram. It is now known to have been written some fifty years after Wolfram's death, and the author is identified as one Albrecht, perhaps the Albrecht von Scharfenberg cited by Ulrich Füetrer as one of his sources in the collection of medieval stories he compiled and printed in the sixteenth century; even this identification has been disputed, but the designation is used by the recent editor of the text.

The concluding lines of *Parzival* gave a further hint in the name of Parzival's son Loherangrin and the sketch of his mission to Brabant; this provided the main impetus for the anonymous stanzaic poem of *Lohengrin*. Heinrich von dem Türlin's *Diu Krone*, written in the 1220's, and so known from an allusion by Rudolf von Ems, is indebted to Wolfram to the extent of being an anti-Parzival, offering a rival completion of the unfinished story Wolfram had before him by allowing Gawan to become Grail king. Another text by the same author, *Der Mantel*, takes up a theme otherwise connected with the story of Lancelot, a magic coat which is a chastity-diviner. The kind of anecdotal treatment to which this theme lends itself is also characteristic of his superficial handling of the Grail theme.

Continuations of Gottfried's *Tristan* were apparently less

widely distributed than completions and imitations of Wolfram, and there appears to have been no disposition to confuse Gottfried's continuators with the canon of the original text. There were, however, two separate completions of *Tristan*, one composed about 1235 by Ulrich von Türheim, the author of *Rennewart*, the other about 1290 by Heinrich von Freiberg. Neither of these texts solves the problems left unsolved by Gottfried; they do not even follow the same source, Thomas of Britanny, but go back to the more primitive text of Béroul. Ulrich, indeed, reveals an additional indebtedness to Eilhart; Heinrich, with some disingenuity (even this is not original) claims Thomas as his source, but clearly follows Béroul, though his version shows competence within his limitations.

The direction of Gottfried, as far as content is concerned, found few followers. Perhaps the most notable is the love story of *Floire und Blanscheflur* by Konrad Fleck (about 1220). The love of the two is not illicit but furtive, and overcomes obstacles by subterfuge. Floire und Blanscheflur has some appeal purely as a tale of intrigue, as did the earlier Tristan stories; but it differs from them in having a happy ending, brought about touchingly as a reward for a display of extreme selfless devotion in the face of death. Few of the incidents are distinctive enough to suggest that the tale was much more than a compilation of popular elements; nevertheless this version was a reworking just after the classical age of a story which had already been told once in German, and has the advantages of straightforward narration and a lavish and exotic setting. It looks as though this story circulated as a kind of appendix to the Tristan material, for there was also a version written shortly after the earlier German Tristan romance.

Konrad Fleck was, like Gottfried, of educated burgher stock. By the middle of the thirteenth century there begin to be cross-currents of burgher authors producing romances, and at the same time drawing on fresh sources for their writing. An author of such mixed output is Der Stricker, who was active between 1220 and 1250. It is perhaps convenient to regard *Daniel von dem blühenden Tal*, a chivalrous romance, as an early work; in his *Karl* he turns to the history and legend of Charlemagne, renewing the matter of the *Rolandslied.* His most striking new contribution to literature is, however, the *bîspel* or anecdotal fable. These very brief, diverting stories draw on an international stock of incidents, and can either stand independently, or be collected together as the deeds of one fictional person, as they are in *Pfaffe Amis.* This type of episodic narration was to become very popular in the later Middle Ages in *Schwänke* and the literature of Folly.

In the decades after Der Stricker, Der Pleier was writing lengthy romances of chivalry which were little more than assemblages of motifs drawn from the successful works of the previous generation. Der Pleier extrapolates intelligently from known themes, attaching independent adventures to secondary figures from other works. *Garel von dem blühenden Tal* (the very name is warrant of the success of Der Stricker's *Daniel*) derives in part from the tale of the abduction of Guinevere by Meljakanz, an episode often narrated in the course of earlier romances. *Meleranz* draws on a popular tale of a water-sprite as well as on earlier Arthurian sources. *Tandareis und Flordibel* is associated with *Parzival* in that Tandareis is the son of Antikonie; the second name, like the theme of the captive knight incarcerated in a tower, appears to derive from the Floris romances.

The most prolific and versatile writers of this age are Rudolf von Ems and Konrad von Würzburg, both of whom in some measure extended the range of subject-matter of what may still be generally called courtly literature. Rudolf von Ems (Hohenems, near Bregenz) seems from the evidence of dedications and documentary references to his patrons to have been writing between 1220 and 1254. He tells us a certain amount about himself, for there are passages in two of his later works, modelled on the passage of literary criticism in Gottfried von Strassburg, in which he passes in review the literature of his day, including his own works. The lists are, of course, more extensive than Gottfried's, especially as they are written more with a view to imparting information than to indulging in polemic against his contemporaries. They tell us of several unknown texts, including his own legend of St Eustace. The nearest approach to a Saint's Life in his extant works is *Der gute Gerhart*, but this is rather an edifying tale, or courtly legend, loosely associated with the emperor Otto I, who is directed by a heavenly voice to seek out Gerhart as a model of true virtue; the story of Gerhart enclosed within this framework is, however, an independent fiction. *Barlaam und Josaphat*, a much more lengthy text, goes back to a legendary life of the Buddha. Much space is given to moral teaching, carried out in the form of parables, in which the *ad hoc* allegories are explained in great detail, recalling in spirit the technique of an earlier age, but representing more specifically the persistence of habits of thought. It is notable that this text is prefaced by penitent remarks about giving up the composition of worldly literature. This may have some bearing on the chronology of his works, if it is, in fact, more than a literary formula introducing an acknowledged serious subject. Other works of Rudolf's, while serious in subject-matter, are not specifically describable as legends. The history of *Alexander* is a retelling of a story that had been current in several versions in Latin and the European vernaculars, including the piously inclined twelfth-century German one. The disposal of Rudolf's text is generous—ten books were planned, of which only five survive entire. The beginnings of books are marked out from the rest of the text by the form of the verse, and contain some extraneous matter, including, as the introduction to the second book, the first of the literary digressions. Narrative passages tend to be prolix, perhaps in the endeavour to outbid the mellifluous and rather expansive style of the acknowledged model Gottfried, but tending as well to irrelevancy. The text is evidence for a continuing interest in what passed for history, alongside the avowedly fictional romances of chivalry. In this latter genre, Rudolf left one essay, *Willehalm von Orlens*, which is completely fictional, in spite of an attempted identification of the heroine as the daughter of the King of England. The text is interesting more for its inclusion of the second literary review than anything else. The last work of Rudolf's to be preserved is the *Weltchronik*, which has not even completed the events of the Old Testament when it breaks off after 30,000 lines. The matter was popular enough to prompt completions within a short time. The volume of Rudolf's output and the variety of its subject-matter is something of a novelty in medieval German literature; he wrote for a variety of patrons, and the choice of his themes is no doubt a reflection of the taste of patron rather than author—but Rudolf was capable of turning his hand to any narrative material and producing a well-phrased product without any great profundity or differentiation of style from one theme to another. The trend of his work is one away from pure fiction to didacticism.

Konrad von Würzburg (c. 1230–87) was also a follower of Gottfried, and like Gottfried, he came of non-aristocratic stock. His active life was spent first in Strassburg, and then, for the last seventeen years, in Basle. His first work, *Das Turnier von Nantheiz* (Nantes), datable to 1257 from the occasion for which it was written, is concerned with the details of chivalrous practice; the only one of his works which is strictly a romance is his version of the story of Lohengrin, in continuous verse, and incompletely preserved. Konrad's most successful works are probably the shorter texts, and of these, the best is *Engelhart*, which tells of the loyalty of two brother-knights, including such improbable circumstances as a misleading oath sworn in deliberate exploitation of mistaken identity, a miraculous cure from leprosy, and a miraculous revival of two beheaded children, with the touching particular that each ever after had a narrow red band round the neck to mark the join. Reference to themes of earlier successful literary works is apparent.

Daz Herzmaere is a verse *Novelle* of similar compass based on the widely distributed theme of the unwitting eating of the heart of a child; *Der Welt Lohn* touches another horror theme with graphic description (the poem contains little else) of the elegant and prosperous front of Frau Welt, concealing corruption which becomes apparent as she turns her back—a contrast foreshadowed in one of Walther's poems, and recurrent in sculpture as well as in later literature.

The view of the contrast of reality and appearance is one which recalls the austerity of some twelfth-century writings and the mood of later ages when disaster was rife; its reappearance now shows an awareness of the precariousness of existence which is an undercurrent even at a time when the greatest proportion of literary output was worldly. Persistence of earlier ways of thought is also shown in *Die goldene Schmiede*, an apt name for an ornamental collection of the attributes of the Virgin Mary, strung together, inevitably with no kind of progression, and excelling earlier examples of *Mariendichtung* only by the exhaustiveness of its references and the elaboration of its language. The shorter works also include legends from the Basle years—*Alexius*, *Silvester*, *Pantaleon*—and give evidence of the continued interest in earlier literary forms alongside the products of the age of chivalry. There is one short text of different quality: *Otte mit dem Barte* compresses into the compass of a *Schwank* a period of exile lasting some ten years for an offence of *lèse-majesté* which is purged by a brave (and rather comic) act in saving the offended king's life. The comedy here lies partly in the situation itself, partly in the adoption of a rather artless form of diction. Continuing taste for romances was catered for by the lengthy *Partenopier und Meliur*, based for good measure on two French sources. Finally, the taste for didacticism finds a reflection in the voluminous treatment of *Der Trojanische Krieg*.

A similarly varied output, though a less extensive one, is accredited to Ulrich von Eschenbach or Etzenbach. The former version of the name led to the supposition that Ulrich was a kinsman of Wolfram, but this has not been upheld. He was not a knight, and he appears to have had a thorough formal education. He lived in German-speaking Bohemia, and was born about the middle of the thirteenth century. He, too, wrote an *Alexander* (dedicated to Ottokar II, and datable between 1271 and 1286), based in the main on the *Alexandreis* of Walter of Chatillon, but adducing also the *Historia de Proeliis*. A recension of the popular story of Herzog Ernst (*Herzog Ernst* D) is also attributed to him, although he does not in fact name himself. His *Wilhelm von Wenden*, written between 1287 and 1297, adapts a theme otherwise known from the legend of St Eustace, but applied to the ancestry of his patron.

Ulrich von Lichtenstein's *Frauendienst* (1255) is also a novelty, even unique in Middle High German literature, since it is a romance of fantastic adventure told in the first person, and interspersed with lyrics purporting to emerge from the various situations portrayed. The lyrics belong technically to the most elaborate form of Minnesang, and the adventures described all derive from devotion to a mistress, carried, apparently in all earnest, to such excesses as self-mutilation.

Not all writing continued to express admiration for chivalrous ideals without a glance at their manifestations in real life. The most attractive story, expressive of a realistic, or rather a disillusioned and satirical view of the life of the mid-thirteenth century is the *Novelle*-length poem *Meier Helmbrecht*, the work of a not very closely identifiable Wernher der Gartenære, written some time in the third quarter of the thirteenth century in Austria or Bavaria. This is not even ostensibly a tale of chivalry, for Helmbrecht is obviously no knight, but a peasant who develops ambitions above his station; his chivalry takes the form of joining a robber band led by a nobleman, and after an arrogant return home and further discreditable exploits he is virtually lynched by the villagers he had been too proud to acknowledge. The text is a tract against social climbing and strongly in favour of the *status quo*. We are given a careful description of Helmbrecht's most flamboyant transgression of the sumptuary laws—a cap decorated with impossibly intricate embroidery, in keeping in its way with Hartmann's elaborate account of Enite's horse. The description is disproportionate enough to turn this part of the poem into a literary parody of the ornately descriptive style which appears to have found a ready audience in and after the golden age, as well as a diatribe against social pretensions. The fact that it could be written was an indication that social changes were afoot. Basically similar views are expressed in the texts collectively known as *Seifried Helbling* from a character named in one of them, and written towards the end of the century. A century later still, peasant grossness was still a sufficient theme for crude mirth in a text like the Swiss Heinrich Witenwiler's *Ring*.

The Lyric after Walther

The situation of the upstart peasant is also the theme of what for want of a better term may be called lyric poetry—the works of Neidhart von Reuental. In time and in place he is the direct successor of Walther; indeed, a complaint Walther made about the decadence of courtly song appears to refer to a context in Neidhart. In the quantity of his output, Neidhart may be compared with Walther, but examination of his poems reveals a much smaller range of subject-matter as well as a change in spirit. Indeed, the mere enumeration of peasant names and description of peasant activities bulks so large in the poems that it is easy at first sight to overlook the continuity between Neidhart and the traditions of Minnesang. Yet he belongs to the first half of the thirteenth century; an allusion to Neidhart suggests that he must have been writing by 1217, and his silence on the death of his patron, Duke Friederich II of Austria, in 1246 suggests that he had stopped writing by then. He seems to have been of Bavarian origin, but his birthplace is as difficult to identify as Walther's, for both 'Vogelweide' and 'Reuental' lend themselves equally well to allusive etymology. The name Neidhart is supplied by superscriptions and cross-references, and the manuscript headings call him 'Her'; and it is as a knight exposed to the insolence of an advancing peasant class that he most frequently presents himself. His poems are traditionally divided into *Sommerlieder* and *Winterlieder*; the song accompanies and describes a dance, in the open in summer and indoors in winter. In the summer songs Neidhart is represented, in the third person, as a successful lover, often observed through the eyes of a girl talking to her mother or to a friend. In the winter songs the knight watches with displeasure and chagrin the object of his affection being taken away by a despised peasant who can impress by the length of his purse and expresses his financial advantage unashamedly by flaunting gaudy clothes. Two adjacent stanzas from a *Winterlied* are typical of the way his poems begin:

> Now tell me, summer, where will you go to escape the winter? If you will allow me I will come with you. I will retire from my jubilant song. My opponents are in league with the devil—they permit me no success in my dear pursuit. That adds insult to injury. Giselbolt and Engelram spoil my song for me.
>
> These two are of a kind with Engelmar, who snatched Friderûne's mirror away by force. They are scornful and defiant in all their ways, these two yokels. Giselbolt and Engelram, Erkenfried and curly Uozeman are in it with them: the four of them intend to drive me out. If she were given a foolish notion by them, that would be a grief to me.

The 'foolish notion' of the last sentence is a *tumber wân*, a set expression in the vocabulary of Minnesang for fond hopes or foolish longing, but the words apply in this context in a literal sense as well. The enumeration of names here is a mark of the intrusion of narrative into an originally lyrical form, and the grotesque names, formed, indeed, according to the best principles of the structure of German names, are in themselves an indictment of peasant pretentiousness. But the narrative element does not obtrude so much in this poem as it does in some others where the barn dance develops into a free-for-all; nor is description so advanced here as it is in some other cases, which anticipate Wernher der Gartenære's lampoons of peasant dress. The episode of Engelmar and Friderûne is one to which Neidhart returns several times, without ever narrating it in its own right. His poems are populated by a set of grotesques known to the audience only from a series of allusions, but established in their minds as imagined figures of fun. In spite of some posturing as an unhappy lover, the attitude of Neidhart's poems reflects the scorn of an aristocratic audience for the ambitions of the lower orders. It would be wrong, however, to dismiss Neidhart's poems as nothing but satire. Whole stanzas show themselves to be rooted in the traditions of high Minnesang:

> Now I mourn the flowers and the shining hours and resplendent days of summer. In addition I have another complaint which has secretly taken many a joy from me, that a woman defies me so long whom I so long have served with unrewarded hope. I can never have the joy I ask of her since her heart holds no woman-kindness, and yet she accepts service in the guise of woman. Is there anyone whom this complaint would not grieve? I am astonished that my singing and my service bring no success.

The criticism of the obdurate mistress is more outspoken, perhaps, than a more conventional Minnesinger would have allowed himself, but the situation harks back to Reinmar, and the diction, especially the invocation of summer, to earlier poets. The stanza introduces a poem which contains others of similar tenor, but also further ones which paint a scene of peasant festivity of the kind expected from Neidhart. This raises once again the question whether all stanzas in the same measure necessarily belong to one and the same poem. It also raises the question whether Neidhart, the satirist of peasant pretension, was not also the parodist of courtly attitudinizing. Neidhart's occasional references to his own situation or to current events include a very disillusioned crusading song composed in connection with the 1227 expedition. There is little thought for the eternal glory to be won; instead, concern with temporal privations, including the discomforts of living abroad in the heat of August; may God grant, he adds, that we see the dear day when we sail home again. But expressions of conventional regret as a lover or unconventional disillusion as a crusader should not be allowed to obscure the vigour of his language, the exuberance of his verse and the novelty of his matter. His style was original enough to lend itself to imitation. Some stanzas are regarded as interpolations and have been discarded by editors on grounds that are not always clear. Pastiche started in Neidhart's lifetime, and by the fourteenth and fifteenth centuries many pseudo-Neidhart poems were current, conveniently gathered together under the title of *Neidhart Fuchs*, known only from printed texts. Neidhart's foils, like Engelmar, and the *persona* of Neidhart persist. The texts are part of the literature of folly, of the type familiar from the Eulenspiegel stories, in which the peasant is the butt as in Neidhart, or from the *Pfarrer von Kalenberg*, published in Vienna in 1474. In these texts, the lyrical element recedes, leaving only an anecdote; and in such examples of the literature of folly, the stories are usually insipid if they are decent and obscene if they are funny. But all this is rather far from Neidhart, who kept himself aloof from the antics of the peasantry, and contented himself with recording them as objects of derision.

Neidhart was not the only poet to become a legend in his own lifetime, though he is infinitely more rewarding in his own right than some others about whom tales were told. His near contemporary, Tanhûser (Tannhäuser) had already become the subject of fiction in the middle ages; his stay in the mountain of Venus is perhaps a corruption of a report that in the course of his travels on the same Crusade as Neidhart he was wrecked on the island of Cyprus. His output includes six *Leiche*, nine long poems in regular stanzas, and a collection of one-stanza riddles. In the *Leiche* there is heavy and (deliberately?) inaccurate allusion to prominent beauties of literature in the interest of proclaiming his beloved the fairest of them all. There are two pastourelles, one of which makes great play with foreign words in its rhymes—a practice common enough in romances, but otherwise eschewed in the lyric. Something of genuine feeling is found in the crusading poem in which he, like Neidhart, looks back to a happy life at home. The poem is full of self-pity, but for once there seems to be more to it than technical achievement.

The fiction that Tannhäuser took part in the contest of poets known as the *Wartburgkrieg* no doubt owes continued currency to Richard Wagner; but the contest itself was a medieval invention; it is legendary, but it tells us something of the reputation medieval poets had among their near-contemporaries. The *Wartburgkrieg* is composed of some half a dozen verse texts in two distinct metrical forms; there is no narrative progression in the work, for the stanzas are in fact more or less independent *Sprüche*. The *Fürstenlob*, written in the longer of the two measures (the *Thüringer Herrenton*) introduces as its central character the shadowy figure of Heinrich von Ofterdingen. At the end of this text, Heinrich is saved from defeat in the contest and disgrace by the intervention of Klingsor, a figure of fiction. The other major text, the *Rätselspiel* (in the *schwarzer Ton*), develops largely into a battle of wits between Klingsor and his creator, Wolfram von Eschenbach. Among the contestants in the *Fürstenlob* is a Reinmar, here specifically identified as Reinmar von Zweter; but it seems possible that one element in the genesis of the *Wartburgkrieg* was the known rivalry between Walther and Reinmar der Alte, and another element was the implication of a passage in *Parzival* that Walther and Wolfram were at one time at the Wartburg together. The dialogues of this text give an interesting sidelight on medieval ideas about the personalities of some of the major poets of the age, even if the historicity of the events portrayed—and the quality of the poetry—may be called into question. The whole work appears to be an elaborate charade, a form of impersonation which anticipates the catalogue of characters in the *Narrenschiff* or the processions of characters in some of the earlier *Fastnachtspiele*.

Minnesingers who are not themselves the products of a legend or do not become the subjects of one tend after the golden age to produce little more than elegant variations on the essential theme of unrequited love, varied in part by an excessive use of rhetorical devices, in part by an elaboration of verse forms, including frequent use of internal rhymes. In a poet like Gottfried von Neifen, diction becomes highly conventionalized. All the elegant expressions of his predecessors are there, but so concentrated as to become tautological, e.g. *fröidebernde wünne* ('joy-giving bliss'); *fröit sich manges senden herzen muot* (approximately 'the soul of many a longing heart rejoices'). Some of his poems, however, show greater originality, though their authenticity has been doubted; but they form a sizeable proportion of those attributed to him in manuscript C. The stanza forms are simpler, and the content moves away from the stately conventions of the courtly lyric towards the primeval situations of the folk-song, like the short poem which hints at a meeting by the well, or a particularly effective evocation of the situation of the dawn-song, which mentions the coming of day in a refrain at the end of each stanza; but the words accompany the rocking of a cradle, and a touchingly sentimental scene is sketched in with considerable delicacy. Gottfried von Neifen may be contrasted with a near-contemporary, Ulrich von Winterstetten, who shows rather more classical attitudinizing in his poems, including allusions *à la* Reinmar to the task of the poet. But his *Leiche* end in village dances, which recall the robustness of Neidhart, as do, indeed, some of his rhymes. His diction is on the whole more studied than Neifen's, and his imagery is occasionally striking, as when 'the sun pierces the green shield of May', though the effect is rather impaired by complex syntax. Like Neifen, Ulrich too uses the theme of the dawn-song, but his otherwise conventional treatment adds a fresh character, in the person of the lady's serving-maid.

Didactic verse was also actively written in the thirteenth century, though the new practitioners had neither the range nor the wit of Walther. Indeed, Reinmar von Zweter seems in some ways to refer back to the simple gnomic verse of the Spervogels. A large proportion of his output is written in an identical verse-form. In one of the manuscripts, the stanzas in the *Frau-Ehren-Ton* are divided systematically according to the subject-matter. In all his writing, Reinmar may be described as conservative—perhaps even Blimpish—in his hankering after the good old days, with expressions of support (not alien to Walther's thought) for a rigidly ordered society:

> Hair and beard trimmed to a monkish cut, and monk's habits cut in monkish fashion: of this I've seen plenty, but I've not seen those who wear them aright. Half fish, half man is neither fish nor man. All-fish is fish, All-man is man, as I see it; but I can't say anything about court monks and monastery knights.

These 'reliable' sentiments are a foretaste of the moral tone of the Meistersinger; the elaborate diction reflects the kind of artificiality which gives rhetoric its bad name. Other poems come out more outspokenly in favour of a paternalistic society, like the parable of a boat-load of egalitarians who get sucked into a millrace for want of an authority to direct them to row away from danger; though other contexts show that authority does not derive from birth alone. Elsewhere, Reinmar reveals the international currency of the jingle which begins, 'For want of a nail the shoe was lost', though there is a moral here: the decisive link in the chain of causation nail, shoe, horse, man, castle, nation, is the man, and the poem calls woe on the man who is found wanting in an emergency.

A wider range of themes is found in the rather later Heinrich von Meissen, commonly called Frauenlob (d. 1318). Like Reinmar von Zweter his most frequent pose is that of the *laudator temporis acti*; the differences lie largely in a more vigorous diction, including an invocation to 'Sir Court':

> If you would 'monk' yourself, let the abbeys 'court' themselves in your place, since all their counsel is 'give and give: you keep the bones, I'll keep the fish for your sins.' Sir Court, if you don't change, your falcon will become a raven.

Coinages like *munchen* for 'turn yourself into a monk' and *hoven* for 'courtlify yourself' have the force of conciseness, and the references of the last line appear to be particularly rich. Frauenlob's didactic streak even accompanies his love-lyrics: he is less concerned with the expression of experience than with the presentation of a situation seen from the outside. He consoles himself for his misfortunes with a list of the injuries done by woman to Adam, Samson, David, Solomon, Absolom, Alexander, Virgil, Holofernes, Aristotle, the city of Troy, Achilles, King Arthur and Parzival. The sufferings of the biblical figures are still well-known, and in the Middle Ages there was no need to rehearse the indignities imposed on Virgil, Aristotle and Alexander as *Minnenarren*. The fictional figure of Parzival takes his place with biblical and historical characters, further evidence of the esteem in which Wolfram continued to be held; but Frauenlob's indebtedness does not stop at literary allusion; in some of his poems the exuberance of his language seems to be modelled on Wolfram, most notably, perhaps in his elegy for Konrad von Würzburg, where allusion to jewellery suggests that the primary reference is to the *Goldene Schmiede*. Frauenlob himself contributed to the genre of *Mariendichtung* a notable *Leich*, which goes over into the first person and becomes, so to speak, an extended Magnificat. From such a work he may derive his nickname, if this does not, indeed, come from a more worldly source, his championship of *frouwe* against *wip* in competition with his contemporary Regenbogen, and in contrast with the position taken up by Walther.

The collected manuscripts of the medieval German lyric contain poems by a hundred or so named writers, so that there is room to deal only with the most significant or the most prolific. The burgher Johannes Hadlaub of Zurich deserves consideration probably on the latter count, and there is a possibility, or at least a legend, that his poems owe their preservation to his being the scribe of MS. C, the one manuscript in which they were preserved. However, they give some ideal of further developments in the lyric in non-aristocratic hands. Some of the poems breathe the didactic spirit which has become more and more apparent in the later poets, but the most significant novelty of his verse is probably the tendency away from reflection towards narration in stanzaic verse. His poems are still concerned with the individual, but they no longer purport to give an individual's view of events; instead, they relate the events themselves. This is rather different from Ulrich von Lichtenstein's romance in the first person. Hadlaub's lyrics are concerned with trivial incidents which Ulrich would have dismissed in narrative. When the Meistersinger took over the stanza form of the Minnesinger, they, too, used them for narrative, but their narrative dispensed even with the formal link with the pure lyric implicit in the use of the first person.

Even at the end of the fourteenth century, it was still possible for lyric poetry to be practised by aristocrats as well as burghers. Indeed, there are interesting indications of what appear to be cross-influences between an aristocratic art in the hands of a wider circle and more popular forms in the hands of aristocrats. Two of the very last lyric poets in the medieval tradition, Hugo von Montfort and Oswald von Wolkenstein, were descendants of noble families. For once, biographical details for these writers are fairly full; both were public figures involved in the events of their day and widely travelled and experienced. The mark of this in Hugo's poetry is not particularly strong, unless it be that such a practical man had little taste for the greatest artificialities of the art he was practising. The form of his stanzas is simpler, with lines of more regular length and with a less artificial disposition of rhymes. The sentiments also approximate to the more practical wisdom of the *Spruchdichter*; the diction admits words which had long been banished from the vocabulary of the Minnesinger—words expressive of natural affection rather than the distilled abstraction of the courtly code at its height. In other words, an aristocratic poet shares some features with popular verse, which begins to take shape in the fourteenth and fifteenth centuries. Some of the same features are to be seen also in Oswald, though his output is much greater and more varied, including, for example, survivals of the more elaborate metres and some use of traditional diction alongside the new simplicity and directness.

Many of his poems are on edifying themes, and written in elaborate stanzas, in which he reverts several times to the same measure. A characteristic feature of more than one of these is a most effective, rather bludgeoning short first line. In content these *Sprüche* look back to earlier poets, but the grouping of usually odd numbers of stanzas into a complete poem anticipates the practice of the Meistersinger, who usually settle for three. The same type of metrical form accompanies other poems which may be classed as dancing songs, in which lists of epithets, lists of names and the transition from narrative to dialogue have some of the vigour of Neidhart. He uses both simple and complex metres to recount the events of his adventurous career, and turns to simple measures to address his beloved. Here the diction is also simpler, and there is little suggestion of the artificiality of courtly poetry, but rather the reinvigoration of an aristocrat's art by the infusion of material akin to the folk-song. It may be assumed that simple rhymes and melodies had always had an oral currency, though few efforts appear to have been made to collect them and write them down until the fifteenth century, for only then did literacy begin to spread and the production of manuscripts become cheaper with the widespread use of paper instead of parchment. A particularly rich source of anonymous poems is the *Liederbuch* of the nun Klara Hätzlerin (1471). Not all the poems in the collection are anonymous, but many are. These are usually built up of a few short stanzas, expressing fairly simple emotions. It cannot be claimed that the poems show any great antiquity; the vocabulary shows a blend of derivations from courtly usage with more widely-used terms, giving the collection the air in many places of popularized versions of the attitudes which had been adopted in aristocratic literature in the previous century. It is perhaps surprising to find avowedly secular love-songs written down by a nun; but the *Liederbuch* contains also its devotional poems, including adaptations of secular themes, including even the dawn song, interpreted as a call to the soul to wake.

Didactic and Religious Verse

The streak of didacticism which found its way into lyrical verse from the thirteenth century onwards was not, of course, an isolated phenomenon. It is most conveniently traced back to the single-stanza *Sprüche* which were current from the time of the earliest lyrics onwards. But there were also more extensive texts of proverbial wisdom, though the earlier ones of these tend to be composed in short stanzas not unlike those of the Spervogels. Among such texts the most notable is the *Winsbeke*, in which a father advises his son in a long series of ten-line stanzas. Textual allusion dates this text shortly after the composition of Wolfram's *Parzival*. The advice is concerned with the practice of chivalry, and its content is by the time of writing virtually self-evident. The authority and popularity of the text is attested by a large number of manuscripts, the existence of a sequel (*Die Winsbekin*, addressed by a mother to her daughter) and additional parodistical stanzas. Indebtedness to Wolfram is shown in the very title of *Tirol und Fridebrant*, for Fridebrant is the name given to a king of Scotland in *Parzival*, Book I. The name is adopted for another giver of advice on the code of chivalry. The appropriate conduct of the knight in more general terms is one of the main themes of Thomasin von Zerclære's *Der wälsche Gast*, which bases its code on the more abstract principles established as the triad of values in Walther's most celebrated *Spruch*, and observable in other authors of the golden age. The arrangement of the book and the appeal to authority mark the scholar; the work is raised above the purely practical considerations which characterize other writings of the same type. Even such a text as Freidank's *Bescheidenheit*, for all the vigour of the separate fables, is concerned with rules of conduct for specific occasions rather than the establishment of general principles. Hugo von Trimberg's *Renner*, written in the last decade of the thirteenth century, is again a compilation from various sources, with a strongly moral purpose in addition to the purely didactic content; the method is the favoured allegorical one. The work is more notable as a repository of current knowledge than as a literary text, but it was influential in its day. Half a century later, Heinrich von Mügeln, in *Der meide kranz*, gives a display of scholarship in an artificial literary form: he creates his own allegories for the various branches of learning he discusses, but his method goes back to a twelfth-century model, the widely-read Latin *Anticlaudianus* of Alanus de Insulis. Like Hugo von Trimberg, Heinrich von Mügeln is fully aware of the tradition of scholarship behind him; yet in lyrical writings he shows himself, like his contemporary Frauenlob, to be an intermediary between the old art of the court and the new art of the townsfolk. In a way there is, indeed, a continuity between the seven Liberal Arts and the mastery of a craft; in both, achievement is based on precept and precedent, and knowledge of the Liberal Arts, especially of the arts of language, the Trivium, is one of the constant facts of medieval culture. The artificial courtly society of the high middle age marks only an apparent exception.

None of these didactic works is primarily a literary text. They are interesting in the main as social documents, evidence of the state of knowledge or belief at the time. The same may be said of vernacular chronicles, which continued to be written throughout the thirteenth and fourteenth centuries on the model of the *Kaiserchronik* of the twelfth.

Saints' Lives continued to be written in the thirteenth century as before; in general the fascination with the apocryphal gospels continued, and they were the sources of further accounts of the life of the Virgin Mary. Konrad von Heimesfurt wrote a *Himmelfahrt Mariae* about 1225 in which the stylistic influences are Gottfried von Strassburg and Konrad von Fussesbrunnen, whose narration of the infancy gospel had in turn been indebted to the narrative art of Hartmann. Another anonymous German life of the Virgin Mary was based on the Latin *Vita beatae Mariae rhythmica*, an early thirteenth-century text itself notable for adopting the rhythmical patterns of German verse to Latin. Konrad von Heimesfurt's interest in the New Testament apocrypha is further shown by his treating the Harrowing of Hell in the *Urstende*. Reinbot von Durne's legend of St George, written in the 1230's, shows the interpenetration of courtly and religious by the adoption, as in so many secular texts of the time, of the mannerisms of Wolfram.

A work of more general application is *Die Erlösung*, written in the first quarter of the fourteenth century. The author seems to have been a learned cleric, with knowledge of classical antiquity, music and architecture. The sources are again the New Testament apocrypha, especially the Gospel of Nicodemus. The narrative falls easily into sections, which anticipate the scenes of Passion Plays. Heinrich von Neustadt, known to have been living in Vienna in 1314, wrote secular as well as religious texts; but his major work, *Von gotes Zůkunft*, is concerned with the redemption of mankind, and draws heavily on the medieval method of allegory. A more specialized work sometimes attributed to the same author is the *Visio Philiberti*. The impact of encyclopaedism on the modest tradition of Saints' Lives was ultimately a collected work like the *Passional*. As the name implies, much space is given to the Life of Christ, going back in the first book as far as the birth of the Virgin Mary and going on to her death in the first book, dealing in the second with the apostles and events down to the fall of Jerusalem, and in the third relating the lives of 75 eminent saints in their sequence in the church year from Advent to Advent. The separate Lives are arranged in the conventional order of life, death (especially martyrdom), and miracles. The author is unknown, but he may have written his text at the end of the thirteenth century in the 'Ordensland', the districts settled by the Teutonic Knights. The matter of the first two books derives from the Gospels and apocryphal Gospels; the third draws on the accepted thirteenth-century compendium of Saints' Lives, the *Golden Legend* of Jacobus a Voragine. The *Passional* was widely read; over seventy manuscripts are known, and it formed the basis of later collections of Saints' Lives in German.

Practical Prose and Visionary Prose

Prose is relatively unimportant in early literature. Prose there was in Old High German, but this was largely 'utility German': statements of a legal code, translations of the Bible and selected parts of the liturgy, works of scholarship. As soon as 'art' or 'magic' came into play, prose gave away to verse. This position continues virtually throughout the Middle Ages. In the thirteenth century prose was again concerned with the codification of law: Eike von Repgow produced his *Sachsenspiegel*, the code of Saxon law, in Low German between 1220 and 1230. Within a few decades a comparable High German text was produced—the *Schwabenspiegel*, which seems thereafter to have been one of the most heavily consulted books of the Middle Ages—350 manuscripts are known. The success of the law texts appears to have prompted the writing of chronicles, first, again, in the north a *Sächsische Weltchronik*, by the author of the *Sachsenspiegel*, again followed a little later in the south by a text which was associated, at least by juxtaposition in the manuscripts, with the *Schwabenspiegel*. These are followed by other prose chronicles. The use of prose for encyclopaedic works made a start, again in the North, with the German version of the *Lucidarius*, probably from the end of the twelfth century. This text book of accepted, and often very unreliable knowledge, handed down as undisputed fact and imparted by means of question and answer, is another of the works which continued to be used throughout the Middle Ages. There seems to have been no strong impetus, however, to produce more vernacular textbooks for another hundred years or so, when Hugo von Langenstein produced his *Mainauer Naturlehre*. Konrad von Megenburg's *Buch der Natur* was not produced until the early years of the fourteenth century; the author is known to have been at the University of Paris and to have taught in what shortly after his retirement was to become the University of Vienna. The work shows, as might be expected, some spirit of enquiry and observation, especially in contrast with the type of information enshrined in the bestiaries.

The use of prose in a thirteenth century version of the romance of *Lanzelet* is unique. This work is voluminous, but it is a demonstration that German prose was fully adequate to the presentation of dialogue and narrative as well as the imparting of facts.

One other form of utilitarian prose comes close to pure literature—the sermon. Specific edicts of Charlemagne are preserved commanding preaching in the vernacular, and a collection of Latin homilies drawn up by Paulus Diaconus may well have been the foundation of the sermon repertoire; certainly the vernacular sermons preserved, sporadically at first, from the twelfth century onwards show at times a family resemblance to this source. Sermons are important because their themes are recurrent, and repetition can hardly fail to have impinged on the minds of the writers of vernacular literature exposed to them. The technique of the sermon is also relevant to the study of medieval literature, since the methods of interpretation—historical, allegorical, mystical—were adopted into purely literary forms. The form in which medieval sermons have come down to us is not always authenticated: possibly a preacher wrote them out after delivering them, possibly we may have to rely on a member of his congregation. This uncertainty applies in the case of a preacher like Berthold von Regensburg, who flourished about the middle of the thirteenth century and swayed great congregations with his oratory. Seventy-one of his German sermons are preserved, in addition to works in Latin. The art of Berthold lies in a combination of traditional exegesis with the born preacher's appeal to the common experience of his hearers. The words of other prominent preachers of the time, notably the preacher of St Georgen, some of whose sermons have been ascribed to Berthold, were also, it has been established, written down by enthusiastic listeners.

The sermon or homily is ultimately an inducement to a congregation to order its life with a view to the will of God; it is a public act, and in that respect the very opposite of the experience of the mystics, which lies essentially in the achievement, often transitory, of the union of the soul with its creator. The writings of the mystics are efforts to express or analyse this condition of heightened perception, and are therefore turned inwards. The seeds of mystical thinking are to be seen, however, in the processes of allegorization, which in themselves could be rationalistic. The interpretation of Old Testament passages as prefigurations of the Virgin Mary is akin in spirit to the ecstasy of the rapt mystic; and a parallel to the more personalized processes of thought involved may be found in the interpretation of the Song of Songs as reference to a mystical union between God and the Soul; this tends to be more systematic than the interpretation of random passages of the Old Testament as attributes of the Virgin. The imagery of the Song of Songs lay ready to hand for some of the earliest accounts in German of mystical experiences, as in Mechthild von Magdeburg's *Das fließende Licht der Gottheit*, not preserved in its original mid-thirteenth century German, but available in Latin translation, and a

German verse translation of this from a hundred years later. This not only gave allegorical interpretations of scripture, but also adopted the special language used by the Minnesinger to express earthly love. In the hands of the German mystics of the fourteenth century, the all-pervading theme of oneness with God is combined with the systematic dialectic of scholasticism; the mystical movement of the fourteenth century is dominated by the Dominican order, who were active preachers and teachers, and also had spiritual and administrative charge, at the operative time, of convents of nuns, which were then particularly numerous in Germany. In view of their public activities, they were more concerned with the use of the vernacular than the enclosed orders were, and their vernacular sermons were directed not only to the public at large, but especially to the nuns.

Meister Eckhart, born in 1260, was himself a Dominican, and eminent in his order; a distinguished scholar, who studied and, for a while, taught in Paris, and was singled out by his order not only as a teacher, but also as an administrator. His works in Latin and the vernacular are numerous, and only now in the process of being brought out in scholarly editions, and freed of false attributions. He started out in the scholastic tradition, and in a sense he always remained in it; but he combines exegesis and analysis with intuitions, not so much about the meaning of a biblical text, though this is often his point of departure, as about its implications for the relationship of the soul to God. He is a product of his time and his training in his reliance on authority even for some of his most challenging statements, including such a fundamental distinction as that between *got* and *gotheit.* The *gotheit* is the divine essence (basis or *grunt*) from which the three persons of the Trinity emerged, not as 'emanations' in a gnostic sense, but as modes in which God is perceived. The term *got* is used of the Christian God, unknowable, and definable only at the expense of being reduced beneath all-being and omnipresence. God transcends the world, but is also immanent in it. The last statement is unexceptionable, but when it is put the other way, that all things are in God, it could lend itself to the allegation that Eckhart had maintained the eternity of created things. To this he replied with the postulation of a 'passive creation', according to which things had pre-existed *in posse* before emerging substantially, explained by the analogy of a speaker's words which pre-exist their utterance. This in fact appears to draw on a distinction long made by scholastics; in German sermons, however, the conception of 'being in God' is expressed in extreme terms suggesting that the speaker—Eckhart—had been eternally present in God and had willed his own existence. It seems to have been the formulation, rather than the content, of the thought which aroused opposition. The human soul contains a highest or most intimate element, a *grunt*, to which Eckhart refers as a *Fünklein* (again, no original conception, and even the term *scintilla animae* had its precedents). This is not accessible even to the persons of the Trinity, because it is inaccessible to modes and powers, but only to the *gotheit*. It is specifically denied, once again, that the *Seelenfünklein* is uncreated; also that the notion of its permeation by God is pantheistic. In the *Fünklein* grace brings about the birth of the word. To receive grace, the soul must acquire receptivity, *gelassenheit*, an emptiness of all else, that allows it to be filled with God. Some intellectual or spiritual effort may be made to receive grace, but as receptivity depends mainly on faith, Eckhart has been understood as a prophet of Protestantism—though the thought itself could be Augustinian, or even Pauline. Eckhart's thought is not expressed as a system, but culled from remarks in sermons and exegetical writings, both Latin and German. Individual contexts are usually sufficient to themselves, but the totality, like all attempts to express the inexpressible, is liable to be understood only by the adept, and not verifiable by any rationalistic process. Yet the arguments are held in dialectical terms, and there is surprisingly little of the allegory of the spiritual marriage.

The boldness of some of Eckhart's formulations brought

him his detractors, and he was arraigned for heresy. This he denied, though he was prepared to accept that he could err, and offered to retract proven misstatements. Some of the charges against him on the basis of his own sayings looked serious only by virtue of being wrenched from the context in which they were uttered, some were invented. Yet Eckhart did not live to hear his beliefs vindicated; after his death, indeed, some of his teachings were condemned.

The extremity of his expression may derive in no small degree from the inadequacies of the German language of his day; there was no ready-made abstract vocabulary, and Eckhart is credited with coining a whole range of special terms and with creating a language for philosophy in German. Characteristic of his usage are the numerous abstract nouns of verbal origin, and this in itself makes his writing expressive of activity and change rather than of an unchanging state; in this way he anticipates, perhaps fortuitously, later developments in German thought and language. His language has disadvantages as well as advantages, however; it does not lend itself readily to definition, and he tends to give wide ranges of meanings to his terms—even important ones like *wesen*—and to use more than one term to satisfy what appear to be similar contexts.

The German works were, in any case, more outspoken than the Latin ones, and with good reason, since the conditions of preaching, especially in the vernacular, preclude careful reference to authority that may be made in a work designed for silent reading, and the need to drive a point home may lead to extreme statement. In one German work, the *Buch der göttlichen Tröstung*, addressed to Queen Agnes of Hungary on the occasion of a bereavement, either in 1309 or 1314, and designed for reading, he was, however, able to develop something of the rigour of argument which is otherwise typical of the Latin works.

Heinrich Suso, or Seuse, was also a Dominican, perhaps actually a pupil of Eckhart's; he did not reach his vision primarily by way of the intellect, so much as by submitting himself to extreme, or even excessive, mortification of the flesh and self-penance. Knowledge of his life comes from an autobiographical account which forms the first of four parts of his works, and from this emerges the beatific nature of his vision. In his more discursive works, the *Büchlein der Wahrheit* (1327) and the *Büchlein der ewigen Weisheit* (1328–32)—the latter further expanded and translated into Latin as the *Horologium*—he develops his intuitive approach in language which calls on some of the worldly terminology of Minnesang in the attempt to express the inexpressible. But such works were not all his life; he was also a preacher and teacher; he defended the impugned doctrines of Eckhart, and may himself have suffered for it; he was a spiritual advisor, and amongst those committed to his care the nun Elsbeth Stagel collected a set of letters, some to herself, which form a compendium of spiritual guidance.

The third great mystic of the time, Johannes Tauler, was a more active and practical preacher. He was deeply concerned at the state of public morals in his day, and his sermons, which are all we have of his works, are a call to repentance. At the same time, he took over some of Eckhart's concepts, in particular that of the *Seelenfünklein*, and was also in contact with the lay mystic movement known as the *Gottesfreunde*. Der Gottesfreund aus Oberland is, in fact, a fictionalized source for the visionary writings of Rulman Merswin, a Strassburg merchant of the second half of the fourteenth century, who retired from the world to found this contemplative movement, which was to become tainted with heresy. It was not the only such movement, nor was it the first; quite apart from the regular enclosed orders, which had especially numerous houses in Germany, there had been for many years such semi-enclosed organizations as the béguines, devoted to contemplation and the good life; the public at large was made more receptive to visionary expression by the precariousness of human existence at a time of interdict and plague.

The mystics and their writings had a wide influence in

their own day, and indeed afterwards; Luther expressed approval of sermons of Tauler which he read, and reissued the anonymous *Theologia Deutsch*, an early fourteenth-century reworking of some of Eckhart's thought, with a commendatory preface. Luther afterwards repudiated connection with the mystics, and in any case their immediate impact had waned. For all their influence, the writings of the mystics are not literature in themselves; rather they express habits of thought which may be observed at various other times in medieval and later literature; indeed, it is characteristic of mystical thought that it can be communicated only by metaphor, which is a literary device, though it does not usually form the substance of a literary work. To what extent these works are philosophy must also be open to question. The eighteenth century treated them with contumely; the nineteenth century rediscovered them, and recent writing expresses acceptance of their views. Clearly, the views of the mystics would not stand up to positivistic analysis; but their adherents would claim that they are exempt from such treatment, precisely because they deal with what is beyond and by inference above comprehension.

Worldly Writings of the Fourteenth Century

Allegory was the mainspring of one novel but relatively unimportant branch of literature current in the fourteenth century. It is hard to determine who would be the audience for such a work as Hadamar von Laber's *Jagd der Minne*, in which the 'huntsmen' give allegorical advice, interspersed with lovers' laments. The anonymous *Minneburg* has a similarly allegorical action; together with *Das Kloster der Minne* they represent the last remains of the ideals of courtly love as expressed in the *Blütezeit*. The last of these texts is in some ways the most interesting of them, for in addition to the rules of the initiates we are presented with a highly allegorical account of the building itself. It has twelve gates, one for each month of the year, and twelve towers crowned with virtues. Its groundplan is circular. It takes up, then, for their own sake, some of the externals of the cave of love in Gottfried's *Tristan*. But this is not all; the number of the gates is reminiscent of earlier religious allegories, and the application of twelve to the months of the year is a characteristic piece of allegorical opportunism. The building also echoes in some way the splendours of the Grail Castle in the *Jüngerer Titurel*. What appears to be an innovation has in fact a long tradition behind it; what had previously been an ornament has become an end in itself, but even this development is unsurprising, in view of the attention given in works of the golden age to description and allegory.

Love allegories were also written by the Viennese poet Peter Suchenwirt, though his most distinctive form was the type known as *Heroldsdichtung*, which takes on the standard form of an encomium of a patron, followed by a description of his armorial bearings, in which the various devices and tinctures are allegorically interpreted. His verse form is the doggerel inherited from the octosyllable of the thirteenth century. There appears to have been a ready market for such occasional verses, or *Reimreden*: that they were more or less made to order is suggested by the career of the Nuremberg brassfounder Hans Schnepperer, who wrote under the name of Rosenplüt, and whose output includes carnival plays in addition to *Wappendichtung*. Suchenwirt's near contemporary Heinrich Teichner was another writer of occasional verse, though he appeals less to the pretensions of his patrons, and indeed extols the simple virtues in his verse tales, which recount incidents of the scope and significance of the *Schwank*. In the modest genre of didactic fables Ulrich Boner's *Edelstein*, written probably about the middle of the century, was well enough known to be one of the first German books to be printed, a hundred years or so later (1461); it continues something of the cautious wisdom of *Bescheidenheit*.

The Fifteenth Century—an Age of Transition

The *Ackermann aus Böhmen* stands alone in the literature of its day as an original prose work dealing movingly with a serious topic, and making its appeal by dialectic rather than allegory. It was written in 1400 by Johannes von Tepl (or von Saaz); and in it the ploughman of the title complains in a dialogue with Death about the loss of his beloved wife. The directness of expression of grief makes it improbable that the text was a literary exercise, yet a dedicatory letter in Latin evaluates its technique in a most detached fashion. The dialogue is a non-progressive form: the ploughman does little in the first half of the work but complain, and only later is he worn down into some semblance of acceptance by reiteration of the position that Death is invincible and inevitable. The ploughman has a 'case' against Death, and the language of the beginning, at least, is very much the formal language of legal pleading; in the end God delivers a judgment, the conclusion of which is what might be expected—Death is adjudged the winner, but plaintiff and defendant alike are commended for their pleading, and censured for their presumption—the ploughman for taking for granted that what he had lost was his by rights, and Death for boasting of his power, which derived from God. In the logic of the decision, unexceptionable as it may be, the spirit of the schools lives again, as it does in the static juxtaposition of claim and counterclaim in the body of the text. But although the presentation of the power of Death is nothing new, and the conclusion of the work is orthodox, the expression of human grief in disciplined but highly-charged language was something not previously attained in German prose, and something which had no immediate successor.

Apart from the *Ackermann aus Böhmen*, there was little original German prose in the fifteenth century, but the language began to acquire greater flexibility as a medium of translation. Albrecht von Eyb's output is largely Latin, no longer in subject matter or in manner the Latin of medieval scholarship, but full of renaissance vigour. His German translations of comedies of Plautus show some freedom of treatment, but the addition to the dialogue of connecting narrative, largely to explain motive, suggests that he did not envisage a stage performance; this is hardly surprising, since there was no adequate German tradition to which he could appeal. In 1478 Niclas von Wyle published a large collected edition of his *Translationen* from renaissance Latin and Italian sources, including Enea Silvio's *Euryalus et Lucretia* and some of the *Facetiae* of Poggio. Others of these were translated by Augustin Tünger, and by Heinrich Steinhöwel. The latter is, however, better known for his translations, prefaced in true renaissance spirit with a biography, of selected fables of Aesop, and for his version of Boccacio's *De claris mulieribus*, under the title *Von den sinnrychen erluchten Wyben*. The *Decameron* reached German in a pseudonymous translation by 'Arigo', who also rendered Tomasso Leoni's *Fiori di Virtù* into prose, though he was anticipated here by the verse of Hans Vintler (*Plüemen der Tugent*, 1411).

The new age of printing also produced prose versions of medieval German texts such as *Wigalois*, and a *Tristan* which goes back for its material not to Gottfried but to the more primitive version of Eilhart. Such publications continued a trend otherwise noticeable in the fifteenth century, when voluminous verse collections of tales of adventure were also compiled, like the *Ehrenbrief* of Jakob Püterich von Reichertzhausen, which recounts a collection of familiar stories in the complicated *Titurel* stanza form. The same metrical model was used again a generation later, in 1492, for Ulrich Füetrer's *Buch der Abenteuer*, a generally similar compilation. These works were informed by the same encyclopaedic urge for completeness as the collection of tales of Charlemagne, collected under the title of *Karlmeinet*, and the rather later compilations of the more popular stories of Dietrich von Bern in the Strassburg and Dresden *Heldenbücher*. The story of Herzog Ernst was also still familiar, and indeed was printed as a *Volksbuch*, as were popular stories from the French like *Die schöne Melusine* and *Die vier Haimonskinder*, for the age of the chapbook had dawned with the invention of the printing press.

Indeed, the introduction of printing in the middle of the

fifteenth century marks a change very nearly as decisive as the almost simultaneous introduction of gunpowder; the latter marked the end of the last vestiges of chivalry, while the former indicated the coming of age of the urban crafts, a new factor in social and cultural life. It cannot be said that the newly-articulate craftsmen had highly developed literary tastes, and their productions are interesting as documents of social history rather than for their intrinsic value. They do, however, show the survival of themes from the earlier literature of the middle ages, indeed of just those themes which were available in the larger collections. The popular literary forms were, however, short-winded; the single anecdote of the *Schwank* type recounted in doggerel is the characteristic form.

Doggerel was also the verse form of the popular drama of the times—the carnival play or Fastnachtspiel. Its performers appear to have been these same craftsmen, but its origin remains obscure. Carnival processions themselves are of great antiquity; they may even go back to pre-christian rites celebrating the return of spring. The earliest type of Fastnachtspiel, including some of those recorded under the names of Rosenplüt or his fellow-citizen Hans Folz, are 'processional', in the sense that each successive speaker addresses the audience without any necessary reference to the other actors present, and gives an account of his own action or folly. The more highly developed type of Fastnachtspiel is a simple sketch—more or less a *Schwank* in dialogue, often a sordid domestic brawl or a townsman's trick on a peasant, but the 'processional' form is archetypal, and even survives vestigially in some of the earlier Fastnachtspiele of Hans Sachs in the next century. A catalogue of this kind appears also to lie behind the list of follies in such a work as Sebastian Brant's *Narrenschiff*, or more humbly, the victims of the Dances of Death.

The Fastnachtspiel was not the only dramatic form known to the middle ages in Germany; but other kinds of drama are rather less richly recorded there than in England or in

France. Comparison is relevant, for the subject matter and the form of the religious drama is international. It originated from the distribution of question and answer parts in the gospel appropriate for certain church festivals. The best known is the Easter trope *Quem quaeritis*, in its simplest form known as an *Osterfeier*, of which examples go back to the tenth century, developed with the accretion of one or two closely allied episodes into the *Osterspiel*, and finally, with extensive additional action, into the *Passionsspiel*. There are also *Weihnachtsspiele* and *Prophetenspiele* for other church festivals. The earliest texts are exclusively in Latin—emphasizing that the *Osterfeier* was a means of bringing a solemn message home more forcibly—but the vernacular comes to be used more and more; there are even some texts where the vernacular echoes the Latin throughout. The earliest and shortest plays were performed in church, but as more and more extraneous material was added, the casts became more and more extensive, and performance began to require several successive days, the plays moved out into the market-place, where a hundred players or more might be present at any one time in full view of their audience, sitting and waiting their turn to come forward and speak their lines on a stage built up with all the properties in position. By the fifteenth century, the actors in the religious plays were men of the city, and in Germany as in England, a particular craft might become associated with its own special part of a cycle of plays.

Profane scenes entered into the religious drama, but it was still a far cry from the basic seriousness of such plays to the often coarse incidents of the Fastnachtspiel, which must have appealed to essentially the same audience, and may indeed have employed the same performers. There is a similar dichotomy in the lyric of the fifteenth and sixteenth centuries. Meistersang was a stilted and mechanical reproduction of the outward forms of Minnesang. The metrical structures were applied, apparently by counting syllables, to narrative material, originally of an edifying nature; for the gatherings of the Meistersinger originally took place in church, though not as part of any service. In its earliest form, composition was confined to the melodies handed down from the twelve 'original' masters—some historical, some fictional; but Folz introduced his own, on the same essential pattern, and it later became the practice for each master to be required to produce his own melody. Even profane subject-matter, of a kind which would have no place in the surroundings of the church, was impeded by the artificialities of the metre, but the same writers and singers were also capable of producing the short *Schwänke* which are the narrative equivalent of the Fastnachtspiel.

Meistersang preserved, in a totally different social environment, the outward forms of the aristocratic Minnesang of the High Middle Ages; its development in the fifteenth century is a foretaste of a wider spread in the sixteenth. Concurrently with it there was a contrary tendency towards a new simplicity in the lyric, which may be said to have started in the writings of a poet like Oswald von Wolkenstein. It is likely that his simple diction drew on an old tradition handed down orally, but little, if any, popular verse can be traced back to the highly literate classical age of medieval German literature; a few ballads may, indeed, be referred to events in the fifteenth century, and isolated poems suggest oral preservation of legendary material of great antiquity, but the folksong, like Meistersang, is more conveniently regarded as a phenomenon of the sixteenth century.

SELECT BIBLIOGRAPHY

CONTENTS

1. GENERAL WORKS OF REFERENCE

P. Merker and W. Stammler (eds), *Reallexikon der deutschen Literaturgeschichte*, 1926–51; 2nd ed., rev. W. Kohlschmidt and W. Mohr, in progress (A–O, two vols, 1955–65). [Articles of varying length and scope, often tracing a theme through all periods of literature.]

W. Stammler (ed.), *Die deutsche Literatur des Mittelalters. Verfasserlexikon*, 1933–55. [Introductions, with bibliographies, to individual authors. The final volume, concluded in 1955, contains more recent information on authors and works dealt with in the previous volumes.]

—— *Deutsche Philologie im Aufriß*, 2nd ed., 1957 ff. [Monographs by eminent scholars on broad themes, e.g. Lyric or Romance, specialized into medieval and modern studies.]

Separate reference to these primary sources of information is not made below.

2. BIBLIOGRAPHICAL AIDS

W. Kosch, *Deutsches Literaturlexikon*, 1947–58.

Germanistik, 1960 ff. [Quarterly, with an annual index; very prompt notice of articles; books briefly reviewed soon after publication.]

Publications of the Modern Language Association of America: Annual Bibliography [from 1922].

The Year's Work in Modern Language Studies, 1931 ff.

3. COLLECTIONS OF TEXTS AND ABBREVIATIONS

ATB — *Altdeutsche Textbibliothek*, 1882 ff. [Independent editions of standard and other medieval authors. The series is continually being revised and extended.]

Bartsch — K. Bartsch and W. Golther, *Deutsche Liederdichter des 12. bis 14. Jahrhunderts*, 8th ed., 1928. [An extensive selection; in some cases the most recent edition available.]

Braune — W. Braune and K. Helm, *Althochdeutsches Lesebuch*, 14th ed., rev. E. A. Ebbinghaus, 1962. [The most important shorter texts and selections from the longer ones; extensive bibliographies.]

Diemer — J. Diemer, *Deutsche Gedichte des 11. und 12. Jahrhunderts*, 1849. [Contains most of the Vorau manuscript.]

DKMA — *Deutsche Klassiker des Mittelalters*, 1864–72, with subsequent reprints. [A small collection for the non-specialist, with introductions and guidance on difficult passages. Many of the texts are out of date, but the series is being revived.]

DL — H. Kindermann (ed.), *Deutsche Literatur. Sammlung literarischer Kunst- und Kulturdenkmäler in Entwicklungsreihen*, 1928 ff. [Only part of the projected series appeared; reprints of extant volumes are being produced. The relevant *Reihen* are: *Geistliche Dichtung des Mittelalters; Drama des Mittelalters; Realistik des Spätmittelalters; Mystik; Das deutsche Volkslied.*]

DNL — J. Kürschner (ed.), *Deutsche National-Litteratur*, 1882 ff. [The first 14 volumes (some in several parts) contain medieval texts. The editions of standard authors are by now obsolete, but some of the other texts are still most readily available here.]

DTMA — *Deutsche Texte des Mittelalters*, 1904 ff.

Henschel — E. Henschel and U. Pretzel, *Die kleinen Denkmäler der Vorauer Handschrift*, 1963.

KLD — Carl von Kraus, *Deutsche Liederdichter des 13. Jahrhunderts*, I (Text), 1952; II (Commentary, ed. Hugo Kuhn), 1958. [Omits individual poets whose works have been recently published in separate editions. C. von Kraus and Hugo Kuhn, *Minnesang des 13. Jahrhunderts*, 2nd ed., 1962, is a selection from this work.]

LV — *Bibliothek des literarischen Vereins in Stuttgart*, 1843 ff.

Maurer — F. Maurer, *Die religiösen Dichtungen des 11. und 12. Jahrhunderts*, 1964–65.

MF — *Des Minnesangs Frühling*, nach K. Lachmann, M. Haupt und F. Vogt neu bearbeitet von Carl von Kraus, 30th ed., 1950.

MGH *Monumenta Germaniae Historica*, 1826 ff. [Includes Latin and vernacular chronicles, etc.]

MSD K. V. Müllenhoff and W. Scherer, *Denkmäler deutscher Poesie und Prosa aus dem 8. bis 12. Jahrhundert*, 3rd ed., rev. E. von Steinmeyer, 1892. [Smaller Old High German and early Middle High German texts.]

MSH F. H. von der Hagen, *Deutsche Liederdichter des 12., 13. und 14. Jahrhunderts*, 1838. [Still not superseded for all texts.]

Steinmeyer E. von Steinmeyer, *Die kleinen althochdeutschen Sprachdenkmäler*, 1916.

Waag A. Waag, *Kleinere deutsche Gedichte des 11. und 12. Jahrhunderts*, 2nd ed., 1916. [Part of ATB.]

Periodicals and Collections of Monographs

Archiv *Archiv für das Studium der neueren Sprachen und Literaturen*, 1845 ff.

DU *Der Deutschunterricht*, 1948 ff.

DVLG *Deutsche Vierteljahrsschrift für Literaturwissenschaft und Geistesgeschichte*, 1923 ff.

EG *Études germaniques*, 1946 ff.

Euph *Euphorion. Zeitschrift für Literaturgeschichte*, 1894 ff.

Germ. Abh. *Germanistische Abhandlungen*, 1882 ff. [Monographs.]

Germ. Stud. *Germanische Studien*, 1919 ff. [Monographs.]

GLL *German Life and Letters*, new series, 1947 ff.

GRM *Germanisch-romanische Monatsschrift*, 1909–43; new series 1950 ff. [Numbered consecutively throughout.]

JEGP *Journal of English and Germanic Philology*, 1897 ff.

MLR *Modern Language Review*, 1906 ff.

PBB *Beiträge zur Geschichte der deutschen Sprache und Literatur*, herausgegeben von H. Paul und W. Braune, 1874 ff. From vol. lxxvii (1955) onwards, two journals with this title have been appearing: *PBB* (*T*) (Tübingen, ed. H. de Boor) and *PBB* (*H*) (Halle, ed. T. Frings).

PMLA *Publications of the Modern Language Association of America*, 1886 ff.

PSQ	*Philologische Studien und Quellen*, 1956 ff. [Monographs.]
QF	*Quellen und Forschungen*, 1874 ff; new series, 1958 ff. [Editions and monographs.]
SG	*Sammlung Göschen*. [Introductory texts and studies; kept up to date in revised editions.]
SM	*Sammlung Metzler*, 1960 ff. [Monographs and studies on individual authors and texts, with full bibliographies and accounts of scholarship.]
UB	*Reclams Universal-Bibliothek*. [Translations of medieval texts, reprints of more modern ones.]
WW	*Wirkendes Wort*, 1950 ff. [Useful summaries of recent scholarship, as well as original articles.]
ZfdA	*Zeitschrift für deutsches Altertum und deutsche Literatur*, 1841 ff.
ZfdP	*Zeitschrift für deutsche Philologie*, 1869 ff.

Abh. or Sb. preceded by a place name indicates respectively *Abhandlungen* or *Sitzungsberichte* (philosophisch-historische Klasse) of the Akademie der Wissenschaften established there (usually under governmental and formerly under royal auspices, as the full title of the institution indicates).

Fs. followed by a personal name indicates a *Festschrift*, or volume of essays presented to the scholar named. They carry a variety of titles, but can usually be located under the name of the recipient.

Names of authors and texts are abbreviated to initials in contexts where they are immediately comprehensible.

In the titles of works cited below, the following abbreviations have been used:

ahd.	althochdeutsch [and inflexions]
(d.) dt.	(der, des, etc.) deutsch [and inflexions]
diss.	dissertation
Ger.	German
Germ.	Germanic, germanisch
Gesch.	Geschichte
Hist.	History
Jh.	Jahrhundert

Ma., mal.	Mittelalter, mittelalterlich
MA	Middle Ages
med.	medieval
mhd., MHG	mittelhochdeutsch, Middle High German
OHG	Old High German
rev.	revised (by)
trans.	translated (by), translation
Zs.	Zeitschrift

4. SUBJECT BIBLIOGRAPHIES

The Early History of the Germanic Peoples

T. Hodgkin, *Theodoric the Goth*, 1891.
—— *Italy and her Invaders*, 2nd ed., 1892–99.
J. B. Bury, *The Invasion of Europe by the Barbarians*, 1928.
E. A. Thompson, *A Hist. of Attila and the Huns*, 1948.
L. Schmidt, *Gesch. d. dt. Stämme bis zum Ausgang der Völkerwanderung*, 1940–41.
W. Ensslin, *Theoderich der Große*, 1947.
E. Schwarz, *Goten, Nordgermanen, Angelsachsen*, 1951.
Early sources:
Tacitus, *Germania* (numerous editions; trans. [with the *Agricola*] H. Mattlingly, *Tacitus on Britain and Germany*, 1948).
Jordanes, *De origine actibusque Getarum*, c. 551 [an abridgement of a more extensive lost work by Cassiodorus, c. 533], ed. T. Mommsen, 1882 (MGH, *Auctores Antiquissimi*, V). Trans. C. C. Mierow, 1915.
Gregory of Tours (538–594), *Historia Francorum*, ed. W. Arndt and B. Krusch, 1883 (MGH, *Scriptores rerum Merovingicarum*, I). Trans. O. M. Dalton, 1927.
Paulus Diaconus (eighth century), *Historia Langobardorum* [down to 744], ed. L. Bethmann and G. Waitz, 1878 (MGH, *Scriptores rerum Langobardicarum*). Trans. W. D. Foulke, 1907.

Early Germanic Culture

J. Hoops (ed.), *Reallexikon der germ. Altertumskunde*, 1911–19.
G. Schütte, *Our Forefathers*, 1933.
G. Neckel, *Kultur der alten Germanen*, 1934.
H. Schneider, *Die Götter der Germanen*, 1938.

H. Schneider, H. de Boor, F. Genzmer, *Germ. Altertumskunde*, 2nd ed., 1951.
D. Talbot Rice (ed.), *The Dark Ages*, 1965. [Brief and popular, but written by experts in various fields of European historical studies, with considerable emphasis on the period of the migrations. Valuable illustrations.]

German History

K. Hampe, *Dt. Kaisergesch. in der Zeit der Salier und Staufer*, ed. F. Baethgen, 7th ed., 1937.
W. Andreas, *Deutschland vor der Reformation*, 2nd ed., 1934.
H. Heimpel, *Deutsches Mittelalter*, 1941.
R. Holtzmann, *Gesch. der sächsischen Kaiserzeit*, 1943.
A. W. A. Leeper, *A Hist. of med. Austria*, 1941.
S. H. Steinberg, *A Short Hist. of Germany*, 1944.
G. Barraclough, *The Origins of Modern Germany*, 2nd ed., 1947.
K. Hampe, *Das Hochmittelalter. Gesch. des Abendlandes von 900 bis 1250*, 5th ed., 1963.
G. Barraclough. *The med. Empire. Idea and Reality*, 1950.
B. Gebhard, *Handbuch d. dt. Geschichte*, I, 8th ed., 1954 ff.
H. Rössler and G. Franz, *Sachwörterbuch zur dt. Gesch.*, 1958.
P. Rassow, *Dt. Geschichte im Überblick*, 2nd ed. 1962.
Sources:
W. Wattenbach, *Deutschlands Geschichtsquellen im Ma.* [*Vorzeit und Karolinger*, ed. W. Levison and H. Löwe, 1952–53; *Dt. Kaiserzeit* (period to 1125), ed. R. and W. Holtzmann, 1938–43.]

Ecclesiastical and Social History

J. Bühler, *Dt. Vergangenheit*, 1923–29. [Documents on political and social history.]
H. Günter, *Das dt. Mittelalter*, 1936–39.
E. Salin, *La civilisation mérovingienne*, 1949–59.
A. Hauck, *Kirchengeschichte Deutschlands*, 1887–1920 [reprinted 1952].
M. Buchberger, *Lexikon für Theologie und Kirche*, 2nd ed., 1957.
S. J. Crawford, *Anglo-Saxon Influence on Western Christendom*, 1933.
W. Levison, *England and the Continent in the eighth century*, 1946.

C. H. Talbot, *The Anglo-Saxon Missionaries in Germany*, 1954. [Translations of lives and correspondence.]
T. Schieffer, *Winfrid-Bonifatius und die christliche Grundlegung Europas*, 1954.
J. Gegenbaur, *Das Kloster Fulda in Karolinger Zeitalter*, 1871–74.
J. M. Clark, *The Abbey of St Gall*, 1926.
M. Bloch, *La société féodale*, 1939–40.
H. Mitteis, *Lehnrecht und Staatsgewalt*, 1933.
—— *Der Staat des hohen Mas.*, 5th ed., 1955.
F. L. Ganshof, *Feudalism*, 1952. [Trans. of *Qu'est-ce que la féodalité*, 1947.]
H. Conrad, *Deutsche Rechtsgeschichte*, 1954.
H. Mitteis and H. Lieberich, *Deutsche Rechtsgesch.*, 3rd ed., 1954.
A. Schultz, *Das höfische Leben zur Zeit der Minnesinger*, 2nd ed., 1889.
—— *Deutsches Leben im 14. und 15. Jh.*, 1892.
Joan Evans (ed.), *The Flowering of the MA*, 1966. [Brief articles by authorities on various fields, with many illustrations.]
H. Naumann and G. Müller, *Höfische Kultur*, 1929.
H. Naumann, *Dt. Kultur im Zeitalter des Rittertums*, 1938–39.
M. Seidlmayer, 'Weltbild und Kultur Deutschlands im Ma.', in O. Brandt, *Handbuch d. dt. Gesch.*, 2nd ed., I, 1953.
G. Ehrismann, 'Die Grundlagen des ritterlichen Tugendsystems', *ZfdA* lvi (1919).
F. Maurer, 'Zum ritterlichen "Tugendsystem"', *DVLG* xxiv (1950), reprinted in *Dichtung und Sprache des Mas.* [collected essays], 1963.
E. Neumann, 'Zum "ritterlichen Tugendsystem"', *WW* iv Sonderheft 1 (1954).
—— 'Der Streit um "das ritterliche Tugendsystem"', *Fs. Helm*, 1951.
Helen Adolf, 'Studies in the med. scale of values', *Fs. Starck*, 1964.
J. Bumke, *Studien zum Ritterbegriff im 12. und 13. Jh.*, 1964.
R. Sohm, *Die Entstehung d. dt. Städtewesens*, 1890.
H. Planitz, *Die deutsche Stadt im Ma.*, 1954.
J. Huizinga, *The Waning of the Middle Ages*, 1924.

Culture, Education and the Arts

W. P. Ker, *The Dark Ages*, 1904. [Reissued 1955.]
H. O. Taylor, *The Medieval Mind*, 4th ed., 1925.

H. Schaller, *Die Weltanschauung des Mas.*, 1934.
E. Gilson, *La philosophie au moyen âge*, 2nd ed., 1944.
G. Leff, *Medieval Thought*, 1958.
Anne Freemantle, *The Age of Belief*, 1954. [Selected texts in English trans., with commentary.]
W. von den Steinen, *Notker der Dichter und seine geistige Welt*, 1948.
P. T. Hoffmann, *Der mal. Mensch, gesehen aus Welt und Umwelt Notkers des Deutschen*, 2nd ed., 1937.
F. A. Specht, *Gesch. des Unterrichtswesens in Deutschland*, 1885.
J. von den Driesch and J. Esterhues, *Gesch. der Erziehung und Bildung*, 1951–52.
K. Burdach, *Vom Ma. zur Reformation*, 1912–35.
A. E. Berger, *Die seelische Struktur des Spätmas.*, 1930. [Introduction to DL, *Reformation*, I.]
W. Stammler, *Von der Mystik zum Barock*, 2nd ed., 1950.
G. Dehio, *Geschichte der deutschen Kunst*, I, 1930.
J. Beckwith, *Early medieval art. Carolingian—Ottonian—Romanesque*, 1964.
H. Jantzen, *Ottonische Kunst*, 1947.
J. Baum, *Die Malerei und Plastik des Mas.*, II. *Deutschland, Frankreich und Britannien*, 1933.
—— *La sculpture figurale en Europe à l'époque mérovingienne*, 1937.
P. Frankl, *Die frühmittelalterliche und romanische Baukunst*, 1926.
E. Lehmann, *Der frühe dt. Kirchenbau*, 1938.
M. Grabmann, *Die Gesch. der scholastischen Methode*, 1909–11.
—— *Mittelalterliches Geistesleben*, 1926–36.
P. von Winterfeld, *Deutsche Dichter des lateinischen Mas.*, 1913.
S. Singer, *Germanisch-romanisches Ma.*, 1935.
E. R. Curtius, *Europäische Literatur und lateinisches Ma.*, 2nd ed., 1954. [English trans. (1953) from 1st ed., 1948.]
W. Fechter, *Lateinische Dichtkunst und dt. Ma.*, 1964 (PSQ 23).
E. H. Zeydel, 'The med. Latin literature of Germany as Ger. literature', *PMLA* lxxx (1965).
P. Salmon, 'Über den Beitrag des grammatischen Unterrichts zur Poetik des Mas.', *Archiv*, cic (1963).
H. Glunz, *Die Literarästhetik des Mas.*, 2nd ed., 1963.

Histories of Literature

G. Ehrismann, *Gesch d. dt. Literatur bis zum Ausgang des Mas.*, 1918–35. [I, *Ahd. Literatur*; II, i, *Frühmhd. Literatur;* II, ii, 1,

Die mhd. Literatur. Blütezeit; II, ii, 2, *Schlußband.* Full bibliographies to date of publication, great detail on factual matters, such as location of manuscripts.]

H. Naumann, *Dt. Dichten und Denken von der germ. bis zur staufischen Zeit. Dt. Literaturgesch. vom 5. bis zum 13. Jh.*, 1938.

J. Schwietering, *Die dt. Dichtung des Mas.*, 1941.

H. Schneider, *Heldendichtung, Geistlichendichtung, Ritterdichtung*, 2nd ed., 1943.

—— *Gesch. d. dt. Dichtung, nach ihren Epochen dargestellt*, 1949–50.

H. de Boor and R. Newald, *Gesch. d. dt. Literatur*, I and II, 5th ed., 1962 (literature to 1250); III, i, 1962 (literature 1250–1350). [Incorporates recent critical views; bibliographies selective, but brought up to date in successive editions.]

H. O. Burger (ed.), *Annalen d. dt. Literatur*, 2nd ed., 1961. [F. Genzmer, 'Vorgeschichtliche und frühgeschichtliche Zeit'; H. de Boor, 'Von der karolingischen und cluniazensischen Epoche'; Hugo Kuhn, 'Die Klassik des Rittertums in der Stauferzeit'; F. Ranke, 'Von der ritterlichen zur bürgerlichen Dichtung'.]

J. G. Robertson, *A Hist. of German Literature*, 5th ed., revised Edna Purdie (and others), 1966.

P. Wapnewski, *Dt. Literatur des Mas. Ein Abriß*, 1960.

W. T. H. Jackson, *The Literature of the MA*, 1961.

M. O'C. Walshe, *Medieval German Literature*, 1962.

E. Erb, *Gesch. d. dt. Literatur von den Anfängen bis 1160*, 1963–64. [The first volume of the hist. of literature produced for the Kollektiv für Literaturgesch. under the general editorship of K. Gysi. Well documented and illustrated; the Marxist standpoint produces some novel and interesting views.]

W. von Unwerth and T. Siebs, *Gesch. der ahd. Literatur bis zur Mitte des 11. Jhs.*, 1920.

J. K. Bostock, *A Handbook on OHG Literature*, 1955.

F. Vogt, *Gesch. der mhd. Literatur*, 2nd ed., 1901. [Part of Hermann Paul's *Grundriß der germ. Philologie*, 2nd ed. Vol. I of a 3rd ed., down to Gottfried von Strassburg, appeared in 1922.]

Language and Writing

Very generally speaking, OHG is distinguished as the stage of the language in which inflexional syllables contain full vowels (e.g.

nimu, nemamēs, nemant), which are reduced to the 'neutral' vowel in MHG (*nime, nemen, nement* respectively). MHG is differentiated from modern German *inter alia* by consistent changes in the long vowels and diphthongs of accented syllables. The time and extent of these changes varies dialectally; some are already marked in the twelfth-century Vorau manuscript, but have still not reached the spoken language of Switzerland.

O. Behaghel, *Gesch. der deutschen Sprache*, 5th ed., 1928.

R. Priebsch and W. E. Collinson, *The German Language*, 6th ed., 1966.

A. Bach, *Gesch. d. dt. Sprache*, 8th ed., 1965.

W. B. Lockwood, *An informal Hist. of the Ger. language*, 1965.

H. Eggers, *Deutsche Sprachgeschichte*; I, *Das Althochdeutsche*, 1963; II, *Das Mittelhochdeutsche*, 1965.

T. Frings, *Grundlegung einer Gesch. d. dt. Sprache*, 2nd ed., 1950. [Particularly useful for its emphasis on dialectology.]

F. Wrede, *Deutscher Sprachatlas*, 1926 ff.

W. Mitzka, *Deutscher Wortatlas*, 1951 ff.

W. Braune and K. Helm, *Ahd. Grammatik*, 10th ed., rev. W. Mitzka, 1961.

J. H. Gallée, *Altsächsische Grammatik*, 2nd ed., 1910.

H. Paul, *Mhd. Grammatik*, 18th ed., rev. W. Mitzka, 1959.

E. G. Graff, *Ahd. Sprachschatz*, 1834–46 [including alphabetical index by H. F. Massmann. Still the most nearly complete specialized dictionary].

Elisabeth Karg-Gasterstädt and T. Frings, *Ahd. Wörterbuch*, 1952 ff. [Still in the earliest stages of the alphabet.]

W. Müller, G. F. Benecke, F. Zarncke, *Mhd. Wörterbuch*, 1854–66.

M. Lexer, *Mhd. Handwörterbuch*, 1870–78, reprinted 1965. [Designed as a supplement and index to the previous item; both have to be consulted for maximum information on usage, dependent on editions available 100 years ago.]

M. Lexer, *Mhd. Taschenwörterbuch*, frequently reprinted; 30th ed., 1962, with appendix. [Incorporates vocabulary from newly-available texts, but does not give references.]

A. Götze, *Frühneuhochdeutsches Glossar*, 6th ed., 1960.

W. Wattenbach, *Das Schriftwesen im Ma.*, 3rd ed., 1896.

E. Petzet and O. Glauning, *Dt. Schrifttafeln des 9. bis 16. Jhs.*, 1910–30.

E. Crous and J. Kirchner, *Die gotischen Schriftarten*, 1928.

G. Baesecke, *Lichtdrucke nach ahd. Handschriften*, 1926.
A. Heusler, *Dt. Versgeschichte*, 1925–28.
J. C. Pope, *The Rhythm of 'Beowulf'*, 1942. [Suggests modifications to Heusler's theories.]
W. P. Lehmann, *The development of Germanic Verse Form*, 1956.
U. Pretzel, *Frühgeschichte d. dt. Reimes*, 1941 (Palaestra, 220).
J. Müller-Blattau, 'Zu Form und Überlieferung der ältesten dt. geistlichen Lieder', *Zs. für Musikwissenschaft*, xvii (1935).

Heroic Literature

W. P. Ker, *Epic and Romance*, 2nd ed., 1908.
A. Heusler, *Lied und Epos in germ. Sagendichtung*, 1905.
H. M. Chadwick, *The Heroic Age*, 1926.
H. Schneider, *Germanische Heldensage*, 1928–34.
—— *Deutsche Heldensage* [abridged from the above], 1932 (SG 32; 2nd ed., rev. Roswitha Wisniewski, 1964; cf. also *Englische und nordgermanische Heldensage*, 1933; SG 1064).
H. M. and K. Chadwick, *The Growth of Literature*, 1932–40.
A. Heusler, *Die altgermanische Dichtung*, 2nd ed., 1932.
H. de Boor, *Das Attila-Bild in Gesch., Legende und heroischer Dichtung*, 1932.
Caroline Brady, *The Legends of Ermanaric*, 1943.
G. Zink, *Les légendes héroiques de Dietrich et d'Ermrich dans les littératures germaniques*, 1950.
C. M. Bowra, *Heroic Poetry*, 1952.
K. Hauck (ed.), *Zur germ. Heldensage*, 1961 [16 essays by various hands 1925–61].
J. de Vries, *Heroic Song and Heroic Legend*, 1963.

Icelandic

Poetic Edda (*Saemundar Edda*), ed. F. Jónsson, 1932; ed. G. Neckel, 4th ed., 1962. German trans. by F. Genzmer [1933]; 2nd ed., I (Heldendichtung), 1963. English trans. by L. M. Hollander, 2nd ed., 1962.
Prose Edda (*Edda Snorra Sturlusonar*), ed., F. Jónsson, 2nd ed., 1924. German trans. by G. Neckel and F. Niedler English trans.: A. G. Brodeur, 1916; Jean Young (selections), 1954.

Thidrekssaga, ed. H. Bertelsen, 1905–11; G. Jónsson, 1951. German trans. by F. Erichsen, 1924.

Völsungasaga, ed. with English trans. by R. G. Finch, 1965.

Early Middle High German Religious Literature

W. Schröder, 'Der Geist von Cluny und die Anfänge des frühmhd. Schrifttums', *PBB* lxxii (1950).

Hugo Kuhn, 'Gestalten und Lebenskräfte der frühmhd. Dichtung', *DVLG* xxvii (1953).

H. Rupp, *Dt. religiöse Dichtungen des 11. und 12. Jhs.*, 1958.

C. Soeteman, *Dt. geistliche Dichtung des 11. und 12. Jhs.*, 1963 (SM 33).

S. Singer, *Die religiöse Lyrik des Mas.*, 1933.

S. Beissel, *Gesch. der Verehrung Marias in Deutschland während des Mas.*, 1909.

R. Cruel, *Gesch. d. dt. Predigt im Ma.*, 1879.

A. E. Schönbach, *Altdeutsche Predigten*, 1886–91.

H. Leyser, *Dt. Predigten des 13. und 14. Jhs.*, 1838.

W. Walther, *Die dt. Bibelübersetzung des Mas.*, 1889–92.

H. Kriedte, *Dt. Bibelfragmente in Prosa des 12. Jhs.*, 1930.

J. F. L. T. Merzdorf, *Die dt. Historienbibeln des Mas.*, 1870 (LV 100–101).

Secular Narratives by Clerical Authors

E. F. Ohly, 'Zum Reichsgedanken d. dt. Rolandsliedes', *ZfdA* lxxvii (1940).

E. Nellmann, *Die Reichsidee in dt. Dichtungen der Salier- und frühen Stauferzeit*, 1962 (PSQ 16).

A. Hübner, 'Alexander der Große in d. dt. Dichtung des Mas.', *Die Antike*, ix (1933).

G. Cary, *The medieval Alexander*, 1956.

E. Klassen, *Geschichts- und Reichsbetrachtung in der Epik des 12. Jhs.*, 1938 (Bonner Beiträge zur dt. Philologie, 7).

Spielmannsepos

H. Naumann, 'Versuch einer Einschränkung des romantischen Begriffs Spielmannsdichtung', *DVLG* ii (1924).

H. Steinger, 'Fahrende Dichter im dt. Ma.', *DVLG* viii (1932).

T. Frings and M. Braun, *Brautwerbung*, 1947 (Leipzig Sb., 96).
P. Wareman, *Spielmannsdichtung*, diss. Amsterdam, 1951.
W. J. Schröder, *Spielmannsepik*, 1962 (SM 19).

The Romance

R. R. Bezzola, *Le sens de l'aventure et de l'amour*, 1947.
J. D. Bruce, *The evolution of Arthurian Romance from the beginnings down to the year 1300*, 1928.
E. Faral, *La légende arthurienne*, 1929.
F. Maurer, 'Die Welt des höfischen Epos', *DU* vi (1954).
R. S. Loomis (ed.), *Arthurian Literature in the MA*, 1959.
Maria Bindschedler, 'Die Dichtung um König Artus und seine Ritter', *DVLG* xxxi (1957).
E. Scheunemann, *Artushof und Abenteuer*, 1937.
K. O. Brogsitter, *Artusepik*, 1965 (SM 38).
A. C. L. Brown, *The origin of the Grail Legend*, 1943.
R. Nelli (ed.), *Lumière du Graal*, 1951.
F. Ranke, *Tristan und Isold*, 1925.
W. Golther, *Tristan und Isolde in den Dichtungen des Mas. und der neuen Zeit*, 1907.
—— *Tristan und Isolde in der französischen und dt. Dichtung des Mas. und der Neuzeit*, 1929.
Estelle Morgan, 'Some Modern English Versions of the legend of Tristan and Isolde', *Die Neueren Sprachen*, new series, i (1952).
H. Küpper, *Bibliographie zur Tristansage*, 1941.
Hannah M. Closs, 'Courtly love in literature and art', *Symposium*, i (1946–47).
B. Mergell, *Tristan und Isold. Ursprung und Entwicklung der Tristansage des Mas.*, 1949.
Gertrude Schoepperle, *Tristan and Isolt. A study of the sources of the romance*, 2nd ed., with additions by R. S. Loomis, 1960.
E. Köhler, *Ideal und Wirklichkeit in der höfischen Epik*, 1956.
M. Wehrli, 'Strukturprobleme des mal. Romans', *WW* x (1960).
F. Ranke, 'Zur Rolle der Minneallegorie in d. dt. Dichtung des ausgehenden Mas.', *Fs. Siebs*, 1933 (= Germ. Abh. 67).
K. Viëtor, 'Die Kunstanschauung der höfischen Epigonen', *PBB* xlvi (1921–22).
O. Lauffer, *Frau Minne in Schrifttum und bildender Kunst d. dt. Mas.*, 1947.

R. Gruenter, 'Bemerkungen zum Problem des Allegorischen in d. dt. "Minneallegorie"', *Euph* li (1957).

—— 'Zum Problem der Landschaftsdarstellung im höfischen Versroman', *Euph* lvi (1962).

(Parallels in other literatures:

Chrétien de Troyes [Kristian von Troyes], *Sämtliche Werke*, I–IV, ed. W. Foerster; V (*Perceval*), ed. A. Hilka, 1884–1932. English trans. of *Erec*, *Cligés*, *Yvain*, *Lancelot* by W. W. Comfort, 1914; German trans. of *Perceval* by K. Sandkühler, 1929.

Mabinogion, trans. Gwyn Jones and T. Jones, 1949.)

The Courtly Lyric

General:

E. Wechssler, *Das Kulturproblem des Minnesangs*, 1909.

H. Brinkmann, *Entstehungsgesch. des Minnesangs*, 1926.

—— *Zu Wesen und Form mal. Dichtung*, 1928.

L. Ecker, *Arabischer, provenzalischer und deutscher Minnesang*, 1934.

A. Moret, *Les débuts du lyrisme en Allemagne des origines à 1350*, 1951.

—— 'Les origines de Minnesang', *EG* ii (1947).

—— 'Qu'est-ce que la Minne?', *EG* iv (1949).

T. Frings, *Die Anfänge der europäischen Liebesdichtung im 11. und 12. Jh.*, Munich Sb., 1950.

—— 'Minnesinger und Troubadours' (1949, reprinted in H. Fromm, *Der dt. Minnesang*, 1961).

A. Jeanroy, *La poésie lyrique des troubadours*, 1934.

I. Frank, *Trouvères et Minnesänger*, 1952.

H. Kolb, *Der Begriff der Minne und das Entstehen der höfischen Lyrik*, 1958 (Hermaea, new series, 4).

C. S. Lewis, *The Allegory of Love*, 1936.

H. Furstner, *Studien zur Wesensbestimmung der höfischen Minne*, diss. Groningen, 1956.

K. Burdach, *Über den Ursprung des mal. Minnesangs*, 1918 (Berlin Sb.).

Hugo Kuhn, *Minnesangs Wende*, 1952 (Hermaea, new series, 1).

(Related texts:

Andreas Capellanus, *De amore libri III*, ed. E. Trojel, 1892.

—— [trans.] *The art of courtly love*, with introduction and notes by J. J. Parry, 1941.

F. Schlösser, *Andreas Capellanus, seine Minnelehre und das christliche Weltbild um 1200*, 1960.

Carmina Burana, ed. A. Hilka and O. Schumann, 1930–41. [Some English translations by Helen Waddell, *Medieval Latin Lyrics*, 4th ed., 1933; reprint (Penguin), 1952.]

Helen Waddell, *The Wandering Scholars*, 7th ed., 1949; reprint (Pelican), 1954.)

Metre and music:

B. Kippenberg, *Der Rhythmus im Minnesang*, 1962.

R. W. Linker, *Music of the Minnesinger and early Meistersinger*, 1962.

E. Jammers, *Ausgewählte Melodien des Minnesangs*, 1963 (ATB, Ergänzungsreihe, 1).

R. J. Taylor, *Die Melodien der weltlichen Lieder des Mas.*, 1964 (SM 34–35).

K. H. Bertau, *Sangverslyrik*, 1964 (Palaestra, 240).

F. Gennrich, *Melodien altdeutscher Lieder*, 1954; and

—— *Mhd. Liedkunst*, 1954 (Musikwissenschaftliche Studienbibliothek, 9–10).

Ursula Aarburg, 'Melodien zum frühen dt. Minnesang', *ZfdA* lxxxvii (1956).

—— *Singweisen zur Liebeslyrik d. dt. Frühe*, 1956. (Appendix to H. Brinkmann, *Liebeslyrik d. dt. Frühe*.)

R. J. Taylor, 'Zur Übertragung der Melodien der Minnesänger', *ZfdA* lxxxvii (1956).

A. H. Touber, 'Zur Einheit von Wort und Weise im Minnesang', *ZfdA* xciii (1964).

K. H. Bertau and R. Stephan, 'Zum sanglichen Vortrag mhd. strophischer Epen', *ZfdA* lxxxvii (1956).

J. A. Huisman, *Neue Wege zur dichterischen und musikalischen Technik Walthers von der Vogelweide*, 1950.

C. Bützler, *Untersuchungen zu den Melodien Walthers*, 1940.

F. Gennrich, 'Melodien Ws. v. d. V.', *ZfdA* lxxix (1942).

K. H. Schirmer, *Die Strophik Ws. v. d. V.*, 1956.

Genres:

F. W. Wentzlaff-Eggebert, *Kreuzzugsdichtung des Mas.*, 1960.

—— 'Kreuzzugsidee und mal. Weltbild', *DVLG* xxx (1956).

—— 'Wandlung der Kreuzzugsidee in der Dichtung vom Hoch- zum Spätma.', *WW* xii (1962).

A. T. Hatto (ed.), *Eos. An Enquiry into the theme of lovers' meeting and parting at dawn in poetry*, 1965. [International collection of texts and translations; section on the German *Tagelied* by the general editor.]

—— 'Das Tagelied in der Weltliteratur', *DVLG* xxxvi (1962).

Mysticism

W. Preger, *Geschichte der deutschen Mystik im Ma.*, 1874–93.

H. Grundmann, *Religiöse Bewegungen im Ma.*, 1935.

F. W. Wentzlaff-Eggebert, *Deutsche Mystik zwischen Ma. und Neuzeit*, 2nd ed., 1947.

J. Quint, 'Mystik' in W. Stammler's *Reallexikon*, 2nd ed., 1962.

W. Stammler, *Von der Mystik zum Barock*, 2nd ed., 1950.

K. Ruh, 'Altdeutsche Mystik. Ein Forschungsbericht', *WW* vii (1957).

F. Pfeiffer, *Deutsche Mystiker des 14. Js.*, 1845–57. [Texts; not fully critical, but not yet completely superseded.]

H. S. Denifle, *Das geistliche Leben. Eine Blumenlese aus d. dt. Mystikern*, 8th ed., rev. F. Schultes, 1926.

W. Stammler, *Gottsuchende Seelen. Prosa und Verse aus d. dt. Mystik des Mas.*, 1948.

J. A. Bizet, *Mystiques allemands du* XIVe *Siècle. Eckhart—Suso—Tauler, choix de textes*, 1957. [With introduction and notes.]

Medieval Drama

E. K. Chambers, *The medieval stage*, 1903.

W. Creizenach, *Gesch. des neueren Dramas*, 2nd ed., 1911–23.

M. J. Rudwin, *A historical and bibliographical survey of the German religious drama*, 1924.

K. Young, *The drama of the med. church*, 1933.

W. Stammler, *Das religiöse Drama d. dt. Mas.*, 1925.

—— *Deutsche Theatergeschichte*, 1925.

H. H. Borcherdt, *Das europäische Theater im Ma. und in der Renaissance*, 1935.

R. Froning, *Das Drama des Mas.*, [1891–93] (DNL 14). [Introduction and texts.]

E. Hartl, *Das Drama des Mas. Sein Wesen und Werden*, 1937 (DL, *Drama des Mas.*, I; texts in I, II and IV—no more issued).

W. Werner, *Studien zu den Passions- und Osterspielen d. dt. Mas. in ihrem Übergang vom Latein zur Volkssprache*, 1963 (PSQ 18).

M. J. Rudwin, *The Origin of the German Carnival Comedy*, 1920.

E. Catholy, *Das Fastnachtspiel des Spätmas.*, 1961 (Hermaea, n.s., 8).

5. NOTES ON INDIVIDUAL TEXTS AND AUTHORS

Many of the earliest literary texts are anonymous; in those cases where the name of an author is known, it is unusual to know more than the barest details of the date and place of his life. Such information is given briefly below, where appropriate. The bibliography aims to give a wide selection of recent works; for fuller details of earlier discussions the reader should turn to the standard reference works.

OLD HIGH GERMAN

Collections of texts: MSD, Steinmeyer, Braune.

Concordance: R.-M. S. Heffner, *A Word-Index to the texts of Steinmeyer*, 1961.

Report on recent research: H. Rupp, 'Forschung zur ahd. Literatur', *DVLG* xxxviii, Sonderheft (1964).

Charms

Merseburger Zaubersprüche: The name indicates the provenance of the manuscript; tenth-century hand on a blank page of a ninth-century missal.

Editions: MSD, Braune.

Commentary:

G. Eis, *Altdeutsche Zaubersprüche*, 1964. [Including a reinterpretation of the first *M.Z.*, and giving examples of survivals in later literature.]

F. Genzmer, 'Germ. Zaubersprüche', *GRM* xxxii (1951).

A. Schirokauer, 'Form und Formel einiger altdt. Zaubersprüche', *ZfdP* lxxiii (1954).

—— 'Der 2. Merseburger Zauberspruch', *Fs. S. Singer*, 1941.

S. Gutenbrunner, 'Der 2. Merseburger Zauberspruch im Lichte nordischer Überlieferungen', *ZfdA* lxxx (1944).

F. Genzmer, 'Die Götter des 2. Merseburger Zauberspruches', *Arkiv för nordisk Filologi*, lxiii (1948). [With late Scandinavian parallels.]

H. W. J. Kroes, 'Die Balderüberlieferungen und der 2. M.Z.', *Neophilologus*, xxxv (1951).

Hans Kuhn, 'Es gibt kein balder "Herr" ', *Fs. Helm*, 1951.

F. R. Schröder, 'Balder und der 2. M.Z.', *GRM* xxxiv (1953).

L. Forster, 'Zum 2. "Merseburger Spruch" ', *Archiv*, cxcii (1956).

W. Krogmann, 'Phol im Merseburger Pferdesegen', *ZfdP* lxxi (1951–52).

K. J. Northcott, 'An interpretation of the second Merseburg Charm', *MLR* liv (1959).

L. Wolff, 'Die Merseburger Zaubersprüche', *Fs. Maurer*, 1963.

E. Erb, *Gesch. d. dt. Literatur*, gives a novel (non-military) interpretation of the first charm, with full documentation.

Variation of the horse-charm: *De hoc quod spurihalz dicunt* (MSD, Braune), manuscript of the ninth–tenth century, Vienna; *Incantatio contra equorum egritudinem, quam nos dicimus spurihalz* (MSD, Braune), late tenth-century; manuscript, Trier. Explicitly christianized version; the participants are Christ and St Stephen; the magic formula is essentially the same as in the Vienna charm. *Ad equum errehet* (Braune), twelfth-century manuscript, Paris, is also christianized, but the beneficiary of Our Lord's incantation is not named. The narration is in verse, but the formula in prose.

Other charms: Tenth-century manuscripts from Vienna and Trier record dialectally different versions of a veterinary charm against worms; *Hundesegen*, tenth-century manuscript, Vienna; bee charm, calling for the return of a swarm, tenth-century hand in ninth-century manuscript, Vatican; charm against bleeding, eleventh-century manuscript, Strassburg (destroyed 1870). All these charms, and some further specimens, in Braune.

The 'Hildebrandslied'

Entered on blank pages of an eighth–ninth-century manuscript; one of two leaves lost, the other restored to Kassel (C. Selmer,

'Wie ich das Hl. in Amerika wiederfand', *WW* vi [1956]). Numerous editions, including Braune and MSD. Earlier scholarship was concerned with the establishment of the text; there are still some unsolved problems of interpretation, owing to the corrupt state of the MS. A Bavarian original probably underlies the present form of the poem, but the ultimate source is unknown; it should have been Langobardic rather than Gothic, and probably goes back to the seventh century.

It has been held that the Hl. represented a vestige of a collection of poems which, according to his biographer (Einhard, see below, p. 200), Charlemagne ordered to be prepared. It is now doubted whether these were heroic texts; cf. most recently G. Meissburger, 'Zum sogenannten Heldenliederbuch Karls des Großen', *GRM* xliv (1963).

Translations:

German: numerous, including Baesecke (cf. below); Ehrismann, *Gesch. d. dt. Literatur*, I.

English: L. Forster, The *Penguin Book of German Verse*, 1959.

Commentary:

G. Baesecke, *Das Hildebrandlied*, 1945 [with facsimiles].

W. Krogmann, *Das Hl. in der langobardischen Urfassung hergestellt*, 1960 (PSQ 6). [Over-confident.]

H. de Boor, 'Die nordische und dt. Hildebrandsage', *ZfdP* l (1923–26).

A. Heusler, 'Das alte und das junge Hl.', *Preußische Jahrbücher*, ccviii (1927).

W. Perrett, 'On the *Hl.*', *MLR* xxxi (1936).

H. Rosenfeld, 'Zur Versfolge im Hl. und seinem seelischen Konflikt', *PBB* lxxv (1953).

—— 'Das Hl.', *DVLG* xxvi (1952).

F. Norman, 'Some problems of the *Hl.*', *London Mediaeval Studies*, i (1939).

J. de Vries, 'Das Motiv des Vater-Sohn-Kampfes im Hl.', *GRM* xxxiv (1953).

W. P. Lehmann, 'Das Hl., ein Spätzeitwerk', *ZfdP* lxxxi (1962).

W. Schröder, 'Hadubrands tragische Blindheit und der Schluß des Hls.', *DVLG* xxxvii (1963).

K. J. Northcott, 'The *Hl.*: a legal process?', *MLR* lvi (1961).

L. L. Hammerich, 'Die Trutzreden Hiltibrants und Hadubrants', *Neophilologus*, xxxiv (1950).

S. Beyschlag, 'Hiltibrant enti Hadubrant untar heriun tuem', *Fs. Hammerich*, 1962.

(*Jüngeres Hildebrandslied:* J. Meier, 'Das j. Hl.', *Jahrbuch für Volksliedforschung*, iv (1934).
'Hildebrands Sterbelied': text in G. Neckel's edition of the *Poetic Edda.*)

The Literature of the Conversion

ISIDORE: Bishop of Seville, d. 636. Best known throughout the Middle Ages for his encyclopaedia (*Etymologiae*), which was repeatedly glossed, rather than for his tract against the Jews. Manuscript of German version from the end of the ninth century, perhaps from Murbach (Alsace), but the language is problematic.
Editions: G. A. Hench, 1893 (QF 72); H. Eggers, 1964 (ATB 63).
Commentary:
Bettina Kirchstein, 'Sprachliche Untersuchungen zur Herkunft der ahd. Isidorübersetzung', *PBB* (*T*) lxxxiv (1962).

The Rule of St Benedict: The Benedictine order was founded early in the sixth century (Monte Cassino), and was particularly strong in France, England and Germany. OHG translation of the Rule: eighth–ninth-century manuscript, St Gall, in the dialect of the region (Alemannic).
Editions: Steinmeyer; Ursula Daab (1959); selections in Braune.
Commentary:
I. Herwegen, *Sinn und Geist der Benediktinerregel*, 1944.
Ursula Daab, *Studien zur ahd. Benediktinerregel*, 1929 (Hermaea, 24).
H. Ibach, 'Zu Wortschatz und Begriffswelt der ahd. Benediktinerregel', *PBB* (*H*) lxxviii–lxxxii (1956–60).

Fragments of St Matthew's Gospel: From an early ninth-century manuscript, mostly in Vienna; Bavarian copy of an original in another dialect.
Edition: G. A. Hench, 1893 (QF 72); selections in MSD.
Commentary:
G. A. Hench, *The Monsee Fragments*, 1891.

Murbach hymns: Early ninth-century manuscript from Murbach, now at Oxford. Alemannic.

Editions: E. Sievers, 1874; Ursula Daab, *Drei Reichenauer Denkmäler der altalemannischen Frühzeit*, 1963 (ATB 57).

Commentary:

W. Bulst, 'Zu den Murbacher Hymnen', *ZfdA* lxxx (1940).

Glosses: Varying dates and dialects, including eighth-century Alemannic copies of a Bavarian original.

Edition: E. von Steinmeyer and E. Sievers, *Die ahd. Glossen*, 1879–1922.

Commentary:

G. Baesecke, *Der dt. Abrogans und die Anfänge d. dt. Schrifttums*, 1931.

—— *Der Vocabularius Sti. Galli in der angelsächsischen Mission*, 1933.

W. Betz, *Der Einfluß des Lateinischen auf den ahd. Sprachschatz*, 1941.

Wessobrunner Gebet: Manuscript, dated 814, from the Abbey of Wessobrunn (founded 753) in Upper Bavaria, now in Munich, otherwise containing theological and didactic material. The problematic heading *De poeta* cannot, apparently, refer to the Creator. Resemblance of lines in this poem to some in *Völuspá* and the *Heliand* probably points to their formulaic quality, though this is itself an indication of antiquity. There is documentary evidence of an injunction to teach the heathen the Christian view of the Creation; cf. Ehrismann.

Editions: MSD, Steinmeyer, Braune.

German translation in Ehrismann, *Gesch. d. dt. Literatur*, I.

Commentary:

G. Eis, *Altdeutsche Handschriften*, 1949.

L. Seiffert, 'The metrical form and composition of the Wessobrunner Gebet', *Medium Aevum*, xxxi (1962).

Muspilli: Ninth-century manuscript, Munich. Entered in a missal presented to Ludwig the German (d. 876), and assumed, notably by the first editor of the poem (J. A. Schmeller, 1832, from whom the title) to have been written down by its first owner; but it may not have been written until the end of the century. Discussion of the poem has been concerned with the meaning of the title-word (*mûð* connected with 'mouth' or 'mundus' + *spill* in the sense 'destroy' or related to 'spell', and having something to do with utterance—the Judgment), and with the assessment as an interpolation of the account of the duel of Satan and Elijah.

Editions: MSD, Steinmeyer, Braune.

Commentary:

G. Baesecke, *Muspilli*, Berlin Sb., 1918.

H. Schneider, 'Muspilli', *ZfdA* lxxiii (1936).

W. Krogmann, 'Der christliche Ursprung des altsächsischen Mūđspelli', *Fs. Borchling* (*Niederdeutsche Jahrbücher* lxxi–lxxiii), 1948–50.

H. Kolb, 'Vora demo muspille', *ZfdP* lxxxiii (1964).

Biblical Narrative in Prose and Verse

TATIAN: The text takes its name from the second-century Syrian compiler of a Greek synoptic version of the life of Christ. This was adapted into Latin, in such a way that the text differs only in respect of minor variants from the relevant words in St Jerome's Latin translation. St Boniface is known to have procured a manuscript of the Latin Tatian in Italy; the earliest one still preserved is that at Fulda. The German version was produced there about 830.

Edition: (Latin and German), E. Sievers, 2nd ed., 1892. (Selections, mainly the Nativity after St Luke, in Braune.)

Heliand: The most extensive German text in alliterative verse, written, in the interests of christianization, at the behest of the (Frankish) King Ludwig the Pious, on an English model. The fragmentary *Old Saxon Genesis* is, however, taken to be the source of the *Old English Genesis B* (E. Sievers, *Der Heliand und die angelsächsische Genesis*, 1894). Early scholarship is concerned with the status of the poet as layman or cleric, and with the ascription of the work to Corvey, Werden or Fulda. Recent work has attempted to demonstrate an elaborate underlying structure, based on the symmetrical disposition of numbers of lines forming significant sections of the text, and on the allegorical interpretation of these numbers.

Editions: J. A. Schmeller, 1830–40 (from whom the title). E. Sievers, 1878. O. Behaghel, 7th ed., rev. W. Mitzka, 1958 (ATB 4).

Glossary:

E. H. Sehrt, *Vollständiges Wörterbuch zum Heliand*, 1925.

Translations:

K. Simrock, 4th ed. (including *Genesis*, translated by A. Heusler), 1933; W. Stapel, 1953; F. Genzmer, 1954.

Commentary:

O. Behaghel, *Der Heliand und der altsächsische Genesis*, 1902.

A. Heusler, 'Heliand. Liedstil und Epenstil', *ZfdA* lvii (1920).

W. Krogmann, *Die Heimatfrage des Heliand im Lichte des Wortschatzes*, 1937.

G. Berron, *Der Heliand als Kunstwerk*, diss. Tübingen, 1940.

R. Drögereit, *Werden und der Heliand*, 1951.

H. Rupp, 'Der Heliand. Hauptanliegen seines Dichters', *DU* viii (1956).

J. Rathofer, *Der Heliand. Theologischer Sinn als tektonische Form*, 1962.

—— 'Zum Aufbau des *Heliand*', *ZfdA* xciii (1964).

W. Krogmann, *Absicht oder Willkür im Aufbau des Heliand*, 1964.

(See also comparative studies under Otfrid).

OTFRID VON WEISSENBURG: From the dedications to historical persons, the date of composition may be estimated to lie between 865 and 871; the Latin dedication to Archbishop Liutpert of Mainz refers to Hrabanus Maurus (in charge of the Fulda monastery school 804–22) as Otfrid's teacher. Otfrid's language, however, shows the South Rhenish Franconian features appropriate to Weissenburg, in Alsace. There are three complete manuscripts, of which that in Vienna may include the author's autograph corrections.

Editions: P. Piper, 1882. O. Erdmann, 4th ed., revised L. Wolff, 1962 (ATB 49).

Translation by R. Fromme, 1928.

Commentary:

H. Bork, *Chronologische Studien zu Otfrid*, 1927 (Palaestra, 157).

W. Köhler, 'Das Christusbild im Heliand', *Archiv. für Kulturgesch.*, xxvi (1936).

C. Soeteman, *Untersuchungen zur Übersetzungstechnik Os.*, 1939.

D. A. McKenzie, *Otfrid von Weissenburg. Narrator or Commentator?*, 1946.

W. Foerste, 'Otfrids literarisches Verhältnis zum Heliand', *Niederdeutsche Jahrbücher*, lxxi–lxxiii (*Fs. Borchling*, 1948–50).

F. P. Pickering, 'Christlicher Erzählstoff bei Otfrid und im Heliand', *ZfdA* lxxxv (1954).

H. Rupp, 'Leid und Sünde im Heliand und in Otfrids Evangelienbuch', *PBB (H)* lxxviii (1956).

W. Krogmann, 'Otfrid und der Heliand', *Niederdeutsche Jahrbücher*, lxxxii (1959).

Hilda Swinburne, 'Numbers in Otfrid's *Evangelienbuch*', *MLR* lii (1957).

J. Rathofer, 'Zum Bauplan von Otfrids *Evangelienbuch*', *ZfdA* xciv (1956).

H. Rupp, 'Otfrid von Weissenburg und die Zahlen', *Archiv*, cci (1965).

Minor Poems in Rhyming Verse

Christus und die Samariterin: Tenth-century manuscript, now in Vienna, perhaps from Reichenau.

Editions: MSD, Steinmeyer, Braune.

Petruslied: Ninth-century manuscript from Freising, now in Munich, including musical notation (neumes).

Editions: MSD, Steinmeyer, Braune.

Psalm 138: Tenth-century Bavarian manuscript, now in Vienna.

Editions: MSD, Steinmeyer, Braune.

Georgslied: Written in a tenth-century hand in the Heidelberg manuscript of Otfrid; Alemannic.

Editions: F. Zarncke, Leipzig Sb, 1874; R. Kögel, *Gesch. d. dt. Literatur*, I, 1894; both reproduced in Braune.

Commentary: F. Tschirsch, 'Wisolf. Eine mal. Schreiberpersönlichkeit', *PBB* lxxiii (1951).

Ludwigslied: Celebrates the Battle of Saucourt (3 August 881) and composed before the death of Louis III (5 August 882). Written down later, as a Latin heading dedicates it to the 'pious memory' of its hero; but the manuscript was written before the end of the ninth century; now at Valenciennes.

Other contents of codex: Legend of St Eulalia, in Latin and in Old French.

Editions: MSD, Steinmeyer, Braune.

Commentary:

H. Naumann, *Das Ludwigslied und die verwandten lateinischen Gedichte*, diss. Halle, 1932.

Ruth Harvey, 'The provenance of the OHG Ludwigslied', *Medium Aevum*, xiv (1945).

W. Schwarz, 'The Ludwigslied: a ninth-century poem', *MLR* xlii (1947).

T. Schuhmacher, 'Uuurdun sum erkorane, sume sâr verlorane', *PBB* (*T*) lxxxv (1963).

De Heinrico: Eleventh-century manuscript, now at Cambridge. The text records a public act of agreement, but says nothing about the quarrel which this ended. The exact date and occasion of the poem have been disputed: perhaps it was put about in the interests of the grandson of the rebellious Heinrich at his accession to the imperial title in 1002.
Editions: MSD, Steinmeyer, Braune.

Old High German Prose

NOTKER DER DEUTSCHE

Born about 950, died 29 June 1022. The third Notker who lived as a monk at St Gall; a nephew and pupil of Ekkehard I, and in turn teacher to Ekkehard IV.

Editions:

E. H. Sehrt and Taylor Starck, *Notkers des Deutschen Werke*, 1933–53 (ATB 32, 34, 37, 40, 43).

Version of the Psalms, ed., R. Heinzel and W. Scherer, 1876.

Glossary:

E. H. Sehrt and W. K. Legher, *Notker-Wortschatz*, rev. ed., 1955.

Commentary:

C. T. Carr, 'Notker's accentuation system', *MLR* xxx (1935).

P. T. Hoffmann, *Der mal. Mensch, gesehen aus Welt und Umwelt Ns. d. Dt.*, 2nd ed., 1937.

Ingeborg Schröbler, *Notker III. von St Gallen als Übersetzer and Kommentator von Boethius, De consolatione philosophie*, 1953 (Hermaea, new series, 2).

(Phrasebooks: The one designed for a Romance speaker is preserved in tenth-century manuscripts in Paris and Rome. The German is glossed into Latin; the language of the learner is deduced from the spelling. Most recent edition: Steinmeyer-Sievers, *Die ahd. Glossen*, V, 1922. Selections in Braune.)

Latin Literature of the Old High German Period

SEQUENCES: The composition of words, originally devotional, to the melodic sequence was adopted and extended by Notker I (Notker Balbulus, d. 912). Secular sequences are preserved from the eleventh century onwards: of these Modus Ottinc (MSD) is an encomium of Otto the Great; Modus Liebing (ibid.) an anecdote about a 'snow-child'; Modus Florum (ibid.) a series of preposterous statements designed to provoke incredulity.

Commentary:

K. Bartsch, *Die lateinischen Sequenzen des Mas.*, 1868.
H. Spanke, 'Aus der Vorgesch. und Frühgesch. der Sequenz', *ZfdA* lxxi (1934).
W. von den Steinen, *Notker der Dichter*, 1948. [Includes texts and modern German trans. of sequences.]
P. Dronke, 'The beginnings of the sequence', *PBB* (*T*) lxxxvii (1965).

Waltharius: Traditionally ascribed to Ekkehard I of St Gall (d. 973), but now held to be an earlier work. Much recent writing on the subject has been concerned with authorship. The text is important as a full account of an international story known otherwise in Old English and MHG fragments, and by allusion in the *Nibelungenlied* and by Walther von der Vogelweide.

Editions: K. Strecker, 1951 (MGH, *Poetae Latini Medii Aevi*, VI). K. Langosch, 1956 (with trans.).

Translations:

German: several, including P. von Winterfeld, *Die lateinischen Dichter d. dt. Mas.*, 1913. F. Genzmer, 1953 (UB).

English: F. P. Magoun and H. M. Smysor, *Walter of Aquitaine*, 1950. [Also translates Old English, MHG and other sources.]

Commentary:

A. Heusler, 'Die Sage von Walter und Hildegund', *Zs. für dt. Bildung*, xi (1935).

W. Lenz, *Der Ausgang der Dichtung von Walther und Hildegunde*, 1939 (Hermaea, 34).

F. Panzer, *Der Kampf am Wasichenstein*, 1948.

K. Strecker, 'Der Walthariusdichter', *Dt. Archiv für Gesch. des Mas.*, iv (1940).

—— 'Vorbemerkungen zu einer Ausgabe des W.', ibid., v (1941).

K. Langosch, 'Der Verfasser des W.', *ZfdP* lxv (1940). [Pro-Ekkehard.]

W. von den Steinen, 'Der W. und sein Dichter', *ZfdA* lxxxiv (1952).

K. Hauck, 'Das Walthariusepos des Bruders Gerold von Eichstätt', *GRM* xxxv (1954).

F. Genzmer, 'Wie der W. entstanden ist', ibid.

N. Fickermann, 'Zum Verfasserproblem des W.', *PBB (T)* lxxxi (1960).

H. W. J. Kroes, 'Die Walthersage', *PBB (H)* lxxvii (1955).

G. Zink, 'Walther et Hildegund', *EG* xi (1956).

Hans Kuhn, 'Zur Gesch. der Walthersage', *Fs. Pretzel*, 1963.

(Old English fragments: ed. F. Norman, 1933. MHG fragments: ed. W. Eckerth, 2nd ed., 1909.)

Ecbasis cuiusdam captivi: Two manuscripts in Brussels, eleventh and twelfth centuries. The place and date of composition have been variously estimated from internal references to historically recurrent royal names: as early, perhaps, as 930, or even 912, but now considered to be an eleventh-century work, written perhaps in the region of Toul, i.e. on the border of French and German-speaking territories. The allegory of the outer narrative is a plea for the security of the monastic life; the inner story is an early account of the enmity of fox and wolf, recounted in such a way as to suggest that a story of this kind was already orally current. There are fragments of a late twelfth-century German fable of Reynard, and a thirteenth-century adaptation by Heinrich der Glîchezære, but the beast epic gained wide currency in Germany only in the later Middle Ages, in a Low German form, printed 1498.

Edition: *Ecbasis cuisdam captivi*, ed. K. Strecker, 1935.

Translations:

German: E. Gressler, 1910; W. Trollitzsch and S. Hoyer (with text and commentary), 1965; English (with text and commentary): E. H. Zeydel, 1964.

(Heinrich der Glîchezære, ed. G. Baesecke, 2nd ed., rev. Ingeborg Schröbler, 1952 [ATB 7].

Ysengrimus, ed. E. Voigt, 1884 [with full introduction].

Roman de Renart, ed. E. Martin, 1882–87.

Reinke de Vos [text of 1498], ed. A. Leitzmann, reprinted 1960 [ATB [8.)

Commentary:

E. Martin, 'Zur Gesch. der Tiersage im Ma.', *Fs. Kelle*, 1908. (Prager deutsche Studien, 8.)

K. Voretzsch, 'Zum mhd. Reinhart Fuchs', *Fs. Baesecke*, 1941.

G. Cordes, 'Reinaert und Reinke, de Vos', in H. Schütt (ed.), *Flandern—Niederdeutschland*, 1939.

A. Graf, *Die Grundlagen des Reinecke Fuchs*, 1920.

W. Ross, 'Die Ecbasis captivi und die Anfänge der mal. Tierdichtung', *GRM* xxxv (1954).

H. R. Jauss, *Untersuchungen zur mal. Tierdichtung*, 1959.

Ruodlieb

Editions: J. Grimm and J. A. Schmeller, *Lateinische Gedichte des 10. und 11. Jhs.*, 1838; F. Seiler, 1882; [with English trans.], E. H. Zeydel, 1959.

Translations:

German: P. von Winterfeld, *Dt. Dichter des lateinischen Mas.*, 1913; K. Langosch (with *Waltharius*), 1956.

English: G. B. Ford, 1965.

Commentary:

S. Singer, *Germanisch-romanisches Ma.*, 1935.

K. Dahinten, 'Zum Problem der literaturhistorischen Stellung des R.' *Historische Vierteljahrsschrift*, xxviii (1933).

K. Langosch, '"Historischer Kern", Entstehungszeit und Grundidee des Ruodlieb', *Fs. K. Strecker*, 1941.

W. Mohr, 'Wandel des Menschenbildes in der mal. Dichtung', *WW* iv, Sonderheft 1 (1953–54).
W. Braun, *Studien zum Ruodlieb*, 1962 (QF, new series, 7).

ROSWITHA: Probably lived from about 935 to 975: has recently received considerable attention on the 1,000th anniversary of her literary début. It has been stressed that she was not an enclosed nun, but a canoness; a member of a religious community, but not bound by final vows of poverty. There is some support for the view that her plays were performed, but early medieval theoretical writings on literary genres, admittedly by members of enclosed orders, show no inkling of knowledge of the nature of drama [cf. P. B. Salmon, 'The "Three Voices" of poetry in medieval literary theory', *Medium Aevum*, xxx (1961)].

Editions: C. Celtes, *Opera Hrosvite* . . ., 1501; P. von Winterfeld, 1902; K. Strecker, 2nd ed., 1930.

Translations:
German: O. Piltz (UB); H. Homeyer, 1936; English: C. St John, 1923; H. J. W. Tillyard, 1923.

Commentary:
Hugo Kuhn, 'Hrotsviths von Gandersheim dichterisches Programm', *DVLG* xxiv (1950).
K. Kronenberg, *Roswitha von Gandersheim, Leben und Werk*, 1962. [Popular account of a local figure.]
B. Nagel, *Hrotsvit von Gandersheim*, 1965 (SM 44).

EINHARD: Born 770, died 840; educated at Fulda.
Vita Karoli Magni, ed. G. Waitz, 6th ed., 1911.

Translations:
German: M. Tangl, 4th ed., 1924; English (most recent): S. E. Turner, 1960.

Commentary:
S. Hellmann, 'Einhards literarische Stellung', *Historische Vierteljahrsschrift*, xxvii (1933).
H. Pyritz, 'Das Karlsbild Einhards', *DVLG* xv (1937).
F. von der Leyen, *Das Heldenliederbuch Karls des Großen. Bestand. Gehalt. Wirkung*, 1954.
G. Meissburger, 'Zum sogenannten Heldenliederbuch Karls des Großen', *GRM* xliv (1963).

EARLY MIDDLE HIGH GERMAN LITERATURE

For collections of texts and general accounts, see pp. 172–74 and 183–84 above.

Merigarto: Title from its first editor (Hoffmann von Fallersleben, *Fundgruben*, II, 1834); correctly formed to imply a 'sea-enclosed' land-mass, in accordance with medieval cosmogonies. Dated to the end of the eleventh century—perhaps a fanciful account of a First Crusade experience.

Editions: MSD, Braune, Maurer.

Physiologus: There are three versions; the earliest, containing 12 of 27 articles, dates from the second half of the eleventh century; the later prose version from the 1120's, and the versified form (Milstätter Handschrift) from the second quarter of the twelfth century.

Editions:

Both prose versions, parallel, ed. F. Wilhelm, *Denkmäler dt. Prosa des 11. und 12. Jhs.*, 1914 (Münchener Texte, 8).

Earlier prose version, MSD; Verse text, Maurer.

Commentary:

M. Wellmann, *Der Physiologus. Eine religionsgeschichtlich-naturwissenschaftliche Untersuchung*, 1930.

The Song of Songs

WILLIRAM: d. 1085 as Abbot of Ebersburg. His version of the Song of Songs is dated about 1065. The *St. Trudperter Hoheslied* draws on this version, omits some parts and extends the allegory.

Editions:

Williram, *Paraphrase des Hohen Liedes*, ed. J. Seemüller, 1878 (QF 28); excerpts in Braune.

St. Trudperter Hohe Lied, ed. H. Menhardt, 1934 (Rheinische Beiträge, 21–22).

Commentary:

F. Hohmann, *Ws. v. Ebersburg Auslegung des Hohen Liedes*, 1930.

Marie-Louise Dittrich, 'Ws. v. Ebersburg Bearbeitung der Cantica Canticorum', *ZfdA* lxxxii (1948).

F. Ohly, *Hohelied-Studien*, 1958.

A. Leitzmann, 'Zum St. Trudperter Hohenlied', *PBB* lxi (1937).

Margot Landgraf, *Das St. Trudperter Hohelied*, 1935.

(For the continuity of the allegorical tradition, cf. Brun von Schönebeck's treatment of the Song of Songs: *Das Hohe Lied*, ed. A. Fischer, 1893 [LV 198].)

Other Allegorical Poems

Das himmlische Jerusalem: Twelfth-century Bavarian; based on the Book of Revelations, with allegorical account of precious stones.

Editions: Waag, Henschel.

Commentary:

Elisabeth Peters, *Quellen und Charakter der Paradiesesvorstellungen in d. dt. Dichtung vom 9. bis 12. Jh.*, 1915 (Germ. Abh. 48).

Von der Siebenzahl: Carinthian, attributed to Priester Arnold, author of a legend of Juliana. Seven Ages of Man; seven Sorrows of Mary, etc.

Editions: Waag; P. F. Ganz, *Geistliche Dichtung des 12. Jhs.*, 1960 (PSQ 7).

FRAU AVA, d. 1197; widow and subsequently nun. Wrote verse narratives, with allegorical interpretations, based on the New Testament: John the Baptist, Life of Christ, Antichrist, Doomsday.

Editions: Diemer; P. Piper, *ZfdP* xix (1886–7).

Commentary:

A. Langguth, *Untersuchungen über die Gedichte der Ava*, 1880.

R. Kienast, 'Ava-Studien', *ZfdA* lxxiv, lxxvii (1937–40).

Vom Rechte and *Die Hochzeit:* Carinthian, about 1160.

Edition: Waag.

Commentary:

C. von Kraus, *Vom Rechte und Die Hochzeit*, 1891 (Vienna Sb. 123).

Ingeborg Schröbler, 'Das mhd. Gedicht vom Recht', *PBB* (*T*) lxxx (1958).

(THE VORAU MANUSCRIPT: Written in the 1150's by the regular

canons of Vorau in Styria. Contents: the *Kaiserchronik* and the following religious poems: Versions of Genesis and Exodus (including a **Marienlob*); **Die Wahrheit; *Summa Theologiae; *Lob Salomos; *Drei Jünglinge im Feuerofen* and **Earlier Judith; Later Judith;* truncated version of the *Alexanderlied; Frau Ava; Sündenklage; *Ezzos Gesang; Siebenzahl; *Das himmlische Jerusalem; *Gebet einer Frau.*

Editions: Diemer (except *Kaiserchronik*); *Henschel.)

Ezzos Gesang: Written in Bamberg by a clerical author, at the instance of Bishop Gunther of Bamberg (1057–65), celebrating the latter's visit to the Holy Sepulchre. Manuscripts: Vorau, Strassburg.

Editions: MSD, Waag, Henschel.

Commentary:

H. Schneider, 'Ezzos Gesang' *ZfdA* lxviii (1931).

H. de Boor, 'Ezzos Gesang', ibid.

Anegenge: written about 1180; deals with the Holy Trinity, the Incarnation and the Fall of Man.

Edition: K. A. Hahn, *Gedichte des 12. und 13. Jhs.*, 1840. Selections in P. F. Ganz, *Geistliche Dichtung des 12. Jhs.*, 1960 (PSQ 7).

Commentary:

E. Schröder, *Das Anegenge*, 1881 (QF 44).

A. Leitzmann, 'Zum Anegenge', *ZfdA* lxxvii (1940).

F. Scheidweiler, 'Studien zum Anegenge', *ZfdA* lxxx (1944).

Asceticism

Memento mori: Alemannic, about 1070. Manuscript from the monastery of Ochsenhausen, now at Strassburg. Discovered and printed with facsimiles by K. A. Barack, 1879; later editions: Braune, Maurer.

Commentary:

W. Schröder, 'Der Geist von Cluny und die Anfänge des frühmhd. Schrifttums', *PBB* lxxii (1950).

R. Schützeichel, *Das altalemannische Memento mori*, 1962.

DER ARME HARTMANN: Wrote his *Rede vom Glouven* (paraphrase of the Creed) about 1140–50.

Edition: Diemer.

Commentary:

F. von der Leyen, *Des armen Hartmann Rede vom Glouven*, 1897 (Germ. Abh. 14).

HEINRICH VON MELK: Lay brother of the monastery of Melk after retreating from the chivalrous world to which he was born. Wrote his poems about 1160.

Edition: R. Heinzel, 1867; reprinted by R. Kienast, 1946.

Commentary:

W. Wilmanns, *Der sogenannte Heinrich von Melk*, 1885.
K. Kochendörffer, 'Erinnerung und Priesterleben', *ZfdA* xxxv (1891).
T. Baunack, 'Beiträge zur Erklärung Heinrichs von Melk', *ZfdA* liv (1913).
H. J. Gernentz, 'H. v. M.', *Weimarer Beiträge*, vi (1960).

TWELFTH-CENTURY SERMONS

Editions:

K. A. Barack, 'Dt. Predigten des 12. Jhs.', *Germania*, x (1865).
A. E. Schönbach, *Altdeutsche Predigten*, 1886–91.
W. Wackernagel, *Altdt. Predigten und Gebete*, ed. M. Rieger, 1876.

Mariendichtung

Litanei: Twelfth-century manuscript, Graz, from St Lamprecht; Strassburg manuscript, 1187, revised and extended. Ed. C. von Kraus, *Mhd. Übungsbuch*, 2nd ed., 1926.

Arnsteiner Marienleich: About 1150. (A *Leich* is a lengthy poem composed of a symmetrical arrangement of variously-shaped stanzas; it probably originated from the sequence (cf. p. 197), but secular forms have also been derived from the accompaniment of a dance.)

Edition: Maurer; Text with commentary by E. Henschel, Fs. Pretzel, 1963.

Melker Marienlied: Early twelfth century; editions: Waag, Maurer.

Vorauer Marienlob: incorporated in the Vorau Pentateuch; editions: Waag, Henschel, Maurer.

Mariensequenz aus St Lamprecht: Twelfth-century manuscript, now at Graz; poem probably composed before 1140. Translated from Latin hymn 'Ave praeclara maris stella'.

Editions: MSD, Maurer, Waag.

Mariensequenz aus Muri: Twelfth-century manuscript from Muri, now at Sarnen; editions: MSD, Waag, Maurer.

Early Middle High German Biblical Narrative and Legend

Vienna Genesis: Twelfth-century Vienna manuscript of Genesis and Exodus in German verse translation. Related texts (more closely so in the case of Exodus) in a mid-twelfth-century Milstatt manuscript (now at Klagenfurt).

Editions:

V. Dollmayr, *Die altdeutsche Genesis*, 1932 (ATB 31).

E. Kossmann, *Die altdeutsche Exodus*, 1886 (QF 57).

Commentary:

S. Beyschlag, *Die Wiener Genesis*, 1942 (Vienna Sb. 220).

R. Gruenter, 'Der paradisus der Wiener Genesis', *Euph* xlix (1955).

K. J. Northcott, 'Paradisiacal love in early MHG literature', *Fs. Starck*, 1964.

VORAU PENTATEUCH: Consists of (i) a *Genesis*, which shows few links with the *Wiener Genesis*; (ii) the story of Joseph; (iii) the story of Moses.

Editions: Diemer, op. cit., and 1864 (Vienna Sb. 47–48).

Judith: Two versions, both in the Vorau manuscript, the shorter preceded by the story of Shadrach, Meschach and Abednego, composed by about 1130; longer version composed about 1140.

Editions:

Ältere Judith: Waag, Maurer.

Jüngere Judith: Die J. J. aus der Vorauer Handschrift, ed. H. Monecke, 1964 (ATB 61).

Commentary:

Edna Purdie, *The Story of Judith in German and English Literature*, 1927.

O. Baltzer, *Judith in d. dt. Literatur*, 1930.

W. Stammler, 'Zur staufischen Judithballade', *ZfdP* lxx (1948–49).

PRIESTER WERNHER: He lived at Augsburg. The *Driu Liet von der Maget*, which are preserved in two versions different enough to make the establishment of a text difficult, are dated 1172.

Edition: C. Wesle, 1927.

Commentary: U. Pretzel, 'Studien zum Marienleben des Priesters Wernher', *ZfdA* lxxv (1938).

(Edition of Pseudo-Matthew in C. de Tischendorf, *Evangelia apocrypha*, 2nd ed., 1876.)

Annolied: chronicle and didactic poem, giving an account of Archbishop Anno of Cologne (1065–75). Probably written shortly after 1100 at Siegburg.

Editions: M. Opitz, 1639; M. Rödiger, 1895 (MGH, *Dt. Chroniken*, I); K. Meisen, 1946.

Commentary:

M. Ittenbach, 'Das Annolied', *Euph* xxxix (1938).

F. R. Whitesell, 'Opitz' Ausgabe des As.', *JEGP* xliii (1944).

Doris Knab, *Das Annolied*, 1962 (Hermaea, new series 11) [on the circumstances and place of composition].

Kaiserchronik: Legendary lives of kings and emperors down to 1147, including some religious legends. Attributed to Priester Konrad of Regensburg, author of the *Rolandslied*, but the date of composition of neither is settled.

Editions: H. F. Massmann, 1849–54; E. Schröder, 1892 (MGH, *Deutsche Chroniken*, I).

Die Kchr. Ausgewählte Erzählungen [*Faustinianus* and *Crescentia*], ed. W. Bulst, 1946.

Commentary:

E. F. Ohly, *Sage und Legende in der Kaiserchronik*, 1940.

E. Klassen, *Geschichts- und Reichsbetrachtung in der Epik des 12. Jhs.*, 1938 (Bonner Beiträge zur dt. Philologie, 7).

W. Mohr, 'Lucretia in der Kchr.', *DVLG* xxvi (1952).

F. Neumann, 'Wann entstanden Kchr. und Rolandslied?', *ZfdA* xci (1962).

F. Urbanek, 'Zur Datierung der Kchr.', *Euph* liii (1959).

E. E. Stengel, 'Die Entstehung der Kchr. und der Anfang der staufishen Zeit', *Dt. Archiv zur Erforschung des Mas.*, xiv (1958).

E. E. Stengel, 'Nochmals die Datierung der Kchr.', ibid. xvi (1960).

G. Zink, 'Rolandslied et Kaiserchronik', *EG* xix (1964).

LEGENDS

Albanus, Patricius, Visio Sancti Pauli, Tnugdalus (*Tundalus*), ed. C. von Kraus, *Deutsche Gedichte des 12. Jhs.*, 1894.

Trier *Silvester:* ed. C. [von] Kraus, 1895 (MGH, *Dt. Chroniken*, I).

Veronica: ed. B. Standring, *Die Gedichte des Wilden Mannes*, 1963 (ATB 59).

Aegidius: ed. K. Bartsch, *Germania* xxvi (1882).

Brandan: ed. C. Schröder, 1871.

Commentary:

A. Leitzmann, 'Zum Trierer Aegidius', *ZfdA* lxxxii (1950).

THE RISE OF SECULAR LITERATURE

Narrative Literature in Clerical Hands

Alexanderlied

The Vorau manuscript preserves the beginning of a translation made about 1140 by Pfaffe Lamprecht of Trier, from a French original of which very little is preserved. This version was reworked some twenty or thirty years later in a version known as the Strassburg *Alexander* (manuscript destroyed in 1870), and there is a third version, the Basel *Alexander*, from the fifteenth century.

Editions: Pfaffe Lamprecht, ed. F. Maurer, 1940 (DL, *Geistliche Dichtung des Mas.*, V); the three texts, with the Old French fragments, ed. K. Kinzel, 1885. See also Rudolf von Ems.

Commentary:

E. Sitte, *Die Datierung von Lamprechts Alexander*, 1940 (Hermaea, 35).

E. Schröder, *Die dt. Alexanderdichtungen des 12. Jhs.*, 1926 (Nachrichten der Gesellschaft der Wissenschaften zu Göttingen).

A. Hübner, 'Alexander der Große in d. dt. Dichtung des Mas.', *Kleine Schriften zur dt. Philologie*, 1940.

C. Minis, 'Handschrift und Dialekt des Vorauer Alexander', *Archiv*, cxc (1954).

C. Minis, 'Paffen Lambrehts Tobias und Alexander', *Neophilologus*, xxxviii (1954).

E. Czerwonka, *Der Basler Alexander*, diss. Berlin (W), 1958.

W. Fischer, *Die Alexanderliedkonzeption des Pfaffen Lambreht*, 1964.

Rolandslied

Translated by the author of the *Kaiserchronik* via a Latin intermediary from the French *Chanson de Roland*, a patriotic *chanson de geste* based on the historical exploits of Charlemagne. The German version tones down the patriotism and enhances the religious fervour. On dating, cf. the controversies over the *Kaiserchronik*.

Editions: K. Bartsch, 1874; C. Wesle, 1928 (2nd ed., 1963); F. Maurer, 1940 (DL, *Geistliche Dichtung des Mas.*, V).

Translation by R. O. Ottmann, 1892 (UB).

(*Chanson de Roland*, ed. J. Bédier, 1924; English trans. by Dorothy L. Sayers, 1957.)

Commentary:

G. Fliegner, *Geistliches und weltliches Rittertum im Rolandslied des Pfaffen Konrad*, diss. Berlin, 1937.

E. F. Ohly, 'Zum Reichsgedanken d. dt. Rolandslieds', *ZfdA* lxxvii (1940).

H. Röhr, 'Die politische Umwelt des dt. Rolandsliedes', *PBB* lxiv (1940).

P. A. Becker, 'Zum dt. Rolandslied', *PBB* lxviii (1946).

P. Wapnewski, 'Der Epilog und die Datierung d. dt. Rolandslieds', *Euph* xlix (1955).

L. Wolff, '... Zur Datierung des Rolandsliedes', *PBB* (*T*) lxxviii (1956).

Elisabeth Mager, 'Zum Rolandslied des Pfaffen Konrad', *PBB* (*H*) lxxxvi (1964).

Spielmannsepen

Oswald

Two versions, both known only from fifteenth-century manuscripts; the longer text (Munich), ed. G. Baesecke, 1907 (Germ. Abh. 28); shorter text (Vienna), ed. G. Baesecke, 1912; Gertrud Fuchs, 1922 (Germ. Abh. 52). In both these texts, the hero uses a raven as his messenger; it has recently been pointed out that Oswald is portrayed with a raven in pictorial representations only from the fourteenth century; doubt has therefore been expressed whether the texts are twelfth-century *Spielmann* texts at all, though there may at that time have existed a Saint's Life more truly appropriate to King Oswald of Northumbria.

Commentary:

M. Curschmann, *Der Münchener Oswald und d. dt. spielmännische Epik*, 1964.

A. Vizkelety, 'Der Budapester Oswald', *PBB* (*H*) lxxxvi (1964) [concerned with a prose version, but deals with the question of dating the Vienna and Munich texts].

Salomon und Markolf

Edition: F. Vogt and W. Hartmann, *Die dt. Dichtungen von S. und M.*, 1880–1934.

Commentary:

H. W. J. Kroes, 'Zum mhd. S. und M.', *Neophilologus*, xxx (1946).

Orendel

Editions: A. E. Berger, 1888; H. Steinger, 1935 (ATB 36).

Translation by K. Simrock, 1845.

Commentary:

R. Heinzel, *Über das Gedicht vom König Orendel*, 1892 (Vienna Sb. 126).

E. Tonnelat, 'Le roi Orendel', *Fs.* (*Mélanges*) *Ch. Andler*, 1924.

S. Singer, 'Dogma und Dichtung des Mas.', *PMLA* lxii (1947).

König Rother

Editions: H. Rückert, 1872 (popular); K. von Bahder, 1884 (ATB 6); J. de Vries, 1922; T. Frings and J. Kuhnt, 2nd ed., 1954.

Translations:

German: H. Zimmer, 1924; G. Legerlotz, 1940; G. Kramer, 1961.

English: R. Lichtenstein, 1962.

Commentary:

T. Frings, 'Rothari—Roger—Rother', *PBB* lxvii (1944).

J. de Vries, 'Die Schuhepisode im K. R.', *ZfdP* lxxx (1960).

Herzog Ernst

The titular hero was one of the most popular legendary figures of the German Middle Ages; there are no fewer than five German and two Latin accounts of his exploits. The German texts are: A, dated from 1170–80, known only from fragments; B, a complete redaction of about 1220, known from two fifteenth-century manuscripts; D, late thirteenth century, by Ulrich von Etzenbach; G, stanzaic poem, early fourteenth century; F, *Volksbuch* in prose (fifteenth century) derived from one of the Latin texts. The Ernst of the legend is a conflation of three historical figures: Ernst I of Bavaria (d. 1065); Liudolf of Swabia (d. 957); Ernst II of Swabia (d. 1030). Liudolf was in rebellion against his father; Ernst II died defending his land in the company of a faithful friend and retainer Werner, in whom traits of Wetzel have been seen. The earliest complete version is significantly later than the early Middle High German period; the influence of courtly literature cannot be ruled out, but the poem appeals to relatively primitive tastes.

Edition of A, B and G: K. Bartsch, 1869.

Commentary:

L. Jordan, 'Quellen und Komposition von H. E.', *Archiv* cxii (1904).

E. Hildebrand, *Über die Stellung des Liedes vom H. E. in der mal. Literaturgesch. und Volkskunde*, diss. Marburg, 1937.

C. Heselhaus, 'Die H. E.-Dichtung', *DVLG* xx (1942).

M. Wetter, *Quellen und Werk des Ernstdichters*, 1941 (Bonner Beiträge zur dt. Philologie, 12).

H. Neumann, 'Die dt. Kernfabel des H.-E.-Epos', *Euph* xlv (1950).

Early Courtly Romances

Graf Rudol,

Editions:

C. von Kraus, *Mhd. Übungsbuch*, 1st ed. only, 1912.

P. F. Ganz (with introduction, notes and bibliography), 1964 (PSQ 19).

Commentary:

G. Holz, 'Zum Grafen Rudolf', *PBB* xviii (1894).

J. Bethmann, *Untersuchungen über die mhd. Dichtung vom Grafen Rudolf*, 1904 (Palaestra 30).

EILHART VON OBERG

Eilhart came of a family of *ministeriales* in the Brunswick-Hildesheim area; it is not known at whose instance the poem was written. A first version is dated to about 1170; the revised text, preserved in fifteenth-century manuscripts, was probably written before the end of the twelfth century.

Editions: (Revised text) F. Lichtenstein, 1877 (QF 19); (fragments of early recension) K. Wagner, 1924.

Commentary:

F. Ranke, *Tristan und Isold*, 1925.

K. Wagner, 'Wirklichkeit und Schicksal im Epos des Eilhart von Oberg', *Archiv*, clxx (1937).

G. Cordes, *Zur Sprache Eilharts von Oberg*, 1939.

H. Eggers, 'Der Liebesmonolog in Es. Tristrant', *Euph* xlv (1950).

H. Stolte, *Eilhart und Gottfried*, 1941.

(Béroul, *Le roman de Tristan*, poème du XIIe siècle, ed. E. Muret, 4th ed., 1937 (Classiques français du moyen âge, 12); A. Ewert, *The Romance of Tristram by Béroul*, a poem of the twelfth century [with introduction and notes], 1939.)

Trierer Floyris: fragments of a late twelfth-century manuscript, for which no source is preserved. Edition by E. von Steinmeyer, *ZfdA* xxi (1877).

Commentary:

L. Ernst, *Floire und Blanscheflur. Studie zur vergleichenden Literaturwissenschaft*, 1912 (QF 118).

HEINRICH VON VELDEKE

Lived at Maastricht, where the bulk of the *Eneide* was composed in a language which has more affinities to Dutch than to German. Text completed under the patronage of Hermann of Thuringia, and adapted in the manuscripts as far as possible to German speech habits. Works include a legend (*Servatius*) and lyrics besides *Eneide*.

Editions:

T. Frings and G. Schieb, *Sente Servas. Sanctus Servatius*, 1956.

—— *Eneide*, I (Introduction and text in parallel manuscript and reconstructed versions) 1964, II (notes) 1965 (DTMA 58–9).

Lyrics: MF (now giving reconstructed text, with manuscript readings in critical apparatus).

Commentary:

T. Frings and G. Schieb, *Heinrich von Veldeke. Die Servatius-Bruchstücke und die Lieder*, 1947 (also *PBB* lxviii–lxxi).

—— *Drei Veldeke-Studien*, Berlin Abh., 1947.

—— 'H. v. V. Die Entwicklung eines Lyrikers', *Fs. Kluckhohn und Schneider*, 1948.

C. Minis, *Textkritische Studien über den Roman d'Eneas und die Eneide von Henric van Veldeke*, 1959.

R. Zitzmann, 'Die Didohandlung in der frühhöfischen Eneasdichtung', *Euph* xlvi (1952).

J. Quint, 'Der *Roman d'Énéas* und Veldekes *Eneit* als frühhöfische Umgestaltungen der *Aeneis* in der "Renaissance" des 12. Jhs.', *ZfdP* lxxiii (1954).

J. Notermans, 'Een kwart eeuw Veldeke-studie', *Levende Talen*, no. 173 (1954).

H. D. Sacker, 'H. v. V.'s conception of the Aeneid', *GLL* x (1957).

Gabriele Schieb, 'Auf den Spuren der Maasländischen Eneide', *Studia germanica Gandensia*, iii (1961).

—— *Henric van Veldeken. Heinrich von Veldeke*, 1965 (SM 42). [Only the more familiar form of the name is on the cover.]

(*Eneas*, ed. J. J. Salverda de Grave, 1925–29.)

The Thuringian School

HERBORT VON FRITZLAR: Born about 1180 at Fritzlar. He is thought to have visited Paris. Works:

Liet von Troye, ed. G. K. Frommann, 1837.

Pilatus, ed. K. Weinhold, *ZfdP* viii (1877).

(Benoît de Ste. Maure, *Roman de Troie*, ed. L. Constans, 1904–12.)

Commentary:

H. Menhart, 'Herbort-Studien', *ZfdA* lxv, lxvi, lxxvii (1928–9, 1940).

F. J. Worstbrock, 'Zur Tradition des Trojastoffes und seiner Gestaltung bei H. v. F.', *ZfdA* xcii (1963).

ALBRECHT VON HALBERSTADT: There are documentary references to a cleric of this name in 1217 and 1218 at the monastery of Jechaburg near Sondershausen. There is no complete manuscript of the *Metamorphosen*, which are known from a sixteenth-century version published by Jörg Wickram.

Editions:

Metamorphosen: fragments, ed. W. Leverkus. *ZfdA* xi (1859); complete reconstructed text, ed. K. Bartsch, *A.v.H. und Ovid im Ma.*, 1861 (with introduction and commentary); Wickram's version: *Georg Wickrams Werke*, VII, ed. J. Bolte, 1905 (LV 237).

Athis und Prophilias (romance of chivalry with classical colouring), ed. C. von Kraus, *Mhd. Übungsbuch*, 2nd ed., 1926.

Commentary:

O. Runge, *Die Metamorphosenverdeutschung As. v. H.*, 1908 (Palaestra 73).

F. Neumann, 'Meister Albrechts und Jörg Wickrams Ovid auf Deutsch', *PBB* lxxvi (1954).

MEISTER OTTE: An educated man, probably a layman with a legal training; *Eraclius* was probably written about 1205–10.

Editions: H. F. Massmann, 1842; H. Graef, 1883 (QF 50).

Commentary:

E. Schröder, *Der Dichter d. dt. Eraclius*, Munich Sb., 1924.

F. Maertens, *Untersuchungen zu Ottes Eraclius*, diss. Göttingen, 1927.

THE ROMANCE IN THE GOLDEN AGE

HARTMANN VON AUE

The 'Aue' he came from has not been identified; he calls himself a Swabian, i.e. a native of south-western Germany, or perhaps northern Switzerland. Date of birth and death are also unknown, but he probably lived between about 1160 and 1210. He took part in a Crusade, but whether this was in 1189 or 1197 has been debated (see below, entry for Hartmann under the Courtly Lyric). Early research on the romances was concerned with identifying Hartmann's sources; a second phase compares his treatment of his subject-matter with that of the sources; the most recent phase interprets the texts in their own right, often seeing religious and mystic implications. Such interpretations are in keeping with medieval notions of allegory, but appear on many occasions to turn romances into sermons.

Editions and translations:

Complete Works, ed. F. Bech, 3rd ed., repr. 1934 (DKMA). Never a standard edition, and largely out of date.

Epische Dichtungen, trans. R. Fink, 1939.

Erec, ed. A. Leitzmann, 3rd ed., rev. L. Wolff, 1963 (ATB 39).

Gregorius, ed. H. Paul, 10th ed., rev. L. Wolff, 1963 (ATB 2), with useful introduction.

—— ed. F. Neumann, 1958 (DKMA, new series, 2).

—— German trans. by B. Kippenberg, 1963 (UB, with text); English trans. by E. H. Zeydel, 1955.

Der arme Heinrich, ed. H. Paul, 12th ed., rev. L. Wolff, 1961 (ATB 3).

—— ed. E. Gierach, 2nd ed., 1925.

—— (Gierach's text with introduction, notes and English glossary), ed. J. K. Bostock, 3rd ed., 1953.

—— (based on Myller's 1784 print of a fourteenth-century manuscript), ed. H. Sacker, 1964 (with grammar and English introduction).

—— German translation with MHG text: H. de Boor, 1963 (Fischer-Bücherei).

English translation: C. H. Bell, *Peasant Life in Old German epics*, 1931; Margaret F. Richey, *H. v. A.*, *Selections* (abridged), 1962.

Iwein, ed. G. F. Benecke and K. Lachmann, 6th ed., rev. L. Wolff, 1959.

—— ed. E. Henrici, 1891–93.

Commentary:

A. E. Schönbach, *Über Hartmann von Aue. Drei Bücher Untersuchungen*, 1894.

H. Sparnaay, *Hartmann von Aue*, 1933–38.

P. Wapnewski, *Hartmann von Aue*, 1962 (SM 17).

F. Neumann, 'Wann dichtete H. v. A.?', *Fs. Panzer*, 1950.

Hugo Kuhn, 'H. v. A. als Dichter', *DU* v (1953).

S. Grosse, 'Beginn und Ende der erzählenden Dichtungen Hs. v. A.', *PBB* (*T*) lxxxiii (1961).

E. Scheunemann, *Artushof und Abenteuer*, 1937 [On *Erec*].
H. Kuhn, 'Erec', *Fs. Kluckhohn und Schneider*, 1948.
A. van der Lee, *Der Stil von Hs. Erec*, diss. Utrecht 1950.
H. Eggers, *Symmetrie und Proportion epischen Erzählens. Studien zur Kunstform Hs. v. A.*, 1956.
H. B. Willson, 'Sin and redemption in H.'s Erec', *Germanic Review*, xxxiii (1958).
A. Hrubý, 'Die Problemstellung in Chrétiens und Hs. *Erec*', *DVLG* xxxviii (1964).
M. O'C. Walshe, 'The Prologue to H.'s *Gregorius*', *London Mediaeval Studies*, ii (1951).
H. W. J. Kroes, 'Die Gregorlegende', *Neophilologus*, xxxviii (1954).
H. B. Willson, 'H.'s *Gregorius* and the Parable of the Good Samaritan', *MLR* liv (1959).
Hildegard Nobel, Schuld und Sühne in Hs. *Gregorius* und in der frühscholastischen Theologie', *ZfdP* lxxvi (1957).
K. C. King, 'Zur Frage der Schuld in Hs. *Gregorius*', *Euph* lvii (1963).
F. Tschirsch, 'Gregorius der Heilære', *Fs. Quint*, 1964.
A. Wolf, *Gregorius bei H. v. A. und Thomas Mann*, 1964.
S. Grosse, 'Wis den wisen gerne bi', *DU* xiv (1962).
A. Schirokauer, 'Zur Interpretation des Armen Heinrich', *ZfdA* lxxxiii (1951–52).
—— 'Die Legende vom Armen Heinrich', *Monatshefte* (Wisconsin), xliii (1951).
B. Nagel, *Der arme Heinrich Hs. v. A. Eine Interpretation*, 1952.
H. B. Willson, 'Symbol and Reality in *Der arme Heinrich*', *MLR* liii (1958).
L. Seiffert, 'The Maiden's Heart', *DVLG* xxxvii (1963).
K. H. Halbach, *Franzosentum und Deutschtum in höfischer Dichtung des Stauferzeitalters* . . . 1939 [on *Iwein*].
H. D. Sacker, 'An interpretation of H.'s *Iwein*', *Germanic Review*, xxxvi (1961).
H. B. Willson, 'Love and charity in H.'s *Iwein*', *MLR* lvii (1962).
—— 'The role of Keii in H.'s *Iwein*', *Medium Aevum*, xxx (1961).
P. Salmon, 'Ignorance and awareness of identity in Hartmann and Wolfram . . .', *PBB (T)* lxxxii (1960).
—— 'The Wild Man in *Iwein* and medieval descriptive technique', *MLR* lvi (1961).

H. Milnes, 'The play of opposites in *Iwein*', *GLL* xiv (1961).
O. Kratins, 'Love and marriage in three versions of *The Knight of the Lion*', *Comparative Literature*, xvi (1964).
A. T. Hatto, '"Der aventiure meine" in H.'s Iwein', *Fs. Norman*, 1965.

ULRICH VON ZATZIKHOVEN: Mentioned as a parish priest at Lommis, Thurgau. *Lanzelet* is derived from an unidentified French source, acquired from a member of the entourage of Richard Coeur de Lion (late 1170's), which may have antedated the differing version by Chrétien.

Edition: K. A. Hahn, 1845; (reprinted with commentary by F. Norman, 1965).
English translation: K. G. T. Webster, rev., with additional notes and introduction by R. S. Loomis, 1951.
Commentary:
W. Richter, *Der Lanzelet des U. v. Z.*, 1934.
M. O'C. Walshe, 'The fabulous geography of *Lanzelet*', *London Mediaeval Studies*, i (1937).
S. Hofer, 'Der Lanzelet des U. v. Z. und seine französische Quelle', *Zs. für romanische Philologie*, lxxv (1959).

WIRNT VON GRAVENBERG: An East Franconian knight from the Nuremberg-Bayreuth region; *Wigalois* was written at Merano between 1204 and 1209.

Editions: A. E. Schönbach, 1877; J. M. N. Kapteyn, 1926.
Commentary:
R. Bauer, *Studien zum Wigalois*, 1936 (Germ. Stud. 180).
W. Mitgau, 'Nachahmung und Selbständigkeit Ws. v. G.', *ZfdP* lxxxii (1963).

Moriz von Craûn: Anonymous text, based on a lost French source.

Editions:
E. Schröder, *Zwei altd. Rittermären*, 2nd ed. (with introduction), 1913; 4th ed. (text), 1929.
U. Pretzel, *Moriz von Craûn*, 2nd (rev.) ed., 1962 (ATB 45).
Commentary:
A. T. Hatto, 'M. v. C.', *London Mediaeval Studies*, i (1938).
Ruth Harvey, *Moriz von Craûn and the chivalric world*, 1961.
K. H. Borck, 'Zur Deutung und Vorgeschichte des M. v. C.', *DVLG* xxxv (1961).

WOLFRAM VON ESCHENBACH

There are scattered allusions in Wolfram's works from which some clues to his life and the date of his works may be deduced. He was born at [Wolframs-] Eschenbach, near Ansbach, came under the patronage of the Lords of Durne—celebrating their castle of Wildenberg in (one derivation of) the name of Munsalvæsche—the Counts of Wertheim and Hermann of Thuringia. At the Wartburg he met Walther von der Vogelweide; he seems also to have visited Styria. Further textual allusions establish the date of *Parzival* in the first decade of the thirteenth century. The nature of Wolfram's subject matter and his allusive treatment of even simple incidents make him particularly amenable to allegorical-mystical interpretation, which occupies much recent writing about him.

Editions:

K. Lachmann, 6th ed., prepared by E. Hartl, 1926.
—— 7th ed., rev. E. Hartl, I, 1952 (*Parzival*).
A. Leitzmann, 5 vols, latest editions 1959–63 (ATB 12–16).
Parzival und Titurel, ed. E. Martin, 1900–03 (with exhaustive notes).
—— ed. K. Bartsch, rev. Marta Marti, 1927–32 (DKMA).
Parzival: Lachmann's text, with *Nacherzählung* by G. Weber, 1963.
Lyrical poems: KLD.

Translations:

German: F. Knorr and R. Fink (*Parzival*, 1943; *Willehalm*, 1944).
English:
Parzival: H. M. Mustard and C. E. Passage, 1961; Margaret F. Richey, *The Story of Parzival and the Graal* . . . (abridged), 1935; E. H. Zeydel and B. Q. Morgan (with notes and connecting summaries), 1951.
Titurel: Margaret F. Richey, *Schionatulander and Sigune* . . ., 2nd ed., 1960 (with commentary).

Concordance:

R.-M. S. Heffner, *Collected Word-Indexes to the works of Wolfram von Eschenbach*, 1961.

Commentary:
A. Schreiber, *Neue Bausteine zu einer Lebensgeschichte Ws. v. E.*, 1922.
Margaret F. Richey, *Studies of W. v. E.*, 1957.
J. Bumke, *W. v. E.*, 1964 (SM 36).
G. Weber, *W. v. E.*, 1928.
H. J. Koppitz, *Wolframs Religiosität*, 1959.
H. Eggers, 'Wolframforschung in der Krise?', *WW* iv (1953).
Margaret F. Richey, *Gahmuret Anschevin*, 1923.
S. Singer, *Neue Parzival-Studien*, 1939.
J. Schwietering, *Wolframs Parzival*, 1941.
Hugo Kuhn, 'Parzival', *DVLG* xxx (1956).
H. Sacker, *An introduction to W.'s Parzival*, 1963.
D. Blamires, *Characterisation and Personality in W.'s Parzival*, 1966.
P. Wapnewski, *Wolframs Parzival. Studien zur Religiosität und Form*, 1955.
B. Mockenhaupt, *Die Frömmigkeit im Parzival*, diss. Bonn, 1942.
W. J. Schröder, *Der Ritter zwischen Welt und Gott*, 1952.
F. R. Schröder, 'Parzivals Schuld', *GRM* xl (1959).
J. Schwietering, 'Parzivals Schuld', *ZfdA* lxxxi (1944).
G. Keferstein, *Parzivals ethischer Weg*, 1937.
Helen Adolf, 'The theological and feudal background of W.'s *zwîvel*', *JEGP* xlix (1950).
H. Hempel, 'Der *zwîvel* bei W. und anderweit', *Fs. Helm*, 1951.
H. Rupp, 'Die Funktion des Wortes *tump* im *Parzival* Ws. v. E.', *GRM* xxxviii (1957).
A. M. Haas, *Parzivals tumpheit*, 1964 (PSQ 21).
W. Deinert, *Ritter und Kosmos im Parzival*, 1960.
Elisabeth Karg-Gasterstädt, *Zur Entstehungsgeschichte des Parzival*, 1925.
F. Panzer, *Gahmuret. Quellenstudien zu Ws. Parzival*, 1939–40 (Heidelberg Sb.).
W. J. Schröder, 'Der Prolog von Ws. Parzival', *ZfdA* lxxxiii (1951–2).
A. T. Hatto, 'Zur Entstehung des Eingangs und der Bücher I und II des Parzival', *ZfdA* lxxxiv (1952–53).
H. Rupp, 'Ws. Parzival-Prolog', *PBB (H)* lxxxii (1960).
W. J. Schröder, 'Der dichterische Plan des Parzivalromans', *PBB* lxxiv (1952).

H. Eggers, 'Strukturprobleme mittelalterlicher Epik, dargestellt am Parzival Ws. v. E.', *Euph* xlvii (1953).
B. Mergell, *W. v. E. und seine französischen Quellen*, 1936.
G. Keferstein, 'Die Gawanhandlung in Ws. Parzival', *GRM* xxv (1937).
Marianne Wynn, 'Parzival and Gâwân—Hero and Counterpart', *PBB (T)*, lxxxiv (1962).
G. Weber, *Parzival. Ringen und Vollendung*, 1948.
F. Maurer, 'Parzivals Sünden', *DVLG* xxiv (1950).
S. Singer, *Wolfram und der Gral*, 1939.
W. Golther, *Parzival und der Gral in der Dichtung des Mas. und der Neuzeit*, 1925.
B. Mergell, 'Der Gral in Ws. Parzival', *PBB* lxxiii (1951).
—— 'W. und der Gral in neuem Licht', *Euph* xliv (1944).
A. T. Hatto, 'On W. v. E.'s conception of the "Graal"', *MLR* xliii (1948).
H. Kolb, *Munsalvæsche*, 1964.
H. and R. Kahane, *The Krater and the Grail*, 1965.
H. B. Willson, '"Mystische Dialektik" in Ws. Parzival', *ZfdP* lxxix (1960).
—— 'Das Fragemotiv in Ws. Parzival', *GRM* xliii (1962).
—— 'Ws. neutrale Engel', *ZfdP* lxxxiii (1964).
W. J. Schröder, *Die Soltane-Erzählung in Ws. Parzival*, 1963.
J. Bumke, 'Parzivals "Schwertleite"', *Fs. Starck*, 1964.
L. Wolff, 'Ws. Schionatulander und Sigune', *Fs. Panzer*, 1950.
J. Fourquet, 'L'ancien et le nouveau Titurel', in R. Nelli (ed.), *Lumière du Graal*, 1951.
Margaret F. Richey, 'The *Titurel* of W. v. E. Structure and character', *MLR* lvi (1961).
S. Singer, *Ws. Willehalm*, 1918.
J. Bumke, *Ws. Willehalm*, 1959.
J. Bédier, *Les légendes épiques; I, Le cycle de Guillaume d'Orange*, 3rd ed., 1926.
R. Kienast, 'Zur Tektonik von Ws. *Willehalm*', *Fs. Panzer*, 1950.

GOTTFRIED VON STRASSBURG

Not a knight, but an obviously well-educated burgher, perhaps occupying an official position in Strassburg. Probably a pupil of a monastery school, and therefore well grounded in theology, but he also shows a surprisingly intimate knowledge of law and has a wide, though not always strictly accurate range of classical allusion. As with other authors of the time, early research was concerned with identifying sources and characterizing the treatment of them; more recently, mystical interpretations have been gaining ground, not only in terms of a quasi-religion of courtly love, but also with Christian implications, although Gottfried seems to have a more secular outlook on life than his contemporaries. The date of *Tristan* (about 1210) is established by allusions in the text and to the text.

Editions:

R. Bechstein, 5th ed., repr. 1930 (DKMA).

F. Ranke, 1930 (plain text; accepted as standard, although the apparatus has never appeared).

A. Closs, 3rd ed., 1958 (text selected from Bechstein's edition, with introduction, notes, bibliography and English glossary).

Translations:

German by K. Pannier (UB); English (verse trans. of selected passages with introductory notes and connecting summaries) by E. H. Zeydel, 1948; (complete trans. in prose, with trans. of the text of Thomas) by A. T. Hatto, 1960.

(*Le Roman de Tristan par Thomas*, ed. J. Bédier, 1902–05; English trans. by R. S. Loomis, *The Romance of Tristram and Ysolt by Thomas of Britain*, 1931; *Tristramssaga ok Ísondar*, ed. and trans. into German by E. Kölbing, 1878.)

Concordance:

M. E. Valk, *A Word-Index to Gottfried's Tristan*, 1958.

Commentary:

G. Weber, *Gs. v. S. Tristan und die Krise des hochmal. Weltbildes um 1200*, 1953.

—— *Gottfried von Strassburg*, 1962 (SM 15).

Maria Bindschedler, 'Der heutige Stand der Forschung über G. v. S.', *DU* v (1953).

H. Fromm, 'Zum gegenwärtigen Stand der Gottfriedforschung', *DVLG* xxviii (1954).

J. Schwietering, *Der Tristan Gs. v. S. und die bernhardinische Mystik*, Berlin Abh., 1943.

F. W. Wodtke, 'Die Allegorie des "Inneren Paradieses" bei Bernhard von Clairvaux, Honorius Augustodunensis, G. v. S. und der dt. Mystik', *Fs. Quint*, 1964.

H. Kolb, 'Der Minnen hus', *Euph* lvi (1962).
M. S. Batts, 'The idealised landscape in G.'s *Tristan*', *Neophilologus*, xlvi (1962).
R. Gruenter, 'Das *wünneclîche tal*', *Euph* lv (1962).
Maria Bindschedler, 'G. v. S. und die höfische Ethik', *PBB* lxxvi (1954).
Olive L. Sayce, 'Der Begriff *edelez herze* im Tristan Gs. v. S.', *DVLG* xxxiii (1959).
W. Spiewok, 'Zum Begriff *edelez herze* bei G. v. S.', *Weimarer Beiträge* (1963).
K. Speckenback, *Studien zum Begriff 'edelez herze' im Tristan Gs. v. S.*, 1965.
W. Mohr, 'Tristan und Isold als Künstlerroman', *Euph* liii (1959).
W. T. H. Jackson, 'Tristan the artist in T.'s poem', *PMLA* lxxvii (1962).
—— 'The role of Brangaene in G.'s Tristan', *Germanic Review*, xxviii (1953).
H. Furstner, 'Der Beginn der Liebe bei Tristan und Isolde in Gottfrieds Epos', *Neophilologus*, xli (1957).
J. H. Fisher, 'Tristan and courtly adultery', *Comparative Literature*, ix (1957).
A. T. Hatto, 'Der minnen vederspil Isot', *Euph* li (1957).
H. B. Willson, 'Gottfried's *Tristan*: the coherence of prologue and narrative', *MLR* lix (1964).
—— ' "Vicissitudes" in G.'s *Tristan*', *MLR* lii (1957).
R. Gruenter, 'Der Favorit', *Euph* lviii (1964).
T. C. van Stockum, *Die Problematik des Gottesbegriffes im Tristan Gs. v. S.*, 1963 (Mededelingen van den koninklijke Nederlandse Akademie der Wetenschappen).
S. Sawicki, *G. v. S. und die Poetik des Mas.*, 1932 (Germ. Stud. 124).
H. Scharschuch, *G. v. S. Stilmittel—Stilästhetik*, 1938 (Germ. Stud. 197).
P. W. Tax, *Wort, Sinnbild und Zahl im Tristan Gs.*, 1961 (PSQ 8).
Rosemary N. Combridge, *Das Recht im Tristan Gs. v. S.*, 1964 (PSQ 15).
A. Witte, 'Der Aufbau der ältesten Tristandichtung', *ZfdA* lxx (1933).

THE COURTLY LYRIC

Major collections of texts and general introductions to international aspects of the courtly love lyric are listed above, pp. 172–74 and 185–87.

The most important manuscripts of medieval German lyrics are:

A, Heidelberg, thirteenth century ('kleine Heidelberger Liederhandschrift'): text ed. F. Pfeiffer, 1844 (LV 9); facsimile ed. C. von Kraus, 1932.

B, Stuttgart, fourteenth century ('Weingartner Handschrift'): text ed. F. Pfeiffer, 1843 (LV 5); facsimile ed. K. Löffler, 1927.

C, Heidelberg, fourteenth century ('große Heidelberger Liederhandschrift', also known as the 'Manessische' and formerly as the 'Pariser Handschrift'): text ed. F. Pfaff, 1909; facsimile, 1926–27. From this manuscript come the familiar minatures of individual poets; a selection of these is available in two volumes of the Insel-Bücherei.

J, Jena, mid-fourteenth-century; the most important single source for the melodies: facsimile ed. F. Gennrich, 1963.

Editions:

MF; KLD (for Wolfram); see also under individual names.
H. Brinkmann, *Liebeslyrik der deutschen Frühe*, 1952.
A. Moret, *Anthologie du Minnesang*, 1949.
M. Wehrli, *Deutsche Lyrik des Mas. Auswahl mit Übersetzungen*, 2nd ed., 1962.

Concordance:

R.-M. S. Heffner and K. Petersen, *A Word-Index to Des Minnesangs Frühling*, 1942.

Commentary on German Minnesang in general:

C. von Kraus, *Unsere älteste Lyrik*, 1930.
—— *Des Minnesangs Frühling. Untersuchungen*, 1939.
M. Ittenbach, *Der frühe deutsche Minnesang. Strophenfügung und Dichtersprache*, 1939.
Margaret F. Richey, *Essays on the med. German love lyric*, 1943.
—— *Medieval German lyrics* [translations], 1958.
A. Closs, *Medusa's Mirror*, 1957; and

A. Closs, *The Genius of the German Lyric*, 2nd ed., 1962 (paperback 1965) contains chapters on the nature and affinities of Minnesang.

F. Gennrich, 'Das Formproblem des Minnesangs', *DVLG* ix (1931).

R. Erckmann, 'Der Einfluß der arabisch-spanischen Kultur auf die Entwicklung des Minnesangs', ibid.

J. Fourquet, 'Thèses sur le Minnesang', *EG* ix, (1954).

W. Mohr, 'Zur Form des mal. dt. Strophenliedes', *DU* v (1953).

—— 'Minnesang als Gesellschaftskunst', *DU* vi (1954).

H. Furstner, *Studien zur Wesenbestimmung der höfischen Minne*, diss. Groningen, 1956.

H. Kolb, *Der Begriff der Minne und das Entstehen der höfischen Lyrik*, 1958 (Hermaea, new series, 4).

R. J. Taylor, 'The musical knowledge of the MHG poet', *MLR* xlix (1954).

A. H. Touber, 'Zur Einheit von Wort und Weise im Minnesang', *ZfdA* xciii (1964).

H. Fromm (ed.), *Der deutsche Minnesang*, 1961. [Collection of earlier essays, some considerably revised, by various hands.]

H. Thomas, 'Die jüngere dt. Minnesangforschung', *WW* vii (1957).

Ruth Harvey, 'Minnesang and the "sweet lyric" ', *GLL* xvii (1963).

A. T. Hatto, 'Folk ritual and the Minnesang', *MLR* lviii (1963).

Translation:

K. E. Meurer, *Deutscher Minnesang*, 1150–1300, 1954. (UB)—selection of texts ed. and introduced by F. Neumann.

There is no 'popular' edition of Minnesang in the sense of one which offers elementary guidance on the poets' use of language, which can at times be very difficult.

DER VON KÜRENBERG

The 'Mill Hill' of his name has been identified with place-names near Linz and near Melk; it is known only from an allusion in the poems, and need not absolutely refer to the author.

Commentary:

F. Panzer, 'Der älteste Troubadour und der erste Minnesinger', *Euph* xl (1938).

C. Wesle, 'Das Falkenlied des Kürenbergers', *ZfdP* lvii (1932).
P. Wapnewski, 'Des Kürenbergers Falkenlied', *Euph* liii (1959).
A. T. Hatto, 'Das Falkenlied des Kürenbergers', ibid.
G. Nordmeyer, 'Zur Auffassung des Kürenbergfalken', *Germanic Review*, xviii (1943).
F. Norman, 'Der von Kürenberg', *London Med. Studies*, ii (1938).
G. Ehrismann, 'Die Kürenberg-Literatur und die Anfänge d. dt. Minnesangs', *GRM* xv (1927).
J. K. Bostock, 'The Falcon Song of D. v. K.', *MLR* xlix (1954).

DIETMAR VON AIST

There is an appropriate baronial family whose home was near the confluence of the Enns with the Danube; documentary references to Dietmar occur in 1145 and 1171, by which latter date he was dead. This date seems rather early for some of the poems, which show dependence in diction and attitude on Romance models; a younger kinsman of the same name is postulated as the author of these poems.

Commentary:
K. Rathke, *Dietmar von Aist*, 1932.
H. Koch, 'Zu Dietmar von Aist', *PBB* lxi (1937).
F. H. Bäuml, 'Notes on the "Wechsel" of D. v. A.', *JEGP* lv (1956).
G. Jungbluth, 'Zu Dietmars Tagelied', *Fs. Pretzel*, 1963.

OTHER EARLY MINNESINGERS

Apart from Kürenberg, Dietmar and Meinloh, a few poems attributed to the emperor Heinrich VI (thought to have been written before his accession in 1190) and some by the Burggrafen von Regensburg and von Rietenburg are close to the assumed earlier native traditions, though the last of these was rather more open to foreign influences.

Commentary:
G. Jungbluth, 'Zu den Liedern Meinlohs von Sevelingen', *Neophilologus*, xxxviii (1954).
E. Sievers, 'Zu den Liedern Kaiser Heinrichs', *PBB* lii (1928).
G. Jungbluth, 'Die Lieder Kaiser Heinrichs', *PBB (T)* lxxxv (1963).
—— 'Zum Text des Burggrafen von Regensburg', *GRM* xxxiv (1953).

SPERVOGEL

The earlier of the Spervogel poets, 'Spervogel Anonymus', or, from the occurrence of the name in one of the stanzas, 'Herger', was probably writing before 1170; he wrote gnomic verses of general application, divided into loosely-connected groups of five stanzas; the later poet, who refers to 'mîn geselle Spervogel' turns to more practical issues like those of securing patronage, and was probably writing towards the end of the twelfth, or even early in the thirteenth century. Both the Spervogel poets are itinerant minstrels, in contrast with the aristocrats who sang of love.

Commentary:

G. Ehrismann, 'Beiträge zur Erklärung der Spervogelsprüche', *Fs. Jellinek*, 1928.

O. Grüters, K. Hauck, T. Frings, 'Der Anonymus Spervogel-Herger', *PBB* lxv (1942).

S. Anholt, 'Spervogel—Walther', *Neophilologus*, xxvii (1942).

B. Mergell, 'Zur zyklischen Form der Spruchdichtung Hergers', *DVLG* xxvii (1953).

FRIEDRICH VON HAUSEN

Born about 1150; a Rhinelander; joined Barbarossa on the 1189–90 Crusade; died in battle, 6 May 1190.

Commentary:

H. Brinkmann, *Friedrich von Hausen*, 1948.

F. Maurer, 'Zu den Liedern Fs. v. H.', *Neuphilologische Mitteilungen*, liii (1952). [Text and commentary.]

G. Jungbluth, 'Mîn herze und mîn lîp diu wellent scheiden', *Euph* xlvii (1953).

H. Sperber, 'Der sumer von Triere', *Monatshefte* (Wisconsin), xlv (1953).

H. B. Willson, 'Der sumer von triere', *MLR* li (1956).

HEINRICH VON RUGGE

A Swabian poet, mentioned in Blaubeuren documents between 1175 and 1178; composed a crusading 'Leich' after the death of Barbarossa.

Commentary:

H. Brinkmann, 'Rugge und die Anfänge Reimars', *Fs. Kluckhohn und Schneider*, 1948.

HEINRICH VON VELDEKE

Commentary:

T. Frings and Gabriele Schieb, 'H. v. V. Die Entwicklung eines Lyrikers', *Fs. Kluckhohn und Schneider*, 1948.

P. B. Wessels, 'Zur Sonderstellung des niederländischen Minnesangs im Germanisch-Romanischen Raum', *Neophilologus*, xxxvii (1953).

RUDOLF VON FENIS

Count Rudolf of Fenis-Neuenburg, on Lake Neuchâtel, to whom there are documentary references between 1158 and 1192. His geographical position made him particularly susceptible to Romance influences. His poems include a direct contrafacture from a Provençal source, and are unusual in German Minnesang for the strength of their visual imagination.

Commentary:

E. Baldinger, *Der Minnesinger Graf Rudolf von Fenis-Neuenburg*, 1923.

R.-H. Blaser, *Le minnesinger Rodolphe de Neuchâtel*, 1955 (including musical transcriptions).

ALBRECHT VON JOHANNSDORF

Bavarian, active between 1185 and 1209; wrote crusading lyrics which, like Hausen's, are concerned with the theme of parting; whether they are to be connected with the campaign of 1189 or of 1197 is undecided.

Commentary:

U. Fülleborn, 'Die Motive Kreuzzug und Minne und das Gestaltungsprinzip in den Liedern As. v. J.', *Euph* lviii (1964).

(For Bligger von [Neckar]steinach, Bernger von Horheim, Hartwig von Raute and Ulrich von Gutenburg, see notes to MF and MF *Untersuchungen.*)

HARTMANN VON AUE

He is printed as the last poet of MF on the strength of the manuscript reading 'und lebte mîn her Salatîn und al sîn her', which presupposes the death of Saladin and the 1197 Crusade. As the death of his feudal master is once specifically associated with taking the cross, and is shown by other contexts to have had a profound effect on Hartmann's view of life, the emendation 'und lebt mîn herre, Salatîn ...', which implies participation in the 1189 Crusade, is reasonably well grounded.

Commentary:

F. Saran, *Hartmann von Aue als Lyriker*, 1889.

H. Stolte, 'Hartmanns sogenannte Witwenklage und sein drittes Kreuzlied', *DVLG* xxv (1951).

H. Sparnaay, 'Zu Hs. Kreuzzugslyrik', *DVLG* xxvi (1952).

G. Jungbluth, 'Das dritte Kreuzlied Hs.', *Euph* xlix (1955).

R. Kienast, *Das Hartmann-Liederbuch C*², 1963 (Berlin Sb.).

HEINRICH VON MORUNGEN

A *ministerialis* of Dietrich von Meissen, the son-in-law of Hermann of Thuringia. A document, probably of 1217, records how a Henricus de Morungen, described as a 'miles emeritus', made over an income to St Thomas' church in Leipzig. At this time he must have been an old man, and it is thought, especially in view of textual dependence on him or allusion to him in early poems of Walther von der Vogelweide, that his writing was mainly done in the 1190's.

Separate edition by C. von Kraus, 1950.

Concordance:

E. J. Morrall, *H. v. M., a complete Word-Index*, 1957.

Commentary:

C. von Kraus, *Zu den Liedern Hs. v. M.*, 1916 (Abh. der Göttinger Gesellschaft der Wissenschaften).

—— *Die Lieder Hs. von M.* [with translation and commentary], 1925.

C. Bützler, 'H. v. M. und der edele Moringer', *ZfdA* lxxix (1942).

K. Ruh, 'Das Tagelied Hs. v. M.', *Trivium*, ii (1944).

J. Schwietering, 'Der Liederzyklus Hs. v. M.', *ZfdA* lxxxii (1948–50).

C. Grünanger, *H. v. M. e il problema del Minnesang*, 1948.

F. Maurer, 'Über das Verhältnis von rhythmischer Gliederung und Gedankenführung in den Strophen Hs. v. M.', *Fs. Trier*, 1954.

E. J. Morrall, 'Light Imagery in H. v. M.', *London Mediaeval Studies*, ii (1951).

—— 'H. v. M.'s conception of love', *GLL* xiii (1959).

REINMAR VON HAGENAU

He is called Reinmar der Alte in the manuscripts; 'von Hagenau' is deduced from Gottfried's encomium of his fellow-Alsatian lyric poet. Reinmar's patron was Leopold V, Duke of Austria, with whom he took part in the 1190 Crusade. His poetry shows full acceptance of Romance attitudes, and complete adoption of the Romance stanza form of two equal *pedes* (or *Stollen*) followed by a *cauda* (*Abgesang*) of different pattern. Nevertheless, some specifically 'Austrian' traits also appear in his lyrics, notably the use of *Frauenstrophen* and *Botenlieder*.

Commentary:

K. Burdach, *Reinmar der Alte und Walther von der Vogelweide*, 2nd ed., 1928.

C. von Kraus, *Die Lieder Reimars des Alten*, 1919 (Munich Abh. 30, nos. 4, 6, 7). [Texts and textual criticism, including Walther's contribution to the Walther-Reinmar dispute.]

W. Bulst, *Wörterbuch zu den Liedern Reinmars*, 1934.

H. W. Nordmeyer, 'Fehde und Minne bei R. v. H.', *JEGP* xxix (1930).

—— 'Der hohe Mut bei R. v. H.', *JEGP* xxxi (1932).

—— 'Hohe Minne bei R. v. H.', *Fs. S. Singer*, 1941.

Marlene Haupt, *Reinmar und Walther von der Vogelweide*, diss. Giessen, 1938.

H. Schneider, 'Die Lieder Rs. des Alten', *DVLG* xvii (1939).

P. Schmid, 'Die Entwicklung der Begriffe "minne" und "liebe" im dt. Minnesang vor Walther', *ZfdP* lxvi (1941).

Lida Kirchberger, 'Gottfried on Reinmar', *Monatshefte* (Wisconsin), lvi (1964).

WOLFRAM VON ESCHENBACH

For biographical details, see entry under 'Romance', p. 217.

Commentary:

A. T. Hatto: 'On beauty of numbers in W.'s dawn songs', *MLR* xlv (1950).

H. Thomas, 'Ws. Tageliedzyklus', *ZfdA* lxxxvii (1956–57).

Irmengard Rauch, 'W.'s dawn-song series: an explication', *Monatshefte* (Wisconsin), lv (1963).

WALTHER VON DER VOGELWEIDE

An Austrian, probably from what is now Lower Austria, though other localities have also claimed to be his birthplace. He states that he learned the art of poetry in Austria, and may be considered to have been a pupil of Reinmar's who outgrew his master. At the accession of Leopold VI as Duke of Austria, Walther failed to find continued patronage, and his life of travel started. Within six months or so, in the autumn, he was in the entourage of Philip of Swabia, urging him to take the crown to preserve order in Germany; poems connected with Philip continue for three years or so. In 1203 he was in the train of Bishop Wolfger of Passau on a visit to Vienna; before the end of the decade he was for a time a suitor for a position at the court of Otto IV, when he, in turn, seemed most likely to bring back some kind of security to Germany; finally he turned his support to Friedrich II, from whom he eventually received a fief. He lived until about 1227.

Editions:

K. Lachmann, *Die Gedichte Ws. v. d. V.*, 12th ed., rev. C. von Kraus, 1959.

W. Wilmanns, *W. v. d. V.*, 4th ed., rev. V. Michels, 1924.

F. Maurer, *Die Lieder Ws. v. d. V.;* I, *Die religiösen und politischen Lieder;* II, *Die Liebeslieder*, 2nd ed., 1960–62 (ATB 43, 47). [Including melodies.]

P. Wapnewski, *W. v. d. V., Mhd. Text und Übertragung*, 1962. [Fischer-Bücherei; selected poems with useful commentary.]

H. Protze, *W. v. d. V. Sprüche und Lieder. Gesamtausgabe*, 1963. [With German glossary and notes to individual poems.]

Margaret F. Richey, *Selected poems by W. v. d. V.*, 3rd ed., rev. H. Sacker, 1965. [English notes and glossary.]

Translations:

German: K. Pannier (UB), W. Bulst and numerous others.

English: I. G. Colvin, *I saw the world*, 1938 (60 poems). E. H. Zeydel and B. Q. Morgan, [Thirty] *Poems of W. v. d. V.*, 1952. [Also includes modern Ger. translations.]

A few in L. Forster, *The Penguin Book of German Verse*, 1959.

Concordance:

R.-M. S. Heffner and W. P. Lehmann, *A Word-Index to the poems of W. v. d. V.*, 1950.

Commentary:

For recent works on the melodies and stanza forms, cf. general bibliography under 'Courtly Lyric', p. 186.

A. E. Schönbach, *W. v. d. V. Ein Dichterleben*, 4th ed., rev. H. Schneider, 1923.

H. Naumann, *Das Bild Ws. v. d. V.*, 1930.

K. K. Klein, *Zur Spruchdichtung und Heimatfrage Ws. v. d. V.*, 1952.

K. Halbach, *W. v. d. V. und die Dichter von MF*, 1927 (Tübinger germ. Arbeiten, 3).

G. Sprengel, 'W. v. d. V. und der staufische Staatsgedanke', *Zs. für dt. Bildung*, viii (1932).

K. Burdach, *Reinmar der Alte und W. v. d. V.*, 2nd ed., 1928.

Marlene Haupt, *Reinmar der Alte und W.*, diss. Giessen, 1938.

C. von Kraus, *W. v. d. V. Untersuchungen*, 1935.

H. Brinkmann, 'Studien zu W. v. d. V.', *PBB* lxiii (1939).

F. Maurer, *Die politischen Lieder Ws. v. d. V.*, 2nd ed., 1964. [Text and commentary.]

—— 'Zu den religiösen Liedern Ws. v. d. Vogelweide', *Euph* xlix (1955).

D. von Kralik, *Walther gegen Reinmar*, 1955 (Vienna Sb. 230).

F. Neumann, 'Der Minnesänger W. v. d. V.', *DU* v (1953).

A. T. Hatto, 'W. v. d. V.'s Ottonian poems', *Speculum*, xxiv (1949).

K. H. Halbach, *W. v. d. V.*, 1965 (SM 40).

MIDDLE HIGH GERMAN HEROIC LITERATURE

Nibelungenlied

Principal manuscripts: A, from Hohenems, now in Munich, late thirteenth century; B, St Gall, 1250 or slightly later; C, from Hohenems, now at Donaueschingen, first half of the thirteenth century. After the investigations of Bartsch and Braune, it has been generally agreed that the text represented by A is an abridgement, and C an expansion, of that given in B. The date of composition may be estimated from literary allusions to lie within the early years of the thirteenth century. The whole question of the manuscript tradition has recently been reopened, and there is now some doubt whether relationships between manuscripts can be worked out deterministically.

Editions:

K. Lachmann, *Der Nibelunge Not mit der Klage*, 6th ed., 1961. [Based on manuscript A, as the shortest and most 'authentic' text.]

K. Bartsch, *Der Nibelunge Not*, 1870–80. [Based on manuscript B; the standard edition, complete with concordance.]

—— *Das Nibelungenlied*, 13th ed., rev. H. de Boor, 1958 (DKMA) [especially valuable for new introduction].

F. Zarncke, *Das Nibelungenlied*, 16th ed. rev. W. Braune, 1920. [Based on manuscript C, representing the most polished version, of which the others are abridgements.]

Manuscript tradition:

W. Braune, *Die Handschriftenverhältnisse des Nls.*, 1900.

H. Brackert, *Beiträge zur Handschriftenkritik des Nls.*, 1963 (QF, new series, 11).

Translations:

German: K. Simrock, 1827 (frequently reprinted); G. Junghans (UB); H. de Boor, 1959, etc.

English: D. G. Mowatt, 1962 (Everyman); F. G. Ryder [in verse], 1962; A. T. Hatto [with full commentary], 1965 (Penguin).

Commentary:

E. Tonnelat, *La chanson des Nibelungen*, 1926.

A. Heusler, *Nibelungensage und Nibelungenlied*, 5th ed., 1955.

H. Schneider, *Die dt. Lieder von Siegfrieds Tod*, 1947.

—— 'Die Quellen des Nls.', *Euph* xlv (1950).

D. von Kralik, *Die Siegfried-Trilogie im Nl. und in der Thidrekssage*, I, 1941.

F. Panzer, *Studien zum Nl.*, 1945.

—— *Das Nl. Entstehung und Gestalt*, 1955.

G. Weber and W. Hoffmann, *Nibelungenlied*, 1961 (SM 7).

K. Wais, *Frühe Epik Westeuropas und die Vorgesch. des Nls.*, 1953.

G. Weber, *Das Nibelungenlied*, 1963.

Mary Thorp, *The Study of the Nl. from 1755 to 1937*, 1940.

Mary Fleet, 'The recent study of the Nl.', *JEGP* lii (1953).

J. F. Röttger, *Das Nl. im Lichte der neuesten Forschung*, 1949.

S. Beyschlag, 'Das Nl. in gegenwärtiger Sicht', *WW* iii (1953).

W. Hoffmann, 'Zur Situation der gegenwärtigen Nibelungenforschung', *WW* xii (1962).

W. A. Mueller, *The Nl. today*, 1962.

D. von Kralik, *Wer war der Dichter des Nls?*, 1954.

O. Höfler, 'Die Anonymität des Nls.', *DVLG* xxix (1955).

W. Krogmann, *Der Dichter des Nls.*, 1962 (PSQ 11) [Far-fetched].

B. Nagel, 'Der Dichter des Nls.', *ZfdP* lxxxiii (1964).

H. Naumann, 'Das Nl. eine staufische Elegie oder ein dt. Nationalepos?', [*Dichtung und Volkstum*, i.e.] *Euph* xlii (1942).

Nelly Dürrenmatt, *Das Nl. im Kreis der höfischen Dichtung*, 1946.

B. Mergell, 'Nl. und höfischer Roman', *Euph* xlv (1950).

G. Zink, 'Pourquoi la *Chanson des Nibelungen* est-elle anonyme?', *EG* x (1955).

F. Maurer, 'Die Einheit des Nls. nach Idee und Form', *DU* v (1953).

W. J. Schröder, 'Das Nl. Versuch einer Deutung', *PBB* lxxvi (1954).

B. Nagel, *Zur Interpretation und Wertung des Nls.*, 1954.

—— *Das Nl. Stoff, Form, Ethos*, 1965.

S. Beyschlag, 'Das Motiv der Macht bei Siegfrieds Tod', *GRM* xxxiii (1951).

Hans Kuhn, 'Kriemhilds Hort und Rache', *Fs. Kluckhohn und Schneider*, 1948.

W. Schröder, 'Die Tragödie Kriemhilts im Nl.', *ZfdA* xc (1960).

B. Wachinger, *Studien zum Nl.*, 1960.

J. K. Bostock, 'The message of the Nl.', *MLR* lv (1960).

—— 'Realism and convention in the Nl.', *MLR* lvi (1961).

K. C. King, 'The message of the Nl.—a reply', *MLR* lvii (1962).

D. G. Mowatt, 'Studies towards an interpretation of the Nl.', *GLL* xiv (1961).

H. B. Willson, 'Blood and wounds in the Nl.', *MLR* lv (1960).

—— '*Ordo* and *inordinatio* in the Nl.', *PBB* (*T*) lxxxv (1963).

P. B. Salmon, 'Why does Hagen die?', *GLL* xvii (1963).

J. Stout, *Unde ouch Hagene*, 1963.

J. Fourquet, 'Zum Aufbau des Nls. und des Kudrunlieds', *ZfdA* lxxxv (1954–5).

K. H. Bertau and R. Stephan, 'Zum sanglichen Vortrag mhd. strophischer Epen', *ZfdA* lxxxvii (1956–7).

S. Beyschlag, 'Langzeilen-Melodien', *ZfdA* xciii (1964).

Die Klage

Editions: K. Bartsch, 1875; A. Edzardi, 1875; incorporated in Lachmann's editions of *Der Nibelunge Not.*

Translation: F. H. von der Hagen, 1852, reprinted 1919.

Commentary:

J. Körner, *Die Klage und das Nibelungenlied*, 1920.

A. Leitzmann, 'Nibelungenklage und höfische Dichtung', *ZfdA* lxi (1924).

E. Schröder, 'Zur Klage', *ZfdA* lxx (1933).

Kudrun

Editions:

K. Bartsch, 4th ed., repr. 1937.

E. Martin, 2nd ed., rev. E. Schröder, 1911.

B. Symons, 4th ed., rev. B. Boesch, 1964 (ATB 5). [With full introduction.]

(Related ballads, 'Südeli', 'Die Meererin' in J. Meier, DL, *Das dt. Volkslied*, I, 1935.)

Commentary:

F. Panzer, *Hilde-Gudrun. Eine sagengeschichtliche Untersuchung*, 1901.

W. Jungandreas, *Die Gudrunsage in den Ober- und Niederlanden*, 1948.

H. Rosenfeld, 'Die K.: Nordseedichtung oder Donaudichtung?', *ZfdP* lxxxi (1962).

S. Gutenbrunner, 'Von Hilde und Kudrun', ibid.

F. R. Schröder, 'Die Sage von Hetel und Hilde', *DVLG* xxxii (1958).

H. W. J. Kroes, 'Kudrunprobleme', *Neophilologus*, xxxviii (1954).

B. Boesch, 'Kudrunepos und Ursprung d. dt. Ballade', *GRM* xxviii (1940).

M. Weege, *Das Kudrunepos, eine Dichtung des Hochmas.*, diss. Mainz, 1953.

J. K. Bostock, 'The structure of the K.', *MLR* liii (1958).

R. Jantzen, 'Zum Aufbau des Kudrunepos', *WW* xii (1962).

W. Hoffmann, 'Die Hauptprobleme der neueren K.-Forschung', *WW* xiv (1964).

A. Beck, 'Die Rache als Motiv und Problem in der K.', *GRM* xxxvii (1956).

H. B. Willson, 'Dialectic, *Passio* and *Compassio* in the K.', *MLR* lviii (1963).
Roswitha Wisniewski, *Kudrun*, 1963 (SM 32).
J. Carles, *Le poème de Kûdrûn*, 1963.

Dukus Horant

Editions:
L. Fuks, *The oldest known literary documents of Yiddish Literature*, 1957. [Premature.]
F. Norman, W. Schwarz and P. F. Ganz, *D. H.*, 1964 (ATB Ergänzungsreihe, 2). [With full bibliography.]

EXPLOITS OF DIETRICH VON BERN

Edition:
O. Jänicke, E. Martin and others in K. Müllenhoff, *Deutsches Heldenbuch*, I, II, V, 1866–70.

Selections:
E. Henrici, *Das Heldenbuch*, [1887], (DNL 7).
G. Zink, *Le cycle de Dietrich, morceaux choisis*, 1953.

Separate texts:
Gedichte vom Rosengarten in Worms, ed. G. Holz, 1893.
Laurin, ed. K. Müllenhoff, 5th ed., 1926; ed. G. Holz, 1897.
Der jüngere Sigenot, ed. A. Schoener, 1928.

Translations:
K. Simrock, *Das kleine Heldenbuch*, 1853 (*Rosengarten*, *Ortnit*, *Hugdietrich*, *Wolfdietrich*). *Das Amelungenlied* (Dietrich poems).
L. Bückmann, *Rabenschlacht; Laurin* 1879 (UB).
L. Scharf, *Laurin*, 1916; R. Zoozmann, *Laurin*, 1924.
K. J. Schroer, *Alpharts Tod* (UB).
H. Junghans, *Rosengarten* (UB).

Commentary:
H. Patzig, *Dietrich von Bern und sein Sagenkreis*, 1917.
R. C. Boer, *Die Sagen von Ermanarich und Dietrich von Bern*, 1910.
Caroline Brady, *The Legends of Ermanaric*, 1943.
H. de Boor, 'Die Heldennamen in der historischen Dietrichdichtung', *ZfdA* lxxviii (1941).
—— 'Dietrich von Bern', *ZfdA* lxxx (1944).
T. Steche, *Das Rabenschlachtgedicht*, *Das Buch von Bern* [i.e. *Dietrichs Flucht*] *und die Entwicklung der Dietrichsage*, 1939.

G. Zink, *Les légendes héroiques de Dietrich et d'Ermrich dans les littératures germaniques*, 1950.

C. Brestowsky, *Der Rosengarten zu Worms*, 1929 (Tübinger germanistische Arbeiten, 7).

J. de Vries, 'Bemerkungen zur Laurindichtung', *PBB* lvi (1932).

W. E. D. Stephens, 'Þiðrikssaga and Eckenlied', *London Mediaeval Studies*, i (1937).

Hugo Kuhn, 'Virginal', *PBB* lxxi (1949).

E. Benedikt, 'Die Überlieferung vom Ende Dietrichs von Bern', *Fs. Kralik*, 1954.

Ortnit, Hugdietrich, Wolfdietrich

Edition: V. A. Amelung and O. Jänicke, in K. Müllenhoff, *Deutsches Heldenbuch*, III–IV (1871–73).

Commentary:

H. Schneider, *Die Gedichte und die Sage von Wolfdietrich*, 1913.

D. Scheludko, 'Versuch neuer Interpretation des Wolfdietrichstoffes', *ZfdP* lv (1930).

J. de Vries, 'Die Sage von Wolfdietrich', *GRM* xxxix (1958).

Linde Baecker, 'Die Sage von Wolfdietrich und das Gedicht Wolfdietrich A', *ZfdA* xcii (1963).

THE POST-CLASSICAL PERIOD IN MEDIEVAL LITERATURE

Romances

ULRICH VON TÜRHEIM

Editions:

Tristan in ed. of Gottfried by H. F. Massmann, 1843. (In selection, with Heinrich von Freiberg, DNL IV, ii, 2.)

Rennewart, ed. A. Hübner, 1938 (DTMA 39).

Commentary:

E. K. Busse, *Ulrich von Türheim*, 1913 (Palaestra 121).

F. Wilhelm, 'Studien zu U. v. T.', *Münchener Museum*, iv (1924).

G. Meissburger, *Die Auffassung der Minne bei Gottfried von Straßburg und U. v. T.*, diss. Basel, 1954.

W. Müller, *Das Weltbild Us. v. T.*, diss. Berlin, 1957.

ULRICH VON DEM TÜRLIN

Edition of *Willehalm* by S. Singer, 1893.

Commentary:

R. Wildenmuth, *Ulrich von Türheim und Ulrich von dem Türlin als Nachahmer Wolframs von Eschenbach*, diss. Tübingen, 1957.

Ursula Hennig, 'Frauenschilderung im Willehalm Us. v. d. T.', *PBB* (*T*) lxxxi (1959).

ALBRECHT (VON SCHARFENBERG)

Edition:

W. Wolf, *As. v. S. Jüngerer Titurel*, I, 1955; II, i, 1964 (DTMA 45, 55).

—— [Selections], 1952 (Altdeutsche Übungstexte, 14).

Commentary:

W. Wolf, 'Grundsätzliches zu einer Ausgabe des jüngeren Titurel', *ZfdA* lxxvi, lxxix (1939–42).

—— 'Wer war der Dichter des j. T.?', *ZfdA* lxxxiv (1952–53).

F. Zarncke, *Der Graltempel*, 1879 (Leipzig Abh. 7).

W. Röll, *Studien zu Text und Überlieferung des sogenannten J. T.*, 1964.

(P. Colin and C. Wisse, *Der neue Parzefal* [interpolations between Books XIV and XV of Wolfram's text, composed between 1331 and 1336; no literary merit, but evidence of the abiding interest of the subject-matter], ed. K. Schorbach, 1888.)

Lohengrin (stanzaic poem)

Two authors have been detected; in the earlier part a Thuringian minstrel, and in the second a Bavarian *ministerialis*. There is also a fifteenth-century version of the story, known as *Lorengel*.

Editions:

Lohengrin, ed. H. Rückert, 1858; trans. H. A. Junghans (UB).

Lorengel, ed. E. von Steinmeyer, *ZfdA* xv (1872).

Commentary:

F. Panzer, *Lohengrin-Studien*, 1894.

A. G. Krüger, *Die Quellen der Schwanrittersage*, 1936.

W. Krogmann, 'Die Schwanrittersage', *Archiv*, clxxi (1937).

HEINRICH VON DEM TÜRLIN

A Carinthian; he names Chrétien as the source for *Der âventiure Krone* (written about 1220).

Editions:

Diu Crone, ed. G. H. F. Scholl, 1882 (LV 27).

Der Mantel, ed. O. Warnatsch, 1883 (Germ. Abh. 2).

Commentary:

E. K. Heller, 'A vindication of H. v. d. T.', *Modern Language Quarterly*, iii (1942).

Rosemary E. Wallbank, 'The composition of Diu Krone', *Fs. Vinaver*, 1965.

KONRAD FLECK

Recorded as 'Her Konrad' by Rudolf von Ems; of Swiss or Alsatian origin, lived near Basel and composed his *Floire* between 1220 and 1230. His claimed French source is lost.

Editions: E. Sommer, Quedlinburg, 1846; W. Golther, [1885] (DNL 4, III). (Extensive fragments ed. C. H. Rischen, 1913. Trans. in UB.)

Commentary:

L. Ernst, *Floire und Blanscheflur*, 1912 (QF 118).

J. Reinhold, 'Floire und Blanscheflur-probleme', *Zs. für romanische Philologie*, xlii (1922).

DER STRICKER

The name suggests a plebeian origin, but it is not certain whether it means 'Landstreicher' or 'Weber'. He was a Rhinelander by birth, but spent his literary career in Austria.

Editions:

Karl [modernization of *Rolandslied*], ed. K. Bartsch, 1857.

Pfaffe Amis, ed. P. Piper, [1893] (DNL 4, Ii, *Höfische Epik*, III).

Daniel, ed. G. Rosenhagen, 1894.

Kleinere Gedichte von dem Stricker, ed. K. A. Hahn, 1835.

Fünfzehn kleine Verserzählungen . . ., ed. H. Fischer, 1960 (ATB 53).

Die bisher unveröffentlichten geistlichen Bispelreden, ed. Ute Schwab, 1959.

Tierbispel, ed. Ute Schwab, 1960 (ATB 54).

Fabeln und Mären, ed. H. Mettke, 1959 (ATB 35).

Commentary:

G. Rosenhagen, 'Der Pfaffe Amis des Strickers', *Fs. Ehrismann*, (1925).

H. Mast, *Stilistische Untersuchungen an den kleinen Gedichten des Ss.*, diss. Vienna, 1930.

H. Fischer, *Strickerstudien*, diss. Munich, 1953.

C. Baier, *Der Bauer in der Dichtung des Strickers*, diss. Tübingen, 1938.

H. de Boor, 'Der Daniel des Stricker und der Garel des Pleier', *PBB* (*T*) lxxix (1957).

Ute Schwab, 'Zur Interpretation der geistlichen Bîspelrede', *Annali dell'istituto universitario orientale* (Naples), i (1958).

DER PLEIER

A commoner from Pleien, near Salzburg; active between 1250 and 1280.

Editions:

Garel von dem blühenden Tal, ed. M. Walz, 1892.

Meleranz, ed. K. Bartsch, 1861 (LV 60).

Tandareis und Flordibel, ed. F. Khull, 1885.

Commentary:

J. L. Riordan, 'A vindication of the Pleier', *JEGP* xlvii (1948).

H. de Boor, 'Der Daniel des Stricker und der Garel des Pleier', *PBB* (*T*) lxxix (1957).

RUDOLF VON EMS

A knight of Hohenems, Vorarlberg, 1200–54. He knew both Latin and French, and was probably educated at a monastery school.

Editions:

Der guote Gêrhart, ed. J. A. Asher, 1962 (ATB 56).

Barlaam und Josaphat, ed. F. Pfeiffer, 1843. [From a Latin source; claimed by Rudolf as a return to serious things after earlier worldly writings.]

Alexander [incomplete], ed. V. Junk, 1928 (LV 272, 274).

Willehalm von Orlens, ed. V. Junk, 1905 (DTMA 2).

Weltchronik, ed. G. Ehrismann, 1915 (DTMA 20).

Commentary:

G. Ehrismann, *Studien über Rudolf von Ems*, 1919 (Heidelberg Sb.).

E. Schröder, 'R. v. E. und sein Literaturkreis', *ZfdA* lxvii (1930).

R. Wisbey, 'R. v. E.', *ZfdA* lxxxv, lxxxvi, lxxxvii (1954–57).
J. A. Asher, *Der gute Gerhart Rs. v. E. in seinem Verhältnis zu Hartmann von Aue*, diss. Basel, 1948.
F. Sengle, 'Die Patrizierdichtung *Der gute Gerhart*', *DVLG* xxiv (1950).
C. von Kraus, *Text und Entstehung von Rs. Alexander*, Munich Sb., 1940.
R. Wisbey, *Das Alexanderbild Rs. v. E.*, 1966 (PSQ 31).
A. Hübner, 'Alexander der Große in d. dt. Dichtung des Mas.', *Die Antike*, ix (1933).
G. Cary, *The medieval Alexander*, 1956.
V. Lüdicke, *Vorgeschichte und Nachleben des Willehalm von Orlens*, 1910 (Hermaea, 8).

KONRAD VON WÜRZBURG

A well-educated man from a family of commoners, 1220–87.

Editions:

Ks. v. W., *Legenden*, ed. P. Gereke, 1925–27 (ATB 19–21). [*Silvester*, *Alexius*, *Pantaleon*.]
Engelhard, ed. P. Gereke, 2nd ed., rev. I. Reiffenstein, 1963 (ATB 17).
Kleinere Dichtungen Ks. v. W., ed. E. Schröder, 1924–26 [including *Herzmære*, *Heinrich von Kempten*, *Der Welt Lohn*, *Turnier von Nantheiz*, *Schwanritter*, *Leiche*, *Lieder*, *Sprüche*].
Goldene Schmiede, ed. E. Schröder, 1926.
Otte mit dem Bart, ed. K. A. Hahn, 1838.
Partenopier und Meliur, ed. K. Bartsch, 1871.
Trojanerkrieg, ed. A. von Keller and K. Bartsch, 1858, 1877 (LV 44, 133).

Commentary:

E. Schröder, *Studien zu K. v. W.*, 1912 (Abh. der Göttinger Gesellschaft der Wissenschaften).
K. H. Halbach, *Gottfried von Strassburg und K. v. W.*, 1930 (Tübinger germanistische Arbeiten, 12).
A. Moret, *Un artiste méconnu: Conrad de Wurzbourg*, 1932.

(For later survival of the theme of *Frau Welt*, cf. A. Closs, *Der Weltlohn*, 1934, where a late thirteenth-century anonymous poem on the same theme is edited, with full commentary.)

ULRICH VON ETZENBACH

A Bohemian by birth; lived in the middle of the thirteenth century at the courts of the Prince-Archbishop of Salzburg and of King Wenzel II of Bohemia.

Editions:

Herzog Ernst, ed. F. H. von der Hagen and J. G. Büsching, *Dt. Gedichte des Mas.*, 1808.

Wilhelm von Wenden, ed. H. F. Rosenfeld, 1957 (DTMA 49).

Alexanderlied, ed. W. Toischer, 1888 (LV 183).

Commentary:

H. F. Rosenfeld, *Herzog Ernst D. und U. v. E.*, 1929.

Margot Hühne, *Die Alexanderepen Rudolfs von Ems und Us. v. E.*, 1939.

BERTHOLD VON HOLLE: born of an aristocratic family in the Brunswick area, and active about 1260.

Works and editions:

[*Crane*], ed. K. Bartsch, 1858.

Demantin, ed. K. Bartsch, 1875 (LV 123).

KONRAD VON STOFFELN: a Swabian yeoman, later canon in Strassburg.

Gauriel und Muntabel, ed. F. Khull, 1885.

Wigamur: anonymous North Bavarian text, late thirteenth century, ed. C. von Kraus, *Mhd. Übungsbuch*, 2nd ed., 1926.

Commentary: G. Sarazzin, *Wigamur*, 1879 (QF 35).

Segremors: anonymous fragment; the name of the hero from *Parzival*, Book VI: ed. K. Regel, 'Bruchstück aus der Artussage', *ZfdA* xi (1859).

Reinfried von Brauschweig (anonymous), ed. K. Bartsch, 1871 (LV 109).

Commentary: P. Gereke, 'Studien zu R. v. B.', *PBB* xxiii (1898).

EGENOLF VON STAUFENBERG: author of a short romance entitled *Peter von Staufenberg*, written about 1300; printed edition from late sixteenth century with preface by J. Fischart. Modern edition by E. Schröder, *Zwei altdeutsche Rittermæren*, 4th ed., 1929.

Die Gute Frau (anonymous): written before 1242 for the Duke of

Zähringen by an Alemannic poet. The story has affinities with *Floire*, the St Eustace legend and *Magelone*.

Edition: E. Sommer, *ZfdA* ii (1848).

Commentary: E. Schröder, 'Der Dichter der Guten Frau', *Fs. Kelle*, 1908 (Prager deutsche Studien, 8).

Vorau Novelle: anonymous story of two novice monks, one of whom leaves the cloister for the world; an anecdote in favour of asceticism which can be traced back to Gregory the Great. Thirteenth-century fragments from Vorau, ed. A. E. Schönbach, 1899 (Vienna Sb. 140).

Commentary: A. Leitzmann, 'Zur Vorauer Novelle', *Fs. Baesecke*, 1941.

Manuel und Amanda: fragmentary Arthurian poem, fourteenth century, ed. O. Zingerle, *ZfdA* xxvi (1882).

ULRICH VON LICHTENSTEIN

Born about 1200 at Lichtenstein in Styria; died 1274 or 1277. Author of *Frauendienst* (1255), a first-person romance, interspersed with lyrical poems in the manner of High Minnesang, for which the narrative is no more than a framework.

Editions:

Frauendienst, ed. K. Lachmann and M. von Karajan, 1841; ed. R. Bechstein, 1888. Poems separately, KLD.

Commentary:

H. Arens, *Us. v. L. Frauendienst*, 1939 (Palaestra 216).

O. Höfler, 'Us. v. L. Venusfahrt und Artusfahrt', *Fs. Panzer*, 1950.

K. L. Schneider, 'Die Selbstdarstellung des Dichters im Frauendienst Us. v. L.', *Fs. Pretzel*, 1963.

H. Milnes, 'U. v. L. and the Minnesang', *GLL* xvii (1963).

WERNHER DER GARTENAERE

Probably lived in what is now Upper Austria as a minstrel, though it has been suggested that he was the superintendent of an abbey garden. His one work, *Meier Helmbrecht*, is an unsparing condemnation of overweening ambitions, but hardly a religious poem; it has been called the first story of village life ('Dorfgeschichte') in German literature. It was written in the second half of the thirteenth century.

Editions:

Die Märe von Helmbrecht, ed. F. Panzer, 6th ed., rev. K. Ruh, 1960 (ATB 11).

Meier Helmbrecht, ed. C. E. Gough, 2nd ed., 1947. [With English introduction, notes and glossary.]

Translations:

German: F. Bergmann, 1920; J. Ninck, repr. 1950 (UB).

English: C. H. Bell, *Peasant Life in Old German Epics*, 1931.

Commentary:

F. Neumann, 'Meier Helmbrecht', *WW* ii (1951–52).

A. Bonawitz, 'Helmbrecht's violation of "Karles reht"', *Monatshefte* (Wisconsin), lvi (1964).

F. G. Banta, 'The arch of action in M. H.', *JEGP* lxiii (1964).

G. Nordmeyer, 'Structure and design in Wernher's M. H.', *PMLA* lxvii (1952).

M. Ittenbach, 'Helmbrechts Haube', *DVLG* x (1932).

Erika A. Wirtz, 'M. H.'s cap', *MLR* xlix (1954).

H. Fischer, 'Gestaltungsschichten im M. H.', *PBB (T)* lxxix (1957).

W. T. H. Jackson, 'The composition of M. H.', *Modern Language Quarterly*, xviii (1957).

Pfarrer von Kalenberg

The author, Philipp Frankfurter, a Viennese writer of verse anecdotes (*Schwänke*), was active in the late fourteenth century. In using one character as the central figure in all the episodes, the *Pfarrer von Kalenberg* follows the pattern of the Stricker's *Pfaffe Amis*; its hostility to the peasants links it with Neidhart and his imitators; its coarseness is characteristic of late medieval popular literature.

Editions:

F. Bobertag, *Narrenbuch* [1888], (DNL 11). [Also includes Neidhart Fuchs.]

V. Dollmayr, 1907 (Neudrucke dt. Literaturwerke des 16. und 17. Jhs., 212–214).

Commentary:

R. M. Meyer, 'Die Neidhartlegende', *ZfdA* xxxi (1887).

E. Schröder, 'Pfarrer von Kalenberg und Neithart Fuchs', *ZfdA* lxxiii (1936).

H. Maschek, 'Die Geschichte des Pfarrers von Kalenberg', ibid.

Seifried Helbling

The name of a character in a series of satires written at the end of the thirteenth century by a knight of Lower Austria; an attack on the decline of manners and the presumption of upstart peasants. Edition by J. Seemüller, 1886.

Commentary:

A. Wallner, 'Seifried Helbling', *ZfdA* lxxii (1935).

HEINRICH WITENWILER

Der Ring, ed. E. Wiessner, 1931 (DL,1 *Realistik des Spätmas*).

Commentary:

F. Martini, 'Heinrich Witenwilers *Ring*', *DVLG* xx (1942).
E. Wiessner, 'Heinrich Witenwiler', *ZfdA* lxxxiv (1952).
R. Brinkmann, 'Zur Deutung von Witenwilers *Ring*', *DVLG* xxx (1956).
P. B. Wessels, 'Ws. *Ring* als Groteske', *WW* x (1960).

[Cf. also *Der Bauern Hochzeitsschwank. Meier Betz und Metzen hochzit*, ed. E. Wiessner, 1956 (ATB 48), and commentary: E. Wiessner, 'Metzen hochzit und H. Ws. Ring', *ZfdA* l (1908).]

Eulenspiegel

Till Eulenspiegel was a fourteenth-century peasant from the district round Brunswick, who died in Schleswig in 1350. Some 1500 tales accrued about his name, in most of which peasant literalism and shrewdness gains the better of would-be clever townsfolk. The stories were collected towards the end of the fifteenth century in North Germany, and were printed in a High German version at Strassburg in 1515.

Commentary:

L. Mackensen, 'Zur Entstehung des Volksbuches vom E.', *GRM* xxiv (1936).

The Lyric after Walther

NEIDHART VON REUENTAL

Editions:

M. Haupt, 3rd ed., rev. E. Wiessner, 1955.

A. T. Hatto and R. J. Taylor, *The Songs of Neidhart von Reuental*, 1958. [Selected poems, with musical transcriptions.]

Translation by K. Pannier (UB).

Commentary:

E. Wiessner, *Vollständiges Wörterbuch zu Ns. Liedern; Kommentar zu Ns. Liedern*, 1954.

E. Rohloff, *Neidharts Sangeweisen*, 1962 (Leipzig Abh., 52).

K. Winkler, *N. v. R., Leben, Lieben, Lieder*, 1956.

S. Singer, *Neidhart-Studien*, 1920.

R. Alewyn, 'Naturalismus bei Neidhart', *ZfdP* lvi (1931).

W. Weidmann, *Studien zur Entwicklung von Ns. Lyrik*, 1947.

H. Naumann, 'Frideruns Spiegel', *ZfdA* lxix (1932).

F. Goldin, 'Friderun's mirror and the exclusion of the knight in N. v. R.', *Monatshefte* (Wisconsin), liv (1962).

TANNHÄUSER

Of knightly birth and Frankish-Bavarian origin. Perhaps acquainted with Neidhart von Reuental at the court of Frederick the Quarrelsome, Duke of Austria.

Editions:

S. Singer, 1922.

J. Siebert, *T.: Leben, Gedichte, Sage*, 1934.

Commentary:

A. Wallner, 'Tannhäuser', *ZfdA* lxxii (1935).

Margarete Lang, *Tannhäuser*, 1936.

G. Rosenhagen, 'Die Leiche des T. und des Ulrich von Winterstetten', *ZfdP* lxi (1936).

V. Junk, *T. in Sage und Dichtung*, 1911.

P. S. Barto, *T. and the Mountain of Venus*, 1916.

F. Rostock, *Mhd. Dichterheldensage*, 1925 (Hermaea, 15).

W. Mohr, 'Ts. Kreuzlied', *DVLG* xxxiv (1960).

Der Wartburgkrieg

The identification of Heinrich von Ofterdingen with Tannhäuser was first made as a piece of romantic medieval scholarship by C. T. L. Lucas (*Über den W.*, 1838), though it obviously reached a much wider public through the theatre.

Editions:

T. A. Rompelman, 1939.

F. Mess, *Heinrich von Ofterdingen*, 1963. [Including a new attempt to identify Heinrich].

Commentary:

P. Riesenfeld, *Heinrich von Ofterdingen in d. dt. Literatur*, 1912.

H. Becker, 'Der W. und Heinrich von Ofterdingen', *Wissenschaftliche Zs. der Universität Jena*, 1954–55.

F. Mess, 'Wartburgkrieg und Sachsenspiegel', *Zs. der Savigny-Stiftung*, lxxiv (1957).

GOTTFRIED VON NEIFEN

Came from the Neufen district near Tübingen; mentioned in documents between 1234 and 1255; in the entourage of King Heinrich VII.

Editions: M. Haupt, 2nd ed., rev. E. Schröder, 1932. (Selections in Bartsch.)

Commentary:

C. M. de Jong, *Gottfried von Neifen*, 1923 [with text].

R. Marleyn, 'G. v. N.'s Minnelieder and Ballads', *Fs. Fiedler*, 1938.

A. H. Touber, *Rhetorik und Form im dt. Minnesang*, 1964.

ULRICH VON WINTERSTETTEN

A canon of Augsburg, mentioned in documents dated 1258 and 1280.

Edition by J. Minor, 1882; KLD.

Commentary:

A. Selge, *Studien über U. v. W.*, 1929 (Germ. Stud. 79).

G. Rosenhagen, 'Die Leiche des Tannhäuser und des U. v. W.', *ZfdP* lxi (1936).

The Tradition of Minnesang in the Thirteenth Century

The forms developed up to the time of Reinmar continued to be used, though there are few poets of great eminence; many are represented in the collected editions only by one or two poems. It is noticeable that the practitioners of Minnesang continue largely to be aristocratic, and, indeed, include several ruling princes among their number.

*Konradin, the son of the last Hohenstaufen king, captured and put to death in Italy, 1268; *King Wenzel II of Bohemia, 1278–1305; Wizlav [IV, Fürst] von Rügen; *Heinrich [Fürst] von Anhalt (d. 1252), supporter in turn of Philip of Swabia, Otto IV and Friedrich II, married a daughter of Hermann of Thuringia; *Heinrich [IV] von Breslau; *Heinrich [Markgraf] von Meissen; *Otto IV von Brandenburg (1260–1308) 'Otte mit dem pfîle'; *Otto von Botenlouben (1180–1244), son of Count Poppo VI of Henneberg, took part in the 1197 Crusade; *Hiltbolt von Schwangou; *Der Tugendhaft Schreiber, probably chancellor to the Landgrave of Thuringia.

Swiss Minnesingers:
**Berthold Steinmar von Klingenau, a retainer of Rudolf of Habsburg; introduced into Minnesang the Autumn song, a subgenre continued by his compatriot Hadloub (q.v.); **Ulrich von Singenberg, active in St Gall in the early thirteenth century; **Wernher von Homberg (Hohenberg), b. 1230, Kanton Basel, d. 1284, perhaps in Italy; **Konrad, der Schenk von Landeck (1277–1306).

Editions: *KLD; **K. Bartsch, *Die Schweizer Minnesänger*, 1886; others in separate editions or MSH.

Commentary and separate editions:

H. Kuhn, *Minnesangs Wende*, 1952 (Hermaea, new series 1).

H. Naumann, 'Die Hohenstaufen als Lyriker', *Euph* xxxvi (1935).

J. Lunzer, 'Zu König Wenzels II. Minnelieder, *ZfdA* liii (1912).

F. Gennrich, 'Zu den Melodien Witzlaws von Rügen', *ZfdA* lxxx (1943).

R. J. Taylor, 'A Song by Prince Wizlav of Rügen', *MLR* xlvi (1951).

E. Gülzow, *Des Fürsten Wizlaw von Rügen Minnelieder und Sprüche*, 1922.

O. von Golmen, *Otto IV. mit dem Pfeile*, 1895.

E. Juethe, *Der Minnesänger Hiltbolt von Schwangau*, 1913 (Germ. Abh. 44).

A. Amrhein, *Magister Henricus Poeta, der tugendhafte Schreiber*, 1933.

Spruchdichtung in the Thirteenth Century

*Reinmar von Zweter (Rhinelander, d. 1252); Rumsland von Sachsen; Rumsland von Schwaben (late thirteenth century); Heinrich von Meissen, genannt Frauenlob (of Mainz, 1250–1318); *Der Wilde Alexander (late thirteenth century, probably of Swabian origin); Herman der Damen (von der Dahme, a tributary of the River Spree; mainly active in northern Germany); Barthel Regenbogen (blacksmith and poet, active about 1300; a precursor of Meistersang; opponent of Frauenlob); Konrad Marner (a minstrel; murdered 1270; one of the founders of the Meistersinger tradition); Meister Sigeher (Bohemian) followed the trend set by Reinmar von Zweter.

Editions: *KLD; others MSH and separate editions.

Editions of individual authors and commentary:

Frauenlob: *Leiche, Sprüche, Streitgedichte und Lieder*, ed. L. Ettmüller, 1843.

—— *Ausgewählte Gedichte mit versgetreuer Übertragung*, ed. B. Nagel, 1951.

—— H. de Boor, 'Fs. Streitgespräch zwischen Minne und Welt', *PBB(T)* lxxxv (1963).

Der Minnesinger F. [Selections in modern German renderings], ed. Margarete Lang, 1951.

Irmentraut Kern, *Das höfische Gut in den Dichtungen Fs.*, 1934 (Germ. Stud. 147).

Brunhild Peter, *Die theologisch-philosophische Gedankenwelt des Heinrich Frauenlob*, 1957.

R. Krayer, *Frauenlob und die Naturallegorese. Stilistische Untersuchungen*, 1960.

Regenbogen: text in K. Bartsch, *Meisterlieder der Kolmarer Handschrift*, 1862 (LV 68).

H. Niewöhner, 'Barthel Regenbogen', *PBB (H)* lxxviii (1956).

HEINRICH VON MÜGELN

From Mügeln near Dresden; active 1340–70 at the courts of the Emperor Charles IV and Duke Rudolf IV of Austria. Author of allegorical works as well as of lyrics.

Editions:

Der meide kranz, ed. W. Jahr, diss. Leipzig, 1909.

Die kleineren Dichtungen, ed. K. Stackmann, 1959 (DTMA 50–52).

Vier Meistergesänge von H. v. M., ed. U. Kube, 1932 (Germ. Stud. 112).

Commentary:

K. Stackmann, *Der Spruchdichter H. v. M.*, 1958.

J. Kibelka, *Der ware meister*, 1963 (PSQ 13).

JOHANNES HADLOUB

A householder of Zürich from 1302 probably until his death in the 1330's. Associated with Rüdiger Manesse, amateur and collector of lyric poetry, but Hadlaub's connection with the Manessische Handschrift may be no more than a romantic fiction.

Edition: K. Bartsch, *Die Schweizer Minnesänger*, 1886. (Selections in Bartsch, *Liederdichter*).

Commentary: Hedwig Lang, *Johannes Hadlaub*, 1959 (PSQ 5).

HUGO VON MONTFORT

Count of Bregenz, b. 1357, d. 1423; a man of action; took part in religious war against the Prussians, 1377; held high official positions in Austria. His poetry shows continuity with the past, but also looks forward to the urban poetry of the Meistersinger.

Editions:

K. Bartsch, 1879 (LV 143).

P. Runge, *Die Lieder des Hugo von Montfort mit den Melodien des Burk Mangolt*, 1906.

Commentary:

H. Walther, *Stilkritische Untersuchungen über Hugo von Montfort*, diss. Marburg, 1936.

OSWALD VON WOLKENSTEIN

A Tyrolean, 1367–1445. Saw service in Prussia, Lithuania and the Holy Land. Compelled by the fortunes of war to find humble employment in the Near East; later entrusted by the emperor Sigismund with confidential missions to Paris and Italy.

Editions:

B. Weber, 1847.

J. Schatz and O. Koller [with melodies], 1902.

K. K. Klein, 1962 (ATB 55). [Selected melodies, ed. W. Salmen.]

O. v. W.: Eine Auswahl aus seinen Liedern [with commentary and translation], ed. B. Wachinger, 1964.

Translations by J. Schrott, 1886; L. Passarge (UB).

Commentary:

K. H. Lester, *Zur literarischen Bedeutung Os. v. W.*, 1949.

N. Mayr, *Die Pilgerfahrt Os. v. W.*, 1959.

—— *Die Reiselieder und Reisen Os. v. W.*, 1961.

H. Emmel, 'Die Selbstdarstellung Os. v. W.', *Fs. H. A. Korff*, 1957.

K. K. Klein, 'O. v. W., ein Dichter, Komponist und Sänger des Spätmas.', *WW* xiii (1963).

KLARA HÄTZLERIN

Compiled her book of poems from various sources in 1471.

Edition:

Das Liederbuch der K. H., ed. K. F. Haltaus, 1840.

Commentary:

K. Geuther, *Studien zum Liederbuch der K. H.*, 1899.

Didactic Verse

Winsbeke, etc.:

Winsbeckische Gedichte nebst Tirol und Fridebrant, ed. Leitzmann, 3rd ed., rev. I. Reiffenstein, 1962 (ATB 9).

Commentary:

H.-F. Rosenfeld, 'Zur Überlieferung des Winsbeken', *ZfdA* lxvi (1929).

—— 'Zu Winsbeke, Winsbekin und Winsbekenparodie', *ZfdA* lxvii (1930).

H. Maync, *Die altdeutschen Fassungen von König Tirol und Fridebrant*, 1910 (Sprache und Dichtung, 1).

THOMASIN VON ZERCLÆRE: d. 1235 as canon of Aquileja; was a member of the entourage of the Patriarch Wolfger, formerly Bishop of Passau; probably acquainted with Walther.

Edition: *Der Wälsche Gast*, ed. H. Rückert, 1852.

Commentary:

H. Teske, *Thomasin von Zerclaere*, 1933.

Catherine T. Rapp, *Burgher and Peasant in the works of T. v. Z.*, 1936.

L. Beirer, *Die Beziehungen Walthers von der Vogelweide zu T. v. Z.*, diss. Innsbruck, 1958.

E. P. Siegert, *Der W. G. des T. v. Z.*, diss. Frankfurt, 1953.

A. Leitzmann, 'Zum Wälschen Gast', *PBB* lxiii (1939).

FREIDANK: A minstrel of burgher stock, perhaps from Bruneck in Tirol. *Bescheidenheit* was written soon after 1229 in imitation of *Der Wälsche Gast*. The work gained great currency in the Middle Ages, and a printed edition was brought out by Sebastian Brant in 1508; this was repeatedly reprinted as a *Volksbuch* until the early part of the nineteenth century.

Scholarly editions by H. E. Bezzenberger, 1872; F. Sandvoss, 1877.

German translations by K. Simrock, 1867; K. Pannier, 1878 (UB).

Commentary:

A. Leitzmann, *Studien zu Freidanks Bescheidenheit*, 1950 (Berlin Sb. [1948]).

F. Neumann, 'Meister Freidank', *WW* i (1951).

HUGO VON TRIMBERG: Born about 1230 at Trimberg near Würzburg; schoolmaster at Bamberg from 1260–1309. *Der Renner*, which opens with an allegory reminiscent in content and spirit of the bestiaries, is an elaboration, composed in the last years of the author's life, of an earlier work entitled *Der Sammler* (1266). Hugo's profession is revealed by a survey in Latin verse of widely-read Latin literary texts.

Editions:

Der Renner, ed. G. Ehrismann, 1908–11 (LV 247–8, 252, 256).

Registrum multorum auctorum, ed. K. Langosch, 1942 (Germ. Stud. 235).

Commentary:

L. Behrendt, *The Ethical Teaching of H. v. T.*, 1926.

F. Götting, *Der Renner Hs. v. T. Studien zur mal. Ethik in nachhöfischer Zeit*, 1932.

E. Seemann, *H. v. T. und die Fabeln seines Renners*, 1926.

Chronicles and Legal Codes

(JANS) JANSEN ENIKEL (= Johannes, the Grandson of Jansen): Probably a member of a Bohemian burgher family settled in Vienna, born about 1230–40, died about 1280.

Edition: *Weltchronik* and *Fürstenbuch*, ed. P. Strauch, 1891–1900 (MGH, *Deutsche Chroniken*, III).

Commentary:

H. Menhardt, 'Zur Weltchronik-Literatur', *PBB* lxi (1937).

OTTOKAR VON STEIER(MARK) (also known as Ottokar ouz der Geul, O. von Horneck): in the service of the Lichtenstein family, 1265–1320. Chronicle written 1301–1319 in the manner of courtly narrative.

Edition: *Österreichische Reimchronik*, ed. J. Seemüller, 1890–93 (MGH, *Dt. Chroniken*, V).

Livländische Reimchronik: Deals with the actions of the Teutonic knights in Livonia until 1290; probably written or commissioned by a member of the order. A later recension dates from the middle of the fourteenth century.

Editions: F. Pfeiffer, 1840 (LV 7); L. Meyer, 1876 (version of 1348 ed. K. Höhlbaum, 1872).

Braunschweigische Reimchronik: Manuscript of the thirteenth–fourteenth century; like other 'local' chronicles, factually more reliable than the general ones.

Edition: L. Weiland, 1877 (MGH, *Deutsche Chroniken*, II).

EBERHARD VON GANDERSHEIM: *Gandersheimer Reimchronik*, completed to 1228.

Editions: L. Weiland, 1877 (MGH, *Deutsche Chroniken*, II); L. Wolff, 1927 (ATB 25).

NIKOLAUS VON JEROSCHIN: *Deutschordenschronik*, ed. F. Pfeiffer, 1854 and E. Strehlke, 1861.

Commentary:

K. Helm and W. Ziesemer, *Die Literatur des deutschen Ritterordens*, 1951 (Gießener Beiträge zur dt. Philologie, 94).

EIKE VON REPGOWE: Yeoman and magistrate, traceable between 1209 and 1233 in the Anhalt district.

Works and editions:

Sächsische Weltchronik, ed. L. Weiland, 1877 (MGH, *Deutsche Chroniken*, II).

Sachsenspiegel, ed., C. G. Homeyer, 3rd ed., 1861.

—— ed. K. A. Eckhardt, I (*Landrecht*), 1955; II (*Lehnrecht*), 1956 (MGH, *Fontes iuris antiquissimi*, new series, IV–V).

Commentary:

K. A. Eckhardt, *Die Entstehungszeit des Sachsenspiegels und der sächsischen Weltchronik*, 1931 (Abh. der Gesellschaft der Wissenschaften zu Göttingen, 23).

W. Möllenberg, *E. v. R. und seine Zeit*, 1934.

Schwabenspiegel (version of *Sachsenspiegel*, with additional matter from canon law).

Editions: F. L. A. von Lassberg, 1840; W. Wackernagel, 1840; K. A. Eckhardt, *Schwabenspiegel. Kurzform*, 1960 (MGH, *Fontes juris antiquissimi*, new series, IV).

Deutschenspiegel (Upper German version of *Schwabenspiegel*):
Edition by K. A. Eckhardt and A. Hübner, 1930.

Religious Literature

KONRAD VON HEIMESFURT

Heimesfurt is the present-day Heinsfart, near Öttingen, on the Franconian border of Bavaria. Konrad came of an aristocratic family, and showed the tastes of the cultivated aristocracy in his writing, modelled stylistically on Konrad von Fussesbrunnen, and indirectly on the courtly romance. The *Himmelfahrt Mariä* was written about 1225.

Works and editions:

Himmelfahrt Mariä, ed. F. Pfeiffer, *ZfdA* viii (1851).

Urstende ['Auferstehung'], ed. K. A. Hahn, *Gedichte des 12. und 13. Jhs.*, 1840.

Source and other related texts:

Vita Beatae Mariae rhythmica ed. A. Vögtlin, 1888 (LV 180).

Konrad von Fussesbrunnen, *Die Kindheit Jesu*, ed. K. Kochendörffer, 1881 (QF 43).

Grazer Marienleben, ed. A. E. Schönbach, *ZfdA* xvii (1874).

Walther von Rheinau, *Marienleben*, ed. Edit Perjus, 1949 (Acta Academiae Aboensis, 17).

Philipp der Kartäuser [d. 1345/6 at Seitz, near Cilli], *Leben Christi und Mariä*, ed. H. Rückert, 1853; F. Bobertag, *Erzählende Dichtung des späteren Mas.*, [1887] (DNL 10).

Wernher der Schweizer, *Marienleben* [written before 1382], ed. M. Päpke and A. Hübner, 1920 (DTMA 27).

Commentary:

E. Schröder, 'Von der Vita beatae Mariae rhythmica', *ZfdA* lxviii (1931).

M. Päpke, *Das Marienleben des Schweizers Wernher*, 1913 (Palaestra 81).

K. Reissenberger, 'Zu Bruder Philipp von Seitz', *PBB* xli (1916).

REINBOT VON DURNE: at the court of Otto the Illustrious of Bavaria in the 1240's. *Der heilige Georg*, ed. C. von Kraus, 1907.

HUGO VON LANGENSTEIN: Swabian, from Mainau on the shores of Lake Constance; entered the Teutonic Order in 1282; wrote Legend of *Heilige Martina* about 1293, which is followed in the manuscript by the didactic writings in prose known as the *Mainauer Naturlehre:*

Martina von H. v. L., ed. A. von Keller, 1856 (LV 38).

Mainauer Naturlehre, ed. W. Wackernagel, 1851 (LV 22).

Heilige Elisabeth: (anonymous) fourteenth-century adaptation of Latin Life by the Dominican Dietrich of Apolda celebrating Elisabeth (1207–31), daughter of King Andrew II of Hungary and widow of Ludwig, Landgrave of Thuringia), ed. M. Rieger, 1868 (LV 90).

Die Erlösung: anonymous; sometimes taken to be the work of the same author as *Die Heilige Elisabeth*, ed. K. Bartsch, 1858; F. Maurer, 1934 (DL, *Geistliche Dichtung des Mas.*, VI).

HEINRICH VON NEUSTADT: author of a version of *Apollonius of Tyre* in addition to his religious writings, *Gottes Zuokunft* and *Visio Philiberti:* [Works], ed. S. Singer, 1906 (DTMA 7).

Passional: Das alte P., written for the Teutonic Order in the third quarter of the thirteenth century:

K. A. Hahn, *Das alte Passional* [Books I and II], 1845.

F. K. Köpke, *Das Passional* [Book III], 1852.

Väterbuch: based on the *Golden Legend* (compiled 1263–73); the largest and most influential MHG legendary after the *Passional*; perhaps an earlier work by the same author, ed. E. K. Reissenberger, 1914 (DTMA 22).

Commentary:

E. Öhmann, 'Reinbots heiliger Georg und die Kindheit Jesu', *ZfdA* lxviii (1931).

F. Maurer, 'Über Gleichsetzung der Verfasser bei anonymen altdeutschen Dichtungen und die Einheit von Erlösung und Elisabeth', *ZfdP* lvi (1931).

A. Bockhoff and S. Singer, *Heinrichs von Neustadt Apollonius und seine Quellen*, 1911 (Sprache und Dichtung, 6).

Marta Marti, *Gottes Zukunft von H. v. N.*, 1911 (Sprache und Dichtung, 7).

M. Geiger, *Die Visio Philiberti des H. v. N.*, 1912 (Sprache und Dichtung, 10).

K. Helm and W. Ziesemer, *Die Literatur d. dt. Ritterordens*, 1951 (Giessener Beiträge zur dt. Philologie, 94).

L. M. Kaiser, '*Das Väterbuch* and the *Legenda Aurea*', *Modern Language Notes*, lxviii (1953).

Prose Texts

Lucidarius

Der große Lucidarius: prose text from the end of the twelfth century: ed. F. Heidlauf, 1915 (DTMA 28).

Commentary:

G. Glogner, *Der mhd. Lucidarius*, 1937.

Marlies Dittrich, 'Zur ältesten Überlieferung d. dt. L.', *ZfdA* lxxvii (1940).

KONRAD VON MEGENBERG

Born 1309 at Mainberg (formerly Meygenberg) near Schweinfurt; studied and taught in Paris and Vienna; retired to Regensburg, where he died in 1374.

Editions:

Buch der Natur, ed. F. Pfeiffer, 1861 (translated by H. Schulz, 1897).

Deutsche Sphaera, ed. O. Matthaei, 1912 (DTMA 23).

Commentary:

H. Ibach, *Leben und Schriften des K. v. M.*, 1938.

(Albertus Magnus, *Omnia Opera*, ed. P. Jammy, 1651, reprinted 1890–99; new edition in progress, 1951 ff.; *De animalibus libri XXVI*, ed. H. Stadler, 1916–21.)

Prose Lanzelet (from a French prose source): Edition by R. Kluge, 1948–63 (DTMA 42, 47).

BERTHOLD VON REGENSBURG

1210–72; born and died at Regensburg. Travelled widely as a Franciscan preacher; drew up Latin versions of his sermons (still unpublished) to discourage the production of pirated editions; there is some question of the authenticity of all the vernacular sermons which have been preserved, but some were probably written down after delivery, and correspond closely in content, if not necessarily word for word, to the form in which they were delivered.

Edition:

B. v. R., Vollständige Ausgabe seiner Predigten, ed. F. Pfeiffer and J. Strobl, 1862–80.

Commentary:

H. Mertens, *Die Form d. dt. Predigt bei B. v. R.*, diss. Bonn, 1936.

OTHER SERMONS: the sermons of Berthold's teacher, David of Augsburg, are not preserved, though other works of his are. The Preacher of St Georgen was active at about the same time as Berthold.

Editions:

David of Augsburg [extant works] ed. F. Pfeiffer, *Deutsche Mystiker des Mas.*, I, 1845.

Der sogenannte St Georgener Prediger, ed. K. Rieder, 1908 (DTMA 10).

Commentary:

A. E. Schönbach, *Studien zur Gesch. der altdt. Predigt*, 1897–1907 (Vienna Sb.).

W. Frühwald, *Der St. Georgener Prediger*, 1963 (QF, new series, 9).

P.-G. Völker, 'Die Überlieferungsformen mal. dt. Predigten', *ZfdA* xcii (1963).

Mystics

A link between the allegorization of the Song of Songs, particularly as expressed in the St Trudpert *Hohes Lied*, and more general mystical attitudes, is provided by Hildegard of Bingen (1098–1179) foundress of the Benedictine convent at Rupertsberg, near Bingen.

(*Ordo virtutum; Scivias:* edition in Migne, *Patrologia Latina*, CXCVII. Translations: [Selections], J. Bühler, 1922; *Wisse die Wege. Scivias* [text and trans.], ed. Maura Böckeler, 5th ed., 1963; *Reigen der Tugenden. Ordo virtutum*, trans. and ed. I. Herwegen, 1927. Cf. H. Liebeschütz, *Das allegorische Weltbild der Heiligen Hildegard von Bingen*, 1930; Bertha Widmer, *Heilsordnung und Zeitgeschehen in der Mystik Hs. v. B.*, 1955.)

MECHTHILD VON MAGDEBURG (1210–85): in about 1230 she entered a community of béguines devoted to prayer and good works, and later took the formal vows of a nun. In her native Low German she wrote a prose work known as *Das fließende Licht der Gottheit*, preserved only in a mid-fourteenth-century verse rendering by Heinrich von Nördlingen, one of the Gottesfreund circle.

Works:

Offenbarung, ed. G. Morel, 1869.

Das fließende Licht der Gottheit, eingeführt von M. Schmidt mit einer Studie von H. Urs von Balthasar, 1956 (English trans. by L. Menzies, 1953).

MEISTER ECKHART

Born 1260 at Hochheim near Gotha; studied at Cologne, and after some years of ministry and administrative duties, went to Paris to study and later to teach. His later teaching was done mainly in Strassburg and Cologne, and it was the Archbishop of Cologne who brought about the examination of Eckhart's works for heresy; his appeal to the Pope was not heard in his lifetime, and after his death some of his teachings were declared heretical.

Editions:

Die deutschen und lateinischen Werke, ed. J. Quint and J. Koch, 1936 ff. (in progress).

Die Predigten und Traktate, ed. and trans. J. Quint, 1955.
[Sermons] P. Pfeiffer, *Dt. Mystiker des 14. Jhs.*, II (1857).
Paradisus anime intelligentis, ed. P. Strauch, 1919 (DTMA 30).
Reden der Unterscheidung, ed. E. Diederichs, 2nd ed., 1925.
Buch der göttlichen Tröstung, ed. J. Quint, 1952.

Translations:
Meister Eckhart. Vom mystischen Leben. Eine Auswahl von Es. schönsten Predigten in neuer Übertragung [with postscript by Maria Bindschedler], 1951.
[Selection of sermons], trans. F. A. S. Noerr, repr. 1963 (UB).
Reden der Unterweisung, trans. J. Quint, 1963.
M. E. Selected Treatises and Sermons, trans. with commentary by J. M. Clark and J. V. Skinner, 1958.

Commentary:
A. Dempf, *Meister Eckhart. Eine Einführung in sein Werk*, 1934.
H. Ebeling, *Meister Eckharts Mystik*, 1941.
J. M. Clark, *The Great German Mystics*, 1949.
—— *M. E. An Introduction to the study of his works, with an anthology of his sermons*, 1957.
E. von Bracken, 'M. E. als Philosoph', *DVLG* xxiv (1950).
Jeanne Ancelet-Hustache, *Maître E. et la mystique rhénane*, 1956. [Also in English translation, 1957.]
R. Fahrner, *Wortsinn und Wortschöpfung bei M. E.*, 1929.
B. Schmoldt, *Die dt. Begriffssprache M. Es.*, 1954.
L. Seppänen, *Studien zur Terminologie des Paradisus anime intelligentis*, 1964 (Mémoires de la société néophilologique de Helsinki, 27).

HEINRICH SUSO

Born at Überlingen, on Lake Constance, in the last years of the thirteenth century (?1296); the son of a wealthy and worldly-minded burgher. Entered the Dominican order under age, became a teacher of theology at Constance. The 'Life of the Servant' is an autobiographical account of his life, written down by Elsbeth Stagel, a mystic in her own right, whose spiritual advisor Suso was.

Editions:
Deutsche Schriften, ed. K. Bihlmeyer, 1907.
Horologium Sapientiae, ed. C. Richstätter, 1929.

Translations:

German, by H. S. Denifle, 1880; by N. Heller, 1926.
English: J. M. Clark, *S. The Life of the Servant*, 1952.
—— *Little Book of Eternal Wisdom, and Little Book of Truth*, 1953.

Commentary:

A. Gebhard, *Die Briefe und Predigten des Mystikers S.*, 1920.
C. Gröber, *Der Mystiker H. Seuse*, 1941.
J. M. Clark, *The Great German Mystics*, 1949.
R. Senn, *Die Echtheit der Vita Susos*, 1930 (Sprache und Dichtung, 45).
J. Bühlmann, *Christuslehre und Christusmystik des H. S.*, 1942.
F. W. Wentzlaff-Eggebert, *Heinrich Seuse, sein Leben und seine Mystik*, 1947.
J. A. Bizet, *Suso et le Minnesang*, 1948.
—— *Suso et le déclin de la scolastique*, 1948.

(Related texts: Elsbeth Stagel, *Das Leben der Schwestern zu Töss*, ed. F. Vetter, 1906 (DTMA 6). Related by inclusion in one of the manuscripts of Suso's works is the anonymous *Christi Leiden in einer Vision geschaut*, ed. (from a manuscript then believed to be unique) by R. Priebsch, 1936; from a different source, and drawing on a fragment which dates the work no later than mid-fourteenth century, by F. P. Pickering, 1952.)

JOHANNES TAULER

1300–61; born and died at Strassburg; active in the cities of Strassburg, Basel and Cologne. A pupil of Eckhart, who took over many of his teacher's views but did not use the extreme formulations which were suspect of pantheism; he turned his preaching mainly against the abuses and heresies of his day. The only authentic works are some 80 sermons.

Editions by F. Vetter, 1910 (DTMA 11) and A. L. Corin, 1924–29.

Selections:

J. Quint, *Textbuch zur Mystik d. dt. Mas.*, 1952.

Translations:

German by W. Lehmann, 1913; F. W. Wentzlaff-Eggebert, *Deutsche Mystik zwischen Ma. und Neuzeit*, 2nd ed., 1947; H. Kunisch, *Meister Eckhart, Johannes Tauler und Heinrich Suso. Ein Textbuch aus der altdt. Mystik*, 1958.

English: A. P. J. Cruikshank, *Meditations* . . . , 1925; J. R. Morell, *The following of Christ*, 1886.

Commentary:

D. Helander, *J. T. als Prediger*, diss. Lund, 1923.

F. W. Wentzlaff-Eggebert, *Studien zur Lebenslehre Ts.*, 1940 (Berlin Abh. [1939]).

J. M. Clark, *The Great German Mystics*, 1949.

P. Wyser, 'Der "Seelengrund" in Taulers Predigten', *Fs. Stammler*, 1958.

I. Weilner, *J. Ts. Bekehrungsweg*, 1961.

DIE GOTTESFREUNDE

A society of mystics formed by the Strassburg merchant Rulman Merswin (1307–82). The members included many laymen, but they were in close touch with Tauler, and also with Cistercian nuns like Margarete Ebener. The name comes from the 'Gottesfreund' into whose mouth Merswin laid his revelations.

Edition:

Schriften aus der Gottesfreundliteratur, ed. P. Strauch, 1927–28 (ATB 22, 27).

English trans.: C. F. Kelley, *The Book of the Poor in Spirit*, 1954.

Commentary:

K. Rieder, *Der Gottesfreund vom Oberland*, 1905.

R. Egenter, *Gottesfreundschaft*, 1928.

—— 'Die Idee der Gottesfreundschaft im 14. J.', *Fs. Grabmann*, 1935.

W. Muschg, *Die Mystik in der Schweiz*, 1935.

Theologia Deutsch

An anonymous work of the latter half of the fourteenth century; the author may have been Heinrich von Bergen, Kustos of the house of the Teutonic Order in Frankfurt. The work obtained wide currency through Luther's edition of 1516, reprinted two years later, and very frequently thereafter.

Modern editions:

F. Pfeiffer, 2nd ed., 1855; reissued under the title *Das Buch vom vollkommenen Leben* by K. F. Riedler, 1947.

W. Uhl, *Der Frankforter*, 1912.

German trans. by R. A. Schröder, 1947; English trans., rev. W. R. Trask, 1950.

Secular Allegorical Writing

HADAMAR VON LABER: takes his name from the Schwarze Laber in the Upper Palatinate; he was a member of the entourage of Ludwig of Bavaria, and wrote *Die Jagd* about 1335. The anonymous *Kloster der Minne* was written at about the same time; its title is a little misleading—the work celebrates a life of chivalrous pleasure, and the monastic rules are directed against the spoilsports. *Die Minneburg*, also anonymous, is given the general date 'fourteenth century'.

Editions:

J. A. Schmeller, *Hadamars von Laber Jagd und drei andere Minnegedichte seiner Zeit und Weise*, 1850 (LV 20). Selections in F. Bobertag, *Lehrhafte Literatur des 14. und 15. Jhs.*, I [1888] (DNL 12, i).

K. Stejskal, *H. v. L.*, 1880.

Kloster der Minne, ed. J. von Lassberg, *Liedersaal*, 2nd ed., 1846.

Die Minneburg, ed. H. Pyritz, 1950 (DTMA 43).

Commentary:

F. Ranke, 'Zur Rolle der Minneallegorie in d. dt. Dichtung des ausgehenden Mas.', *Fs. Siebs*, 1933 (Germ. Abh. 67).

R. Gruenter, 'Bemerkungen zum Problem des Allegorischen in d. dt. "Minneallegorie"', *Euph* li (1957).

E. Bethke, *Über den Stil Hadamars von Laber*, 1892.

Eva E. Hese, *Die Jagd Hs. v. L.*, 1936.

G. Richter, *Beiträge zur Interpretation und Textrekonstruktion des mhd. Gedichts Kloster der Minne*, diss. Berlin, 1895.

E. Schaus, 'Das Kloster der Minne', *ZfdA* xxxviii (1894).

G. Ehrismann, 'Untersuchungen über das mhd. Gedicht von der Minneburg', *PBB* xxii (1897).

O. Lauffer, *Frau Minne in Schrifttum und bildender Kunst des Mas.*, 1947.

Burgher Poets

PETER SUCHENWIRT: known to have been writing between 1353 and 1359; went with Duke Albrecht III of Austria in the Prussian campaign of 1377. His works include *Minneallegorien* and *Heroldsdichtung*. Edition by A. Primisser, 1827; selections, ed. F. Bobertag, *Lehrhafte Literatur des 14. und 15. Jhs.* [1888], (DNL 12, i). Cf. O. Weber, *P. S. Studien über sein Wesen und Werk*, 1937.

HEINRICH TEICHNER ('Der Teichner'): Austrian minstrel and friend of Suchenwirt, but reveals totally different attitudes in his writings (datable between 1350 and 1377): *Reimreden*—practical advice on the lines of Freidank or the earlier gnomic poets. Edition by H. Niewöhner, 1953–6 (DTMA 44); selections ed. C. von Kraus, *Mhd. Übungsbuch*, 2nd ed., 1926; F. Bobertag, op. cit.

DER KÖNIG VOM ODENWALD: a citizen of Würzburg, writing about 1430; the term 'König' is probably a nickname for a prominent member of a craft. Edition by E. Schröder, 1900.

MUSKATBLÜT: active in the first half of the fifteenth century; edition by E. von Groote, 1852. Cf. A. Veltmann, *Die politischen Gedichte Ms.*, diss. Bonn, 1902; E. G. Gudde, 'M. and King Sigismund', *Germanic Review*, vii (1932); R. Schimmelpfennig, *Über das Religiöse und Ethische bei dem Meistersinger M.*, 1935.

SUCHENSINN: a minstrel, concerning whom there is an entry in the accounts of Albrecht Buke of Bavaria in 1392. Twenty of his poems are edited by K. Bartsch, *Meisterlieder aus der Kolmarer Handschrift*, 1862 (LV 68). Cf. E. Pflug, *S. und seine Dichtung*, 1908 (Germ. Abh. 32).

ROSENPLÜT: otherwise known as Hans Schnepperer, a Nuremberg brassfounder, was active about the middle of the fifteenth century; as a *Wappendichter* he is an example of the persistence for a century of a restricted form of occasional verse. Edition: A. v. Keller, *Fastnachtspiele des 15. Jhs.*, 1853 (LV 30 [Anhang]).

Didactic Verse

ULRICH BONER: a Dominican, of whom there are documentary records between 1334 and 1349. The *Edelstein* consists of 100 fables in rhyming verse, based on Latin models.

Edition by F. Pfeiffer, 1844. Translation by K. Pannier (UB).

Commentary: R.-H. Blaser, *U.B., un fabuliste suisse du 14ᵉ siècle*, 1949.

The Fifteenth Century

Der Ackermann aus Böhmen

Editions:

J. Knieschek, 1877. [With fifteenth-century Czech parallel.]

A. Bernt and K. Burdach, 1917, 1932 (*Vom Ma. zur Reformation*, III, i and iii).
A Bernt, 1929.
A. Hübner, 2nd ed., 1954.
H. Rupprich, 1938 (DL, *Humanismus und Renaissance*, I).
K. Spalding, 1950. [Introduction and notes in English.]
M. O'C. Walshe, 1951. [English commentary.]
L. L. Hammerich and G. Jungbluth, 1951.
W. Krogmann, 1954 (DKMA, new series, 1).

Translation with introduction and commentary by F. Genzmer, 1951 (UB).

English translation: K. W. Maurer, *Death and the Ploughman*, 1947.

Commentary:

K. Burdach, *Der Dichter des A. a. B. und seine Zeit*, 1917 (*Vom Ma. zur Reformation*, III, i).
A. Hübner, *Das Deutsche im A. a. B.*, 1935 (Berlin Sb., 18).
Renée Brand, *Zur Interpretation des A. a. B.*, [1944].
L. Wolff, 'Der A. a. B.', *WW* i (1950).
W. Krogmann, 'Untersuchungen zum *Ackermann*', *ZfdP* lxxii (1953).
M. O'C. Walshe, 'Der A. a. B. A structural interpretation', *Classica et Medievalia* xv (1954).
—— 'Establishing the text of *Der A. a. B.*', *MLR* liii (1957).
T. C. van Stockum, *Der A.a.B. Herfstij der middeleeuwen of humanistische lente?*, 1953 (Mededelingen der koninklijke Nederlandse Akademie van Wetenschappen, 15).
F. H. Bäuml, *Rhetorical devices and structure in the A. a. B.*, 1960.
G. Eis, 'Zum *A. a. B.*', *Neophilologus*, xlvi (1962).
H. Deinert, 'Der A. a. B.', *JEGP* lxi (1962).
G. Hahn, *Die Einheit des A. a. B.*, 1964 (Münchener Texte und Untersuchungen, 5).
—— *Johann von Saaz, Der A. a. B. Interpretationen*, 1964.

Translators

ALBRECHT VON EYB, 1420–75: received a legal training at Italian universities, became chamberlain to Pope Pius II, and later a canon of Bamberg. Works: *Margarita poetica* [collection of Latin excerpts], compiled 1460, printed 1472; *Ehebüchlein*, 1472; *Spiegel der Sitten*, completed 1474, published posthumously in 1511, together with the Plautus translations.

Edition: *Deutsche Schriften*, ed. M. Herrmann, 1890–91.

Commentary: M. Herrmann, *A. v. E. und die Frühzeit d. dt. Humanismus*, 1893; J. A. Hiller, *A. v. E., Medieval Moralist*, 1939.

NICLAS VON WYLE: born about 1410 at Bremgarten in Aargau, died after 1498, municipal official in Nuremberg and Esslingen, later Chancellor of the Count Eberhard of Württemberg.

Edition: *Translationen*, ed. A. von Keller, 1861 (LV 57).

Commentary: B. Strauss, *Der Übersetzer N. v. W.*, 1912 (Palaestra, 118). W. E. Peuckert, *Die Große Wende*, 1948.

AUGUSTIN TÜNGER: born 1455 at Endingen in Baden, studied at Erfurt, and was in the legal service of the Bishop of Constance.

Edition: *Facetiae*, ed. A. von Keller, 1874 (LV 118).

HEINRICH STEINHÖWEL: born 1412 at Weil in Württemberg; died at Ulm, 1478. Studied at Vienna and Padua; physician at Ulm.

Works and editions:

Von den sinnrychen erluchten Wyben [1473], ed. K. Drescher, 1895 (LV 205).

Äsop [1477], ed. H. Oesterley, 1873 (LV 117).

Apollonius [1471] and *Griseldis* [1473], ed. C. Schröder, 1873.

Commentary:

W. Scherer, *Die Anfänge d. dt. Prosaromans*, 1877 (QF 21).

HANS VINTLER: the date of his birth is not known; at his death in 1419, he held high administrative office in Tirol. The *Pluemen der Tugent* were written about 1411 at Burg Runkelstein, near Bozen. Edition by J. V. Zingerle, 1874.

'ARIGO' has been identified (by G. Baesecke, *ZfdA* xlvii), as the Nuremberg patrician Heinrich Schlüsselfelder. His version of the *Fiori di virtù* is dated at about 1460; he is now accredited with the translation of the *Decameron* formerly attributed to Heinrich Steinhöwel. *Blumen der Tugend*, selections, ed. F. Vogt, *ZfdP* xxviii (1896); *Decameron*, ed. A. von Keller, 1860 (LV 51). Cf. K. Drescher, *Der Verfasser der pseudo-steinhöwelschen Decameron-übersetzung*, 1897, and *A., der Übersetzer des Decameron und des Fiore di virtu*, 1900 (QF 86).

Prose versions of Medieval Romances

The public for this originally aristocratic form was much enlarged by the introduction of printing: prose romances are hardly distinguishable from *Volksbücher*, which were also produced in the fifteenth century, but spread more extensively in the sixteenth century and later. (Cf. Vol. II of these *Introductions*.) The following prints, among others, appeared before 1500:

Wigalois: version written 1472, printed 1493 by Schönsperger of Augsburg.

Tristan: printed by A. Zorn of Augsburg, 1484.

In addition, Ulrich Füetrer's *Buch der Abenteuer* contains a prose Lancelot romance, and there is a fifteenth century Zürich manuscript of a prose *Willehalm*, neither of which was printed until the nineteenth century.

Herzog Ernst: various undated prints, probably produced before the end of the fifteenth century.

Other Chivalrous Texts

JAKOB PÜTERICH VON REICHERTZHAUSEN: son of a Munich patrician, born 1400, died 1469. The *Ehrenbrief* (1462) was written for the duchess Mechthild of Austria.

Edition: A. Goette, 1899; facsimile and text ed. F. Behrend and O. Wolkan, 1920.

ULRICH FÜETRER: active in the latter half of the fifteenth century; died before 1502. The *Buch der Abenteuer* has never been edited in full, though there are recent editions of several individual romances.

Editions:

Albrecht von Scharfenberg: Merlin and Seifrid de Ardemont in der Bearbeitung U. Fs., ed. F. Panzer, 1902 (LV 227).

U. Fs. Prosaroman von Lanzelot, ed. A. Peter, 1885 (LV 175)

Iban, ed. Alice Carlson, diss. Riga, 1937 [with commentary].

Poytislier, ed. Friederike Weber, 1960 (ATB 52).

Persibein, ed. Renate Munz, 1964 (ATB 62).

Die Gralepen in U. Fs. Bearbeitung, ed. K. Nyholm, 1964 (DTMA 57).

Commentary:

J. Boyd, *Ulrich Füetrer's Parzival*, 1936.

E. Hartl, 'Zu U. Fs. Parzival', *ZfdA* lxxv (1938).

Karlmeinet: youthful adventures of Charlemagne. Edition by A. von Keller, 1858 (LV 45).

Commentary:

K. Bartsch, *Über Karlmeinet. Ein Beitrag zur Karlssage*, 1861.

Collected Manuscripts of Narrative Texts ('*Heldenbücher*')

The content of these codices is not confined to texts which are normally classified as heroic, but they also include romances; e.g. the *Ambraser Heldenbuch* (sixteenth century, written to the order of Maximilian I 'Der letzte Ritter') contains the only (almost) complete text of Hartmann's *Erec*.

Dresdner Heldenbuch: compiled by Kaspar von der Roen, 1472; ed. F. H. von der Hagen and G. Büsching, *Deutsche Gedichte des Mas.*, II, 1820).

Strassburger Heldenbuch: a fourteenth-century manuscript containing such texts as *Ortnit*, *Hugdietrich*, *Wolfdietrich*, etc. There was also a Strassburg print of a similar collection of texts made in 1477.

Fastnachtspiele

See also general bibliography, pp. 187–88.

The form seems to have developed particularly strongly in Nuremberg, though plays from other centres are recorded. It was in Nuremberg that Hans Sachs was to develop the tradition of the Fastnachtspiel in the sixteenth century (cf. Vol. II of these *Introductions*), and there that two names of Fastnachtspiel authors are recorded from the fifteenth century—Hans Schnepperer ('Rosenplüt') and Hans Folz. For Rosenplüt, cf. above, p. 261. Hans Folz (1450–1515), born at Worms, followed the trade of a barber at Nuremberg; he wrote *Meisterlieder* and *Fastnachtspiele*.

Editions:

A. von Keller, *Fastnachtspiele aus dem 15. Jh.*, 1853, 1858, (LV 28–30, 46). [This edition includes the plays of Folz and Rosenplüt, as well as anonymous texts.]

Sterzinger Spiele, ed. O. Zingerle, 1886 (Wiener Neudrucke, 9 and 11).

[Lübeck plays], ed. C. Wehrmann, *Niederdeutsche Jahrbücher*, i (1880).

Commentary:

V. Michels, *Studien über die ältesten dt. Fastnachtspiele*, 1896 (QF 77).

E. Catholy, *Das Fastnachtspiel des Spätmas.*, 1961 (Hermaea, new series, 8).

P. B. Salmon, '"Das Hoffgesindt Veneris" and some analogues', *GLL* x (1956). [On relation of Fastnachtspiel to other enumerative genres.]

Medieval Religious Drama

Editions of individual German plays:

Tegernseer Ludus de Antichristo [Latin: the earliest play of this type recorded from Germany, about 1160], ed. F. Wilhelm, 2nd ed., 1930; ed. K. Young, *The Drama of the medieval Church*, II (1933).

Osterspiel von Muri [oldest religious play in German, about 1240–60] and *Redentiner Osterspiel* [fifteenth century] ed. R. Froning, *Das Drama des Mas.*, [1890] (DNL 14).

Osnabrücker Osterspiel, ed. H. H. Breuer, Beiträge zur Gesch. und Kulturgesch. des Bistums O. (1939).

Easter plays from Engelberg, Erlau, Innsbruck, Klosterneuburg, Prague, Trier and Vienna, ed. E. Hartl, 1937 (DL, *Das Drama des Mas.*, II).

Donaueschingen Passion play, ed. E. Hartl, 1942 (DL, *Das Drama des Mas.*, IV).

Passion Plays from Benediktbeuren and St Gall, ed. E. Hartl, 1952 (ATB 41).

—— from Alsfeld, Frankfurt and Vienna, ed. R. Froning, *Das Drama des Mittelalters*, [1890] (DNL 14).

Meistersang and Folk Song

Both forms are only beginning to emerge in the fifteenth century; in the case of the Volkslied it is particularly difficult to establish a categorical date, except in the case of historical Volkslieder, of which only few relate to events antedating the sixteenth century. The quasi-historical *Jüngeres Hildebrandslied* and the stanzaic poems about Young Siegfried (*Der Hürnen Seyfried*, sixteenth-century text, based on an earlier original) and Herzog Ernst suggest a local oral currency.

Meistersang texts:

K. Bartsch, *Meisterlieder aus der Kolmarer Handschrift*, 1862 (LV 68).

Hans Folz, *Meisterlieder*, ed. A. L. Mayer, 1908 (DTMA 12).

Commentary:

B. Nagel, *Der deutsche Meistersang*, 1952.

—— *Meistersang*, 1962 (SM 12).

Volkslied texts:

Die historischen Volkslieder der Deutschen vom 13. bis 16. Jh., ed. R. von Liliencron, 1865–69.

Das Lied vom hürnen Seyfried, ed. W. Golther, 1889.

—— ed. K. C. King, 1958.

Das Lied von Herzog Ernst, ed. [from fifteenth- and sixteenth-century prints] by K. C. King, 1958 (*Texte des späten Mas.* 11). Cf. J. Carles, *La chanson du duc Ernst*, 1964.

Commentary:

E. Wechssler, *Begriff und Wesen des Volksliedes*, 1913.

A. Götze, *Das deutsche Volkslied*, 1929.

W. Wiora, 'Zur Lage d. dt. Volksliedforschung', *ZfdP* lxxiii (1954).

APPENDIX

TEXTUAL REFERENCES AND ALLUSIONS

Some of the passages below are taken from editions which set out to reproduce as faithfully as possible the idiosyncrasies of particuar manuscripts. In such cases a few spellings have been normalized and some punctuation supplied. Lyrical poems are set out in a manner which goes some way towards showing the metrical structure of the stanza, and for this reason the more usual alignment to a left-hand margin has not been adopted. References are given in the conventional way to page and line of early scholarly editions, which are usually followed, or at least noted, by subsequent editors.

p. 16

Thô he gibolgan geng,
swîðo thrîstmôd thegan for is thiodan standen,
hard for is hêrron: ni uuas imu is hugi tuîfli,
blôth an is breostun, ac he is bil atôh,
suerd bi sîdu, slôg imu tegegnes
an thene furiston fîund folmo crafto,
that thô Malchus uuarð mâkeas eggiun,
an thea suîðaron half suerdu gimâlod:
thiu hlust uuarð imu farhauuan, he uuarð an that hôbið uund,
that imu herudrôrag hlear endi ôre
beniuundun brast: blôd aftar sprang,
uuel fan uundun.

Heliand, 4869–80

p. 20

Floug er súnnun pad, stérrono stráza
uuega uuólkono zi deru ítis frono,
Zi édiles fróuun, sélbun scā Máriun:
thie fórdoron bi bárne uuarun chúninga alle.
Gíang er in thia pálinza, fand sia drúrenta,
mit sálteru in hénti, then sáng si unz in énti:
Vuáhero dúacho uuerk uuírkento,
díurero gárno, thaz déda siu io gérno.

Tho sprach er érlicho ubar ál, so man zi fróvuun scal,
so bóto scal io gúater zi drúhtines muater. . . .

Otfrid, I, 5, 5–14

p. 21

thoh ir sagant kicorana thia bita in Hierosolima.

Christus und die Samariterin, line 31

iâ ne niezant, uuize Christ, thie Iudon unsera uuist.

ibid., 8

Thaz óffonot Iohannes thár, bi hiu si só quad in uuár,
bi uuíu si thaz so zélita, thaz drínkan so firságeta:
Uuánta thio zua líuti ni eigun múas gimúati
uuérgin zi iro mázze in éinemo fázze.

Otfrid, II, 14, 19–22

p. 23

Suman thuruhskluog her, Suman thuruhstah her.

Ludwigslied, line 52

p. 29

On the Lion, cf. *Älterer Physiologus:* 'So teta unser trutin to er an der uuerilte mit menischon waz zediu daz ter fient nihet verstunde daz er gotes sun uuare' (Wilhelm, p. 4); *Jüngerer Physiologus:* 'do bedacte er diu vil vernunftiklichen spor siner gotheite; ich meine do er chom in dere magide puosim' (ibid., p. 5)

p. 31

Wir habin gesprockin von einime chussenten brûtegoumen unde von einir gekustir brûte. aber ir beidir chussin, daz ist crist, der dâ chom von deme hôhesten unde fleisch unde bluot nam von der diemuotigesten.

St. Trudperter Hohes Lied, 10, 16–20
(Menhardt, p. 133)

diz kussin daz int[wi]ngit nith zesamene die fleislichen munde, sundir die geistliken willin. diz halsin ist nith der umbefâgenden arme sundir der heiligin gedanken, dâ got mit halsit zallen zîten.

ibid., 11, 14–19

p. 31

Von den anigengin vîrin
got wolti den mennischin zîrin:

er gammi von dem vûri
gisûni vili dûri,
von den luftin hôhirin
daz er mag gihôrin,
von den nidirin daz er gistinckin mag,
von dem wazziri gismag.
der hendi unde der vûzzi birûridi
gilîzz er imo von der erdi.

Summa Theologiae, lines 97–106 (Waag)

32

Ter man ter ist niwit wise, der ist an einer verte,
einen boum vindit er sconen, tar undir gat er ruowen,
so truchit in der slaf ta, so vergizzit er dar er scolta;
als er denne uf springit, wie ser iz in denne riuwit.
Ir bezeichint allo den man. . . . .

Memento mori, lines 115–23 (Maurer)

p. 33

nû sich, wâ sint siniu mûzige wart
dâ mit er der frowen hôhvart
lobet unt säite?
nu sich in wie getâner häite
diu zunge lige in sînem munde
dâ mit er diu troutliet chunde
behagenlîchen singen!
nûne mac si niht fur bringen
daz wort noch die stimme.

Die Erinnerung an den Tod, lines 607–15

p. 35

Tohter davidis,
wech des ewigen lîbis,
irrituomis ende,
tôdes urstende,
lebendigiu brunnâder,
uz der runse floz aller gnâden,
wurze aller guote,
von der der ast erbluote,
der sich wîten hât gibreitet
und siniu zwi gileitet
von der erde durch die himile
unt von dannen her widere
durch das inner abgrunde,
daz er die striche miner sunde
gnædichlichin enbinde,

daz gibiut du frowe dinem chind.
wan du maht ieweder tuon:
gibieten sam diu muoter uber ir sun,
und salt iedoch bitten unde êren
sam diu suozze diu ir herren,
daz er gihuge aller dinge
die er mit dir durch die suntære begienge.

Litanei, 12-century Graz manuscript,
(Kraus, *Übungsbuch*, p. 35)

p. 51

Dô hâte Tristrant einen sete,
des volgete im die vrauwe mete:
swen sie sich gelegetin
und mit ein andir redeten
daz ez in dûchte genûch,
sîn swert er ûz der scheide zôch
und legete ez zwischin sich und sie:
daz en wolde der helt nie
dorch kein ding gelâzen.
wan sie en soldin slâfen,
daz swert en lêge zwischin in.
daz was ein vromder mannes sin
und quam im doch zu heile sît,
wan es quam zu einer zît
ein des koninges weideman
zû der hutten gegân
eines morgenes vrû
heimlîche hin zû.

Eilhart, *Tristrant*, lines 4581–98 (Lichtenstein)

p. 53

Heinrich von Veldeke: on the loss of the source, cf. lines 13429–90.

p. 54

also musten si varen
went ane den virden dach,
dat der wint gelach
unde die starken unden
sachten begunden

Eneide, 216–20

p. 57

Der wechter ûf der zinnen saz,
sîne tageliet er sanc,
daz im sîn stimme erklanc
von grôzme done.
Er sanc 'ez taget schône!
der tag der schînet in den sal.
Wol ûf ritter uber al!
Wol ûf, ez ist tag!'
Do er gesanc sin herze erscrac
sêre unde herte;
er gesach ûf der warte
blicken gegen dem mer wert
halsberg, schilt, helm, swert,
unde die baniren manicfare...

Herbort von Fritzlar, 4178–91

p. 63

und als er rehte daz gesach . . .
daz er was gewæfens blôz,
wie wol her Keiîn genôz
der tugent die Erec hâte.
vil wunderlîchen drâte
daz sper er umbe kêrte
daz er in niht versêrte.
er wante gegen im den schaft
und stach in mit solcher kraft
daz Keiîn rehte sam ein sac
under dem rosse gelac,
nâch sînem rehte
ungelîch einem guoten knehte.
daz ros vuorte Erec dan.
Keiîn, der schalchafte man,
ime vaste nâch lief:
lûte er in ane rief:
'nein, ritter vil guot!
durch dînen tugenthaften muot
daz mir daz ros hie bestê!
oder ich muos es immer mê
geswachet und gehœnet sîn.
jâ enist ez weizgot niht mîn!'

Erec, 4720–43

p. 75

'old grey man': *ein grâ wîse man*, *Parzival*, 127, 21; cf. 162, 30; 163, 16. *irn sult niht vil gevrâgen*, 171, 17.

p. 81

'Genâde und al daz immer maget sol verenden
gein [ir] werdem clâren friunde, daz leist ich, und mac mich des nei man erwenden,
op dîn wille krieget nâch der strangen,
die der bracke zôch ûf der verte, den du mir bræhte gevangen.'

Titurel, stanza 168

p. 85

Deist aller edelen herzen brôt.
hie mite sô lebet ir beider tôt.
wir lesen ir leben, wir lesen ir tôt
und ist uns daz süeze alse brôt.

Tristan, 233–6

p. 86

gelüppeter eit, 15752; shortly after the ordeal scene.

p. 90

rede diu niht des hoves sî, 7958

p. 95

rûmen diu lant, MF 8, 1–8 + 9, 29–36
Kürenberg's *Falkenlied*, MF 8, 33–9, 12.

p. 96

Wie möhte mir mîn herze werden iemer rehte fruot,
daz mir ein edeliu frouwe sô vil ze leide tuot!
der ich vil gedienet hân
als ir wille was getân.
nu wil si niht gedenken der mangen sorgen mîn.
sô hôch ôwi,
sol ich ir lange frömde sîn.

Dietmar von Aist, MF 39, 11–17

p. 98

Wâfenâ, wie hat mich Minne gelâzen! . . .

Friedrich von Hausen, MF 52, 37

p. 99

'too high an aim', MF 217, 5; Hartmann's 'Saladin' poem, 218, 5 ff.

p. 100

Hartmann's *Witwenklage*, MF 217, 14

p. 101

In den aprillen sô dî blûmen springen,
sô louven dî linden ende grûnen dî bûken,
sô heven bit willen dî vogele here singen,
sint sî minne vinden al dâ sî sî sûken,
ane heren genôt . . . . . .

Heinrich von Veldeke, MF 62, 25 ff.

p. 102

Si hât mich verwunt reht aldúrch mîne sêle
ín den vil tôtlichen grunt,
dô ích ir tet kunt daz ich tóbte unde quêle
úmbe ir vil güetlîchen munt.
den bat ich zeiner stúnt daz er mích ze dienste ir bevêle
und dáz er mir stêle
vón ir ein sénftez küssen, sô wêre ich iemer gesunt.

Wie wirde ich gehaz   ir vil rôsevarn munde,
dés ich doch niender vergaz!
noch sô müet mich dáz   daz er mich zeiner stunde
sô mit gewálte versaz.
dés bin ich wórden laz,   alsô dáz ich vil schiere gesunde
in dér helle grunde
brúnne ê ich ir iemer diende,   ine wísse rehte umbe waz.

Heinrich von Morungen, MF 141, 37 ff., accepting the problematic manuscript reading *den bat ich* in line 5 of stanza 1, against Kraus, *den mînen bat ich.*

p. 102

dô sach ich ir werden tugende, ir liehten schîn,
schône und für alle wîp gehêret;
niwan daz ein lützel was versêret
ir vil fröiden rîchez rôtez mündelîn.

MF 145, 13–16

p. 104

Si jehent daz stæte sî ein tugent,
der andern frowe..   sô wol im der si habe!
si hât mir fröide in mîner jugent
mit ir wol schœner zuht gebrochen abe,
daz ich unze an mînen tôt   si niemer mê gelobe.
ich síhe wól, swer nú   vert sêre wüetend alse er tobe,
daz den diu wîp nu minnent ê
dann einen man der des niht kan.
ich ensprach in nie sô nâhe mê.

Ich weiz den wec nu lange wol
der von der liebe gât unz an daz leit.
der ander der mich wîsen sol
ûz leide in liep, derst mir noch unbereit.
daz mir von gedanken ist   alsô unmâzen wê,
des ûberhœre ich vil   und tuon als ich des niht verstê.
gît minne niht wan ungemach
sô müeze minne unsælec sîn:
wan ichs noch ie in bleicher varwe sach.

Des einen und deheines mê
wil ich ein meister sîn die wîle ich lebe;
das lop wil ich daz mir bestê
und mir die kunst diu werlt gemeine gebe,
daz niht mannes siniu leit   sô schône kan getragen.
begât ein wîp an mir   deich tac noch naht niht kan gedagen,
nu hân eht ich sô senften muot
daz ich ir haz ze fröiden nim.
owê wie rehte unsanfte ez mir doch tuot!

MF 162, 25–33; 163, 14–22; 163, 5–13

p. 105

Reinmar's *Falkenlied:* MF 156, 10; allusion to the *Tagelied:*

So ez iender nâhet deme tage,
so getar ich niht gevrâgen 'ist ez tac?' . . .
Im ist vil wol, der mac gesagen
daz er sîn liep in senenden sorgen lie. . . .
ez taget mir leider selten nâch dem willen mîn.

MF 154, 32–3; 155, 5–6; 155, 26

p. 107

Mich hœhet daz mich lange hœhen sol,
daz ich nie wîp mit rede verlôs.
sprach in iemen anders danne wol,
daz was ein schult deich nie verkôs.
in wart nie man sô rehte unmære
der ir lop gerner hôrte und dem ie ir genâde lieber wære.
doch habent si den dienest mîn:
wan al mîn trôst und al mîn leben
daz muoz an eime wîbe sîn.

MF 163, 23–31

p. 109

Si frâgent unde frâgent aber alze vil
von mîner frowen, wer si sî.
daz müet mich sô daz ichs in allen nennen wil:
sô lânt si mich doch danne frî.
genâde unde ungenâde, dise zwêne namen
hât mîn frowe beide. die sint ungelîch:
der ein ist arm, der ander rîch.
der mich des rîchen irre,
der müeze sich des armen schamen.

Swie wol diu heide in manicvalter varwe stât,
sô wil ich doch dem walde jehen
daz er vil mêre wünneclîcher dinge hât:
noch ist dem velde baz geschehen.
sô wol dir, sumer, sus getâner hövescheit!
sumer, daz ich iemer lobe dîne tage,
trôst, sô trœste mîne klage.
ich sage dir waz mir wirret:
daz mir ist liep, dem bin ich leit.

Walther von der Vogelweide [Lachmann] 63, 32–64, 3;
64, 13–21

p. 110

Reinmar: *si ist mîn ôsterlîcher tac*, MF 170, 19. Cf. *Ich wirbe umb allez daz ein man* . . . (159, 1 ff.), especially *sist an der stat/dâs ûz wîplîchen tugenden nie fuoz getrat* (159, 7–8) and *Und ist daz mirs mîn sælde gân/deich abe ir redenden ein küssen mac versteln* (159, 37–8).

p. 110

Reinmar: *Waz ich nu niuwer mære sage / desn darf mich nieman frâgen: ich enbin niht vrô* (MF 165, 10–11); *Sô wol dir, wîp, wie reine ein nam!* (165, 28). Walther: (*in dem dône Ich wirbe umb allez daz ein man*): *Ein man verbiutet âne pfliht / ein spil, des nieman in wol volgen kan . / er gihet, swenne ein wîp ersiht / sîn ouge, ir sî mat sîn ôsterlîcher tac* ([Lachmann] 111, 22–6); *Ir sult sprechen willekomen: / der iu mære bringet, daz bin ich* (56, 14–15).

p. 111

'Ich saz ûf eime steine', Walther, 8, 4
'Ich hôrte ein wazzer diezen', 8, 28

p. 112

'Hêr bâbest . . .', 'Hêr keiser . . .', Walther, 11, 6–13, 4

p. 113

Walther's *pastourelle:* 39, 11; 'So die bluomen . . .': 45, 37

p. 140

Walther on *Frau Welt*, 100, 24–101, 22, especially 101, 5–13.

p. 142

Walther, 65, 13: *ich enwil niht werben zuo der mül* may refer to Neidhart, 69, 38: *deist gehärpfet in der mül*, if the latter is not, as has also been suggested, an idiomatic expression.

p. 143

Nu sage an, sumer, war wiltû den winter hine fliehen?
geruochestû sîn gerne, ich leiste dir geselleschaft:
ich wil mich von mînem üppeclîchen sange ziehen.
mîne widerwinnen mit dem tievel sint behaft:
die enlâzent mir an mînem liebe niht gelingen:
daz ist ein schade bî der scham
Gîselbolt und Engelram
die leident mir mîn singen.

Die selben zwêne die gehellent hin nâch Engelmâren,
der gewalticlîchen Friderûne ir spiegel nam:
tretzic unde hœnic sints an allem ir gebâren,
die selben zwêne dörper, Gîselbolt und Engelram.
des wil helfen Erkenfrit und Uozeman der reide:
die viere dringent mich hin dan.
gwunnes einen tumben wân
gein in, daz wær mir leide.

Neidhart, 57, 24–39

p. 144

Nû klag ich die bluomen und die liehten sumerzît
und die wünneclîchen tage.
dâ bî hân ich eine klage,
diu mir tougenlîche manege fröude hât benomen,
daz ein wîp so lange haldet wider mich ir strît,
der ich vil gedienet hân
ûf genâdelôsen wân.
ich kan mînes willen ninder gein ir zende komen,
sît si niht enhât
in ir herze wîbes güete
unde ir doch dar under dienen lât.
wer wær, der den kumber niht enmüete?
mich wundert, daz mîn dienest und mîn singen niht vervât.

Neidhart, 69, 25 ff

p. 147

Sumer, dîner fröidebernden wunne
fröit sich manges senden herzen muot . . .

Gottfried von Neifen 4, 27–8 (the opening lines of poem II in KLD. Neifen's *Tagelied* is no. L)

p. 148

Hâr unde bart nâch klôstersiten
und klôsterlîch gewant nâch klôsterlîchen siten gesniten
des vinde ich genuoc: in vinde ab der niht vil diez rehte tragen.
Halp visch halp man ist visch noch man,
gar visch ist visch, gar man ist man, als ichz erkennen kan.
von hovemünchen und von klôsterrittern kan ich niht gesagen.

Reinmar von Zweter, MSH II, 184 (Bartsch, p. 220)

p. 149

Her Hof, mugt ir ûch munchen, lât
die klôster hoven an ûwerr stat,
sît ir rât
niht anders gât
wan 'gip und gip! habt ir den grât,
ich nim den visch vur missetât.'
her Hof, lât ir niht abe, û wirt der valke zeime rappen.

Frauenlob, ed. Ettmüller, p. 57 (Bartsch, p. 311)

INDEX

References are confined to medieval authors and texts, historical and legendary figures who have a bearing on medieval German literature and literary genres particularly characteristic of the Middle Ages. Figures in parentheses indicate an indirect or allusive reference; figures in bold face indicate direct bibliographical information.